Perspectiv

eek

PERSPECTIVES ON TOURISM POLICY

Edited by
Peter Johnson and Barry Thomas

MANSELL

338. 4791 p

First published in 1992 by
Mansell Publishing Limited, *A Cassell Imprint*
Wellington House, 125 Strand, London WC2R 0BB , England
387 Park Avenue South, New York, NY 10016–8810, USA

Reprinted in paperback, 1993
Reprinted 1995

© Peter Johnson, Barry Thomas and the contributors, 1992

All rights reserved. No part of this publication may be reproduced or
transmitted in any form or by any means, electronic or mechanical
including photocopying, recording or any information storage or retrieval
system, without prior permission in writing from the publishers or their
appointed agents.

British Library Cataloguing in Publication Data
Perspectives on tourism policy.
I. Johnson, Peter   II. Thomas, Barry
338.4791

ISBN 0–7201–2121–3 (Hardback)
ISBN 0–7201–2164–7 (Paperback)

Library of Congress Cataloging-in-Publication Data
Perspectives on tourism policy/edited by Peter Johnson and Barry
    Thomas.
        p.   cm.
    Includes bibliographical references and index.
    ISBN 0–7201–2121–3 (Hardback)
    ISBN 0–7201–2164–7 (Paperback)
    1. Tourist trade.   I. Johnson, P.S.   II. Thomas. Barry, 1941– .
G155.A1P39   1992
338.4'791–dc20   91–31208
                                                              CIP

Typeset by Colset Private Ltd, Singapore
Printed and bound in Great Britain by
Biddles Ltd, Guildford and King's Lynn

26 JUN 1997

Contents

Notes on Contributors

Gary Akehurst is a currently a senior consultant with Touche Ross
Management Consultants, Greene Belfield-Smith Division (the
specialist tourism, hotel and leisure division). Before joining
Touche Ross, he was Professor and Head of the National Centre
for Hotel Management, South Bank Polytechnic, London, and
Professor and Head of the Department of Catering and Hotel
Management, Dorset Institute, and held faculty positions at
Surrey University, Cardiff Business School, University of Wales
and Manchester Polytechnic. He is a founding editor of the
Service Industries Journal and was a member of the CNAA Com-
mittee for Consumer and Leisure Studies.

Guido De Brabander holds a PhD in Applied Economics. He is
Professor of Economic Geography, Regional and Urban Eco-
nomics and the Economics of Tourism in the Faculty of Applied
Economics of UFSIA–University of Antwerp.

Lino Briguglio has a PhD in Economics from the University
of Exeter and is Professor of Economics and Chairman of the
Board of Studies of Banking and Finance at the University of
Malta. He is also the co-ordinator of the Islands and Small States
Programme at the Foundation for International Studies of the
University of Malta. He has written extensively on the Maltese
economy and has been the convenor of two international confer-
ences on small economies, held in Malta in 1985 and 1991.

David Bruce is a Senior Lecturer in Tourism at the Bristol
Business School. He graduated in Economics from St Andrews

and in Town Planning from Edinburgh and then worked in transportation planning and marketing with the National Bus Company before joining Bristol Polytechnic. He lectures on the environmental impact and transport implications of tourism as well as on postgraduate tourism courses at the University of Wales College of Cardiff. He is Vice-Chairman of the Western Section of the Chartered Institute of Transport and is on the committee of the Association of Teachers and Trainers of Tourism (Tourism Society)

Steve Curry is a Lecturer and Director of Research and Postgraduate Programmes at the Development and Project Planning Centre, Bradford University, UK. He has been involved in research in the tourism sector for twenty years, particularly whilst living and working in Jamaica and Tanzania. His contribution to this volume is part of an on-going research project on tourism and economic policy, for which field-work has been conducted in both Jamaica and Turkey.

James Deegan is a Lecturer in Economics at the University of Limerick. Having graduated from University College Dublin in 1983 with a Masters degree in Economics, he immediately took up an appointment as an Assistant Lecturer of Economics in Dublin City University. He moved to the University of Limerick in 1985. In 1986 he was seconded to teach international economics at the University of Zambia. His major research areas are in international economics and public sector economics. His most recent work and publications have been in the area of tourism policy and associated environmental issues. Over the past seven years he has undertaken assignments for government departments and economic consultancy firms. He is a council and executive member of HEDOO, the body in Ireland that co-ordinates the work of third level colleges involved with economic development in less developed countries.

Donal Dineen is Professor of Economics at the University of Limerick where he is Head of the Department of Business Studies. He joined the faculty at the university in 1973 and has been closely involved in the development of the Business School there since its foundation. His research interests include employment and unemployment analysis, small firms policy and local economic and employment development. He has undertaken several assignments for government departments, local and regional development agencies and worked on a number of studies for the European Commission. Among his publications are *Changing Employment Patterns in Ireland: Recent Trends and Future Prospects* (1989); *Local Innovation and Technological Development – Strategies to Generate Employment Growth* (1988); and *Evaluation of Policy Measures Taken by the Member States and the Community to Create and Develop Small and Medium-sized Enterprises* (1989). In 1990 he was awarded the ERASMUS Prize for Ireland by the European Commission in recognition of his outstanding contribution to the development of student mobility throughout the European Community.

Mary Fish is a Professor of Economics at the University of Alabama. She received her BBA from the University of Minnesota, MBA from Texas Technological College, and PhD in Economics from the University of Oklahoma. She has taught in the business schools of five universities, and was a Fulbright Senior Lecturer in Africa. She has worked for the Gambian government, the US Army forces in Tokyo, and the states of California and Iowa. She has co-authored a book, contributed to anthologies and published over 60 articles in business and economic journals.

Brian Goodall is Professor of Geography, Dean of the Faculty of Urban and Regional Studies, and Consultant Director of the NERC Unit for Thematic Information Systems at the University of Reading. His research focuses on impacts of tourism development, resort evolution, environmental auditing for tourism, and tourism marketing. Recent publications include *The Impact of Tourism Development on Disadvantaged Regions* (1985); *Marketing in the Tourism Industry* (1988); *Marketing Tourism Places* (1990); and theme issues of *Built Environment* on 'Tourism and regional development' (1988) and 'Tourism accommodation' (1989).

Howard Green is Professor of Urban Planning in the School of the Environment, Leeds Polytechnic. Currently he is also Assistant Dean within the school. His research is concerned with the local economy, particularly enterprise development and property and the associated environmental impact. He has undertaken parallel work in France and has written and lectured extensively on France.

Keith Hartley is Professor of Economics and Director of the Institute for Research in the Social Sciences and of the Centre for Defence Economics, University of York.

Nicholas Hooper is Senior Research Fellow at the Centre for Defence Economics, University of York. With Professor Hartley he worked on an EC study of tourism, jointly with Professor Howard Green of Leeds Polytechnic.

Ray Hudson is Professor of Geography and Director of the Centre for European Studies at the University of Durham. His main research interests are in the relationships between economic restructuring, state policies and spatial change, especially within Europe. He has authored, co-authored or edited 12 books, the latest of which include *Wrecking a Region: State Policies, Party Politics and Regional Change* (1989) and *A Tale of Two Industries:The Contraction of Coal and Steel in North East England* (1991) with Huw Beynon and David Sadler.

Colin Hunter is a Senior Lecturer in the School of the Environment, Leeds Polytechnic. By training an environmental scientist, with a PhD in Physical Geography, he has a wide range of research interests including hydrology and water quality, sustainable development and environmental impact assessment, with specific reference to tourism developments. He has worked on a number of research and consultancy contracts for local, national and international organizations, including the OECD and EC.

Marion Jackson is Principal Lecturer in the School of Economics at Bristol Polytechnic. After graduating from Oxford University in 1963 she joined the Research Unit in Agricultural Economics at Bristol University where she worked on a number of research projects in England and Malaya. A career break dictated by family responsibilities followed and she took up her present appointment in 1980. Since then she has developed a strong interest in the economics of tourism and has undertaken research on the economic impact of tourism on regional and local economies. She is Director of the Local Economy Research Unit at Bristol Polytechnic, editor of the *Bristol Economic Bulletin* and a member of the Tourism Society.

Peter Johnson is Reader in Economics at the University of Durham. In recent years, his research interests have focused on the economics of small business and on the employment impact of tourism. He has recently completed (in collaboration with Barry Thomas) a substantial project on the effect of a major tourist attraction in the North-east of England on the local economy. He has acted as a consultant to a number of agencies and has published a wide range of books and articles.

Mike Stabler is Lecturer in Economics at the University of Reading, specializing in urban and regional studies. His research concentrates on the economics of tourism, emphasizing structural changes in the industry. His publications include: 'Timeshare: a new dimension in tourism', *Built Environment*, 1989 (with B. Goodall); 'Modelling the tourism industry: the concept of opportunity sets', in *Tourism and Leisure: Models and Theories* (1990); 'Financial management and leisure provision', in *Management and Planning in the Leisure Industries* (1990); and *The Tourism Industry: An International Analysis* (1991).

Barry Thomas is Senior Lecturer in Economics at the University of Durham. His main research interests are in labour economics and in the evaluation of the impact of tourism. He has acted as consultant to local and national government and to European organizations. He has written a number of books and articles on economics.

Alan Townsend is a Reader in Geography at the University of Durham. He has a long-standing interest in the location and growth of tourism which has been rekindled by its increased relative role in British labour market change in the 1980s, and by his joining the editors of this volume on the steering group for their work on Beamish Industrial Museum. He is a qualified town planner and, like Professor Hudson, a Director of the National Online Manpower Information System. He has produced three books, the latest being *Contemporary Britain* (1990), of which he was co-author.

Stephen Wanhill is Professor of Tourism at the University of Wales College of Cardiff. He has worked in tourism for some 20 years, his initial contact coming through airport planning. He has undertaken numerous tourism projects in the UK and around the world. More recently he has acted as a Parliamentary Adviser on tourism to the Committee on Welsh Affairs. His main interest is in quantitative techniques for tourism planning and development.

Dirk Yzewyn is an economist and holds a Master's degree in physical planning. He is Junior Research Assistant at the Department of Economic and Social Sciences (SESO) of UFSIA–University of Antwerp, where he is presently occupied with urban studies and with economic and physical aspects of tourism.

Preface

This book, and its sister volume *Choice and Demand in Tourism*, also edited by us and published by Mansell, grew out of an international conference on tourism research held at Durham University.

The conference was held because it was felt that, although there had been a considerable expansion of tourism research in recent years, the effort was rather fragmented and dispersed. One reason for this is that many tourism researchers usually operate within traditional disciplinary boundaries, with only limited opportunities for contact with others working in similar fields. A primary purpose of the conference was thus to foster contact between researchers, to enable them to present the results of recently completed work and to receive feedback. It was also seen as an opportunity to review the strengths and weaknesses of current research and to identify potentially fruitful avenues for future work. Another objective of the conference was to encourage contact between researchers and users of research.

Nearly 150 delegates, drawn from all over the world and from a variety of disciplines, attended the conference. About two-thirds of the delegates came from academic institutions; the rest were mainly from central and local government and from the tourism agencies.

The conference papers covered a wide range of topics. However, many were directly relevant to the analysis of tourism policy. Given the relative paucity of literature on this topic and its significance, it was decided to edit a selection of the relevant papers to form the basis for this volume. A primary requirement for selection was that papers should contribute to the book's overall cohesiveness and each paper included here has been revised to take into account comments made at or after the conference. Material has been updated where necessary.

Tourism policy is of course a big theme and a book of this scale makes no pretence to be comprehensive. However, it does provide a useful range of perspectives on policy-relevant issues, as well as offering some insights into the preoccupations of researchers and into some of the strengths and weaknesses of current efforts. The book should be of value not only to researchers and policy-makers, but also to those on undergraduate and postgraduate courses on tourism and related subjects.

We owe a considerable debt to a number of organizations and individuals. Sponsorship for the conference was provided by the Bank of England, the Joseph Rowntree Foundation, Newcastle Breweries, British Rail and Peat Marwick McLintock. Our own Department of Economics also gave generous assistance. The help of these organizations is readily acknowledged. Without it, the conference would not have been possible. Particular thanks are due to Dr Janet Lewis, Research Director of the Joseph Rowntree Foundation, who supported this conference from its inception and who was a constant source of encouragement. Thanks are also due to the conference delegates, many of whom contributed vigorously to the seminar discussions.

We would not have been able to produce this book without the willing and full co-operation of its contributors, all of whom responded so readily to editorial nagging. Julie Bushby, Kathryn Cowton and Lovaine Ord all provided excellent secretarial services and we are grateful to them.

Peter Johnson and Barry Thomas
Durham 1992

1 Tourism Research and Policy: An Overview

Peter Johnson and Barry Thomas

1.1 THE GROWTH OF TOURISM

The past few decades have seen a steady expansion of tourism activity throughout the world. International tourism flows have shown considerable growth: Steve Curry points out in Chapter 12 that arrivals at international borders rose by about 4 per cent per annum in the 1980s. They now stand at over 400 million. The reasons behind this expansion are complex but certain key influences may be identified. On the supply side, the development of wide-bodied aircraft, and the increase in fuel efficiency, have led to a fall in the real cost of air transport (Edwards (1990) estimates that real international air fares fell by about 4 per cent per annum in the mid-1980s). Organizational developments, most notably the package tour, have also reduced the cost of international tourism. On the demand side, the high income elasticity of demand for leisure activities has ensured that the rise in per capita incomes in the developed countries (roughly 3 per cent per annum over the past 20 years or so) has led to a more than proportionate increase in tourism. (For a summary of the evidence on income elasticities for foreign holidays, see Johnson and Ashworth (1990) and Colin Crouch's contribution in *Choice and Demand in Tourism*.) Furthermore, the increasing ease of international communications has played a part in generating new consumer tastes in world travel. *Business* tourism, which grew at about 5 per cent per annum in the 1980s,[1] has been

1

stimulated by the expansion in world trade.

International tourism is of course only one element in tourism activity. Intra-country tourism and leisure day trips – the latter are usually excluded from the standard definitions of tourism used in official statistics, but are clearly very closely related to it – are quantitatively very significant. For example it is estimated that in 1989 UK residents spent £10 865 million on staying trips in the UK and around £4500 million on day and half-day leisure trips.[2] These figures compare with earnings from visits to the UK by overseas residents of £6945 million and overseas expenditure by UK residents of £9357 million. Not surprisingly, in the USA domestic tourism is overwhelmingly important, accounting for 90 per cent of all travel expenditure (Economist Intelligence Unit, 1991).

1.2 THE CASE FOR A TOURISM POLICY

The development of tourism raises substantial policy issues. Two reasons for this are that tourism may generate significant externalities and that it is of considerable economic importance as an activity. Each of these reasons is examined below. It is probably true to say that the emphasis in tourism research to date has been on the measurement and evaluation of the economic importance of tourism. This emphasis is reflected in the balance of topics dealt with in the following chapters. However, the externalities generated by tourism have recently attracted increasing attention (see Chapter 3); they are therefore given relatively more weight in the following discussion. (There are of course other relevant policy considerations. For example, tourism raises a range of issues about consumer protection – Brian Goodall and Mike Stabler provide an excellent case study in Chapter 11 – but it is not possible to deal with these topics here.)

1.3 EXTERNALITIES

1.3.1 Types of Externality

Externalities may be positive or negative. Positive externalities may arise (for example) because tourism puts an area 'on the map'. Another reason may be that attractions that are only viable as a result of visits by tourists may satisfy the 'option demand' of those who value the existence of the attraction because it pre-serves their *option* to visit at some future date, even though in the event they may never exercise that option. Non-visitors may also attach a positive 'existence value' to an attraction because they derive benefit from the fact that it exists, quite apart from whether or not they have visited it or might do so. (For a discussion of option and existence values in the context of environmental economics, see Pearce and Turner, 1990, pp. 132–40.)

It is the negative aspects which have received most attention and which are therefore the main focus here. Tourism may impose costs on others that are not fully reflected in the market prices paid by tourists. The presence of such externalities means *inter alia* that, even in a competitive market, buyers of tourism services do not always pay a price that reflects the true cost of the provision of those services – because suppliers do not have to meet all the costs incurred by their activity – and that as a result 'the market' generates a socially inefficient level of tourism activity.

1.3.2 Negative Externalities and the Environment

A BROAD VIEW OF THE ENVIRONMENT
A key mechanism through which negative externalities arise is the degradation of the environment. As Howard Green and Colin Hunter point out in Chapter 3, it is helpful to take a very broad view of what constitutes the 'environment'. The term may be taken as referring not only to the atmosphere and the natural environment (e.g. mountains, countryside and coast) but also to social relationships, the cultural heritage and the built environment. Thus where tourism leads to the destruction of, say, centuries-old social customs or ties, or to the wearing out of ancient buildings, it may be said to be destroying the environment. In some cases tourism may develop to such an extent that it destroys the very phenomena (e.g. uncrowded beaches, solitude in the country) from which it was originally designed to benefit; see Mishan (1967, p. 105) for an early graphic treatment of this issue.

INTER-GENERATIONAL ISSUES
The adverse environmental impact of tourism may be felt not only by the current generation, but also by future generations. Thus if this generation's tourists wear out a staircase in an

ancient building, future generations will be denied *for ever* the chance of using that same staircase. Replicas may of course be used to replace the original staircase, either before it is worn out, thereby enabling it to be removed to a place of safety, or after it has reached that stage. This in turn raises questions about the relative merits of usage and observation of 'the real thing', and about how the needs of one generation of tourists are to be traded off against those of another. Such a trade-off is far from straight-forward as it is not known whether (for example) an artefact or experience valued by the current generation will in fact be similarly valued by a future generation. By the same token, some-thing that is considered worthless today may be highly valued tomorrow. One response to this uncertainty is to preserve as much as possible *in case* it is valued later. For an example of this approach in museum collecting see Atkinson (1985). How-ever, preservation is not a costless activity. As a result, the ques-tion that arises is: to what extent should this generation incur resource costs to preserve the environment (in its widest sense) for others? Given scarce resources some ranking of priorities is inevitable. In some cases the maintenance of the original facility may not be valued highly. Here, replacement or restoration may be an appropriate response and raise no question over which generation should benefit from the original, although it will never be certain that fashions will not change and that no subsequent generation will value the original. However, it is likely that few visitors will object to a path being resurfaced with stones brought from elsewhere, unless of course the path happens to be along Hadrian's Wall. Where restoration is an appropriate policy, ques-tions of the generational distribution of the costs and benefits still have to be resolved.

THE SUSTAINABILITY OF TOURISM
In recent years considerable attention has focused on the *sustain-ability* of the environment (see, for example, Pearce *et al.*, 1989), a concept that has been applied to tourism development (English Tourist Board/Department of Employment, 1991). A key element in such sustainability is that the future enjoyment of an environ-mental resource should not be prejudiced by current activities, i.e. the present generation should pass on the resource intact to the next generation. Such a concept, involving as it does the notion of trusteeship, is intuitively appealing, but it does raise important issues of resource allocation: as indicated previously, it requires decisions on *what* and *how much* to preserve. The

inherent attractiveness of the idea of sustainability does not of itself generate additional resources.

1.3.3 Externalities and Property Rights

The presence of negative externalities (and indeed of their positive counterparts) raises important questions over the allocation of property rights between tourists, local residents and other interest groups. For example, should tourists have the 'right' to impose noise and congestion on local residents when they visit a beauty spot, and should the local residents have a 'right' to an environment free of congestion and noise? Should developers be free to destroy a good skyline by the insensitive development of multi-storey hotels, or should residents have a right to the protection of their skyline? Do tourists visiting a cathedral have the 'right' to restrict the activities or access of regular worshippers or do the latter have precedence? Clearly, how property rights are allocated will determine the distribution of the gains and losses arising from tourism activity, although it may be argued, following Coase (1960), that an efficient level of tourism activity will result, whatever the allocation of rights, provided this allocation is clearly defined and bargaining between the parties is costless. (For a further discussion of property rights in tourism, see Chapter 2.)

1.3.4 Externalities: The Policy Response

In assessing the scale of tourism externalities and what policy responses might be made towards them, it may be helpful to bear the following points in mind. Firstly, some of what may at first sight appear to be external effects may be reflected to a greater or lesser extent in market prices. For example, higher traffic congestion will tend to raise costs and hence prices. Again, if land and facilities become more scarce their prices will rise. Of course, increased congestion and more built-up areas may also reduce demand (at each price), in which case prices could *fall*.

Secondly, the existence of a negative externality may not always lead to 'free riding' on the part of those organizations and individuals who generate them, but who are not, for various reasons, contractually liable for them. They may be willing to 'pay' something towards the costs of restoring facilities that they have played a part in destroying, either by donations or by taking voluntary corrective action. Indeed the more pressure that is put on economic actors to behave 'responsibly' towards the environment, the more externalities will become internalized. It is interesting to note that the more competitive a market is, the less likely it is that any one firm in the market will be able to contribute unilaterally to the costs of restoration for which they have no legal responsibility.

Thirdly, the existence of market 'failure' arising from the existence of externalities does not of itself necessarily mean that the case for some form of government intervention has automatically been made. Such intervention itself involves resources. It may also generate further distortions because of *government* 'failure', derived, for example, from government officials pursuing their own objectives, which may not be compatible with the achievement of a socially optimal level of tourism activity, or from unanticipated side-effects of policy. Keith Hartley and Nicholas Hooper address some of these problems in Chapter 2.

Faced with the existence of externalities, the government has a number of policy options that it could explore. Possibilities include: moral pressure; legislation which restricts certain activities, defines property rights more fully or imposes compliance costs on firms or individuals; subsidies; public ownership; or taxation. Little work has been done on the relative merits of the different options.

1.4 THE ECONOMIC IMPORTANCE OF TOURISM

The second reason why tourism raises important policy issues is the scale and nature of the economic activity involved. There has been much debate about the appropriate boundaries for tourism employment (for a review, see Johnson and Thomas, 1990). However, if the figures presented by Gary Akehurst in Chapter 13 are taken as a broad guide, tourism is clearly a significant employer, accounting for between 5 and 10 per cent of all employment in ten European Community member countries. There has also been substantial growth in recent years. Ray Hudson and Alan Townsend estimate that there was an increase of nearly a quarter in direct tourism employment in the UK between 1981 and 1989. As these authors point out, the encouragement of tourism is often seen by policy-makers as a particularly useful way of combating unemployment because many of the jobs have a relatively low skill requirement and may be especially suited to young people. Furthermore, parts of the industry are relatively labour intensive; this is likely to mean that a given amount of assistance towards capital investment in the industry will generate more jobs than elsewhere. There is a further reason why tourism appears attractive as a vehicle for alleviating unemployment. Some tourism development may be footloose in the sense that it could be located in any of a number of possible locations. It may therefore be possible to locate such development in areas where the employment effects are most beneficial. Whether the employment (or indeed any other) characteristics of tourism *justify* policy intervention is another matter.

Tourism employment is also economically important in terms of GNP and the balance of payments. Akehurst's figures suggest that in nine of the eleven European Community countries for which data are available, tourism accounts for 4 per cent or more of GNP. And in eight of these countries the percentage share of travel receipts in total export earnings is over 5 per cent (in three, it is over 15 per cent).

There is a further characteristic of tourism connected with its economic importance that deserves mention. While, as indicated earlier, the high income elasticity of demand for tourism means that such demand will grow more rapidly than incomes, it also means that tourism is likely to be relatively sensitive to economic fluctuations. This in turn will generate problems, particularly in downturns.

1.5 THE STUDIES IN THIS VOLUME

It is in the context of the significance of tourism for policy that this book has been produced. The papers brought together in this book are in four main groups. Chapters 2, 3 and 4 deal with broad policy issues. It is appropriate that in the first of these, Keith Hartley and Nicholas Hooper should address a range of fundamental questions on the role of public policy in tourism. A particularly interesting question is whether market failure in the tourism field might be most appropriately dealt with via general policy measures, given that similar types of failure exist in other economic activities, rather than through a specifically *tourism* policy. They also point out that the self-interests of particular groups, including government officials and politicians, may lead to *government* failure. Their analysis is particularly refreshing in that it raises important issues that have received scant attention in the tourism literature, although they have been the subject of considerable treatment in other contexts.

In Chapter 3, Howard Green and Colin Hunter broaden the policy discussion with a detailed consideration of the relationship between tourism and the environment in its broadest sense. They also examine the way in which a formal environmental impact assessment (EIA) can be used to aid decisions over tourism developments. They apply EIA in a case study which utilizes the Delphi technique to assess 'expert' views. It would be helpful to see how a rigorous environmental evaluation of this kind could be incorporated into an *overall* appraisal of tourism developments. How, for example, might environmental factors be compared with the economic characteristics (e.g. employment and incomes) of a project?

In the last chapter in this grouping, Ray Hudson and Alan Townsend focus on the characteristics of tourism employment – a preoccupation of policy-makers – and the implications of tourism development for policy at the local level. The first part of their chapter provides a critical review of tourism employment statistics available in the UK. It shows how misleading a superficial treatment of these statistics can be. The second examines local authority decision making processes with regard to tourism and the role of employment statistics in those decisions. It is striking that many authorities are basing policies on a slim or non-existent research and database. The authors also raise the question of the extent to which tourism-promoting agencies at the local level are playing a zero sum game.

The emphasis of the next group of chapters – 5, 6 and 7 – is on different methodological approaches to the estimation of the impact of tourism. In Chapter 5, Lino Briguglio calculates tourism multipliers for the Maltese economy using both a Keynesian model of the economy and input–output data (the advantage of the latter is that it enables sectoral breakdowns to be made). This study provides policy-makers with a means of estimating the impact on the economy as a whole, and on particular sectors, of a change in the level of tourism activity. The chapter shows that considerable and painstaking effort is often required before official published statistics can be used for this purpose. Furthermore, care must be taken to bear all the limitations of the exercise firmly in mind.

In Chapter 6, Stephen Wanhill considers manpower planning in tourism and utilizes an input–output model for Nepal as a basis for such planning in that country. Interestingly, the data as far as tourism is concerned appear much richer for Nepal than for Malta. Wanhill shows how the resultant manpower forecasts can be used as an input into the formulation of an educational strategy for the sector. The results are of course only as good as the assumptions and data on which they are based. However, they are superior to the available alternatives. Provided the figures are used for guidance rather than followed slavishly, they can be of considerable value in stimulating a more rigorous approach to tourism policy.

The third chapter in this group, by Marion Jackson and David Bruce, is in one sense much more narrowly focused than the preceding two in that it examines tourism in a fairly small market town in the UK. In another sense it is more wide-ranging in its assessment of impact, since it considers the environmental and other non-economic aspects of that impact. There are two particularly distinctive features of the study reported by Jackson and Bruce. Firstly, it is part of an *ongoing* monitoring of a tourism development programme, the results of which are to be fed into the planning of subsequent phases of the programme. Such close interaction between research and policy is rare. Secondly, it pays attention to the explicit specification of the objectives behind the programme. Clearly stated objectives are an essential prerequisite for any evaluation.

Chapters 8, 9 and 10 make up the third group. These chapters are primarily concerned with the magnitude of the economic impact of tourism in a variety of locations. Mary Fish's concern in Chapter 8 is with evaluating the impact of some university football games on the local economy (Tuscaloosa County, Alabama). Her study draws on previous work at other universities and on an established econometric model for the economy to derive employment and income estimates. These estimates are directly relevant for decisions on the future capacity of the university's stadiums, which are currently unable to cope with the demand.

In Chapter 9, James Deegan and Donal Dineen report on an impact study of three tourist attractions in Ireland. Their paper demonstrates the formidable difficulties involved in estimating the full effect of tourism at the micro level. The extent to which employment and incomes generated by expenditure *outside the boundaries* of the attractions by visitors to those attractions can be attributed to the existence of the latter is a particularly thorny problem. Another difficulty is the estimation of the extent to which demand, and hence employment, is simply diverted to the attractions from elsewhere. Two conclusions of the study are worth noting. Firstly, it shows that visitors' 'associated' spending, i.e. that taking place outside the attractions, is very significant in determining the economic impact. Thus the measurement of 'attribution' may be vital to the assessment of economic impact. Secondly, Deegan and Dineen emphasize the importance of the displacement factor. In considering whether to provide public support for a project, policy-makers must always be aware of possible negative 'knock-on' effects.

The economic impact of tourism in the Province of Antwerp is the topic of Chapter 10 by Dirk Yzewyn and Guido De Brabander. These authors use a variety of approaches and data – all of which have limitations, as the authors are careful to make clear – to estimate this impact. Not surprisingly, they identify wide variations in the average daily expenditure of different categories of tourist. Their study further highlights the importance of short visits not involving an overnight stay, a category of visit often excluded from conventional definitions of tourism.

The last three chapters move away from impact analysis and address some wider policy issues. The first of these, by Brian Goodall and Mike Stabler, provides a detailed treatment of the policy implications of a specific recent development, that of timeshare. Their chapter shows that these implications are complex, involving a wide range of considerations, including consumer protection and care of the environment. It also raises some fundamental questions – for example in relation to why the competitive process does not itself lead to the elimination of 'sharp' practice – which need further investigation.

In Chapter 12, Steve Curry examines the way in which economic policy has affected the tourism sector in Jamaica. His particular concern is with the effects of structural adjustment policies introduced as a condition of assistance from international agencies. He is especially interested in the hotel sector. Curry's contribution provides some helpful insights into the variety of ways in which economic policy can affect the tourism industry. It also shows how the component parts of a particular sector, such as hotels, can be affected differentially by economic policy.

In the last chapter Gary Akehurst takes an altogether broader perspective, and looks at the development of tourism policy in the European Community. As he shows, this development has been slow. One possible reason for this has been the lack of clarity on precisely what role (if any) a supra-national organization such as the European Community has to play in this area. Akehurst is right to stress the importance of basing any policy on sound statistical information and on an intimate knowledge of the industry itself.

1.6 CONCLUSION

This book provides an indication of some of the concerns of researchers working in the tourism field. It also offers a basis, albeit a partial one, for considering possible future directions for research. As far as the economic perspective is concerned, it is probably fair to say that the 'impact' literature is now reasonably well established. Economic impact studies, using a variety of methodologies and data sources, will continue to be undertaken, and in increasing numbers as tourism grows in significance. Although much more attention needs to be paid to the concepts and measurement of attribution and demand diversion in the analysis of the impact of particular attractions, it is unlikely that the basic framework for such studies will change in any dramatic way. However, this framework could be extended to deal with a number of questions which are of direct policy relevance but which have not been addressed in any sustained way. For example, relatively little is known about the way in which tourism activity is affected *at the margin* by changes in policy or public funding. Impact studies do not typically ask what would happen if, say, public assistance were to *change* by x per cent.

There are also more fundamental economic questions to be asked about tourism policy. For example, little detailed analysis has been made of the underlying economic rationale for the public funding of tourism promotion and development. It is not self-evident that governments should be involved (at least to the extent and in the way that they currently are) in this area. In this context it would be helpful to have more firm evidence on the effects of public policy and institutions, and to explore more fully the kinds of issues raised in Chapter 2. Another area in which work could usefully be done is in the relationships between individual (publicly financed) local promoters of tourism (regional tourist boards and local authorities): to what extent are they involved in a zero sum game? The same question is relevant when relationships between local and national bodies are considered. A further issue of direct concern to the appropriateness of public assistance for tourism is the extent to which the economic actors involved do in fact utilise mechanisms other than commercial transactions to 'pay' for negative externalities that they generate.

Although the methodologies of economic impact studies of the conventional kind may be fairly well developed, the same cannot be said for studies which take a broader view of the effects of tourism. Given the growing concern with the environment (in its broadest sense), there are likely to be considerable gains from adopting a multi-, or inter-, disciplinary approach to impact analysis. Such an approach would present some major methodological challenges, not least those relating to the way in which different 'costs' and 'benefits' might be weighted in any overall assessment of the effects of tourism. Economists have made considerable strides in recent years in attempting to value costs and benefits for which appropriate market values do not exist – recreation and the arts have been an important area of study – but the perspectives of other disciplines would be vital in this kind of study.

There is clearly much policy-relevant tourism research to be undertaken, much of it involving the application of established methodologies from other disciplines, such as geography, psychology and sociology. If this book has implicitly or explicitly helped to identify potentially fruitful areas for future work, it will have succeeded.

Notes

1 This growth rate is based on data on international business arrivals for the period 1984 to 1988 in the World Tourism Organization's *Compendium of Tourism Statistics*, 10th edition (Madrid).

2 Data for UK spending by UK residents is taken from *The UK Tourist: Statistics 1989* (published by the four national tourist boards, 1990), Summary Table 1, p. 3. The estimates for day and half-day leisure trips come from *Leisure Day Visits in Britain: Market Profile* (published by the British Tourist Authority and the English Tourist Board, 1989), p. 5. The estimates relate to trips by British residents in Britain. An earlier estimate by the Department of Employment (*Tourism '88*, p. 6) put British spending on day trips in 1987 at £3000 million, but this estimate was made on a different basis. The overseas earnings and expenditure figures come from Business Monitor, MS6 *Overseas Travel and Tourism* (HMSO, 1989), Table 1.

References

Atkinson, F. (1985) The unselective collector. *Museums Journal*, **85**, 9–11.

Coase, R. (1960) The problem of social cost. *Journal of Law and Economics*, **3**, 1–44.

Economist Intelligence Unit (1991) *International Tourism Reports*, no. 2, p. 35.

Edwards, A. (1990) Changes in real air fares and their impact on travel. *Travel and Tourism Analyst*, **2**, 76–85.

English Tourist Board/Department of Employment (1991) *Tourism and the Environment: Maintaining the Balance*. London: ETB/DE.

Johnson, P.S. and Ashworth, J. A. (1990) Modelling tourism demand: a summary review. *Leisure Studies*, **9**, 145–60.

Johnson, P.S. and Thomas, R.B. (1990) Employment in tourism: a review. *Industrial Relations Journal*, **21**, 36–48.

Mishan, E.J. (1967) *The Costs of Economic Growth*. London: Staples.

Pearce, D.W. and Turner, R.K. (1990) *Economics of Natural Resources and the Environment*. London: Harvester Wheatsheaf.

Pearce, D.W., Markandya, A. and Barbier, E.B. (1989) *Blueprint for a Green Economy*. London: Earthscan.

2 Tourism Policy: Market Failure and Public Choice

Keith Hartley and Nicholas Hooper

2.1 INTRODUCTION: THE NEED FOR A CRITIQUE

Tourism is often presented as the solution to some of the UK's and EC's regional problems. Declining agricultural, industrial and inner-city areas are seen as the likely beneficiaries from tourism. In the UK, the result has been a proliferation of heritage trails, industrial museums, marinas, conference and leisure centres and theme parks (e.g. Alton Towers, Herriot Country, Wigan Pier). To its supporters tourism creates jobs, maintains and improves the environment, and promotes regional economic development. For a nation, tourism is supposed to contribute to the balance of payments and enhance international understanding, mutual respect and toleration. Critics disagree. They point to large influxes of foreigners causing traffic congestion, damaging the environment, destroying a nation's cultural heritage (e.g. churches becoming tourist shrines rather than places of worship) and creating international tension (e.g. football hooligans). Indeed, some critics view tourism policy both locally and nationally as designed to benefit producer interest groups.

Clearly, the various arguments used by the supporters and opponents of tourism are often dominated by myths and emotion, lacking both critical analysis and supporting evidence. The field is rich in its potential for applying economic analysis and the more recent developments in public choice theory. Questions arise as to whether tourism is different from other industries;

whether the tourist market is failing to work properly; and what, if any, is the appropriate role for public policy at the local, national and international levels (e.g. the EC).

2.2 CHOICES AND MARKETS

Economics is the study of choice. Scarcity means that choices have to be made between tourism and other activities and between different types of tourism. For example, if government allocates resources to museums and art galleries, they cannot be used for reducing NHS waiting lists; and within tourism, choices are needed between, say, business and leisure tourists and between caravan and hotel tourists. Societies have to decide who will make these choices: individuals or groups acting collectively in such forms as local or central government.

For many activities, society might agree to leave individuals to their self-interest, accepting the outcome of *private markets*. In this context, tourism is like any other private market and economic activity. It involves an exchange process between buyers and sellers of goods and services, especially of services. Some of the results of this exchange in international tourist markets are shown in Table 2.1. During the 1980s, there was substantial growth in the numbers of foreigners visiting the UK and in UK residents travelling abroad, mostly to Western Europe. The outflow of British citizens reflects rising real incomes, lower relative prices for foreign holidays, changing preferences and greater leisure, including earlier retirement. In 1989, UK residents travelling abroad spent an average of some £300 per person while overseas visitors to the UK spent about £400 per person. During most of the 1980s, the outcome was a negative balance (deficit) on the international payments account. In addition to international tourism, there was substantial domestic tourism, some of it leading to the saving of overseas expenditure.

Spending by tourists creates and supports jobs. Table 2.2 shows estimates of the total employees in tourism (these estimates exclude the self-employed). Total employment exceeding 1.4 million in tourism appears impressive: but how many of these jobs are the result of expenditure by UK citizens in their consumption, leisure or work activities? (For a fuller and critical treatment of tourism employment statistics, and for estimates derived from the latest Census of Employment, see Chapter 4.) In addition to private spending, there is public-sector support

Table 2.1 UK tourism

	Visits to UK by overseas residents (thousands)			Visits abroad by UK residents (thousands)			Income and expenditure (£ million, current prices)		
	All areas	North America	West Europe	All areas	North America	West Europe	Overseas visitors to UK	UK visitors abroad	Balance
1981	11 452	2 105	7 055	19 046	1 514	15 862	2 970	3 272	−302
1989	17 338	3 481	10 689	31 030	2 218	26 128	6 945	9 357	−2 412

Source: Department of Employment (1991).

Table 2.2 Employment in tourism

Employees employed in 'tourism-related' industries in Great Britain (thousands)

	Restaurants cafes, etc.	Public houses	Night clubs and licensed clubs	Hotels – accommodation	Libraries, museums, recreation	Total
1985 (June)	222.8	266.4	139.7	268.5	373.0	1 270.4
1990 (June)	284.5	288.3	144.7	293.6	418.6	1 429.7

The above figures exclude the self-employed.

Source: Department of Employment (1991).

for tourism. During the late 1980s, the Department of Employment provided about £50 million per annum of public funds specifically for tourism (e.g. grants to the British Tourist Authority and the English Tourist Board). The Department of Employment programme aims to promote the development, growth and international competitiveness of tourism, which is viewed as 'an important creator of wealth and employment opportunities' (Cmnd 288–II, 1988, p. 101). There are, though, other expenditures by central and local government on activities which are directly or indirectly tourist-related. Examples include public expenditure on the arts and libraries, roads, regional assistance, environmental services, leisure and conference facilities as well as on law and order. These public expenditures are substantial and it has to be asked whether they represent 'good value for money'. Is there any economic logic for state intervention in the UK tourist market?

The performance of the tourist market can be assessed by how well and how efficiently it satisfies diverse and changing consumer demands. Consumers in the UK are able to express their changing preferences for holidays and leisure (see Table 2.1). As a result, Florida and Spain have replaced Blackpool; walking, boating and sporting activities have replaced the annual fortnight at the seaside. And the UK tourist industry's response to changing consumer demands and technical progress (e.g. cheap air travel) reflects its relative competitiveness. Of course, such adjustments to market change are not unique to the tourist industry: other UK industries have shown varying degrees of success in responding to change and competition (e.g. motor cars, steel and textiles). If the tourist market is like any other market, questions arise as to how well the market is working and whether there is a role for public policy.

2.3 MARKETS AND PUBLIC POLICY

Left to themselves, market forces will determine the size of the UK tourist sector. However, economic analysis suggests that private markets might fail to work properly, because of imperfections (e.g. monopoly, entry barriers) and beneficial or harmful externalities, including public goods (e.g. noise, traffic congestion, street lighting, information). On this basis, some form of state intervention is often proposed to 'correct' market failure and ensure that markets fully and accurately respond to consumer

HOICE

ey and Hooper, 1990). But how far are such
unique to tourist markets: are they a general
s of the UK economy? For example, there
ry barriers associated with leisure indus-
, brewing and tied public houses; but these
re the focus of UK competition policy which is
with monopolies, mergers and restrictive practices
ughout the economy. Similarly, these are regulatory restrictions on Sunday trading, on international travel and on landing
rights for airlines, all of which have wider implications than
tourism and all of which are policy-created: they could be removed
by changing public policy (e.g. deregulation).

Tourist markets are likely to be characterized by externalities,
with a region whose comparative advantage depends on outstanding natural beauty attracting 'too many' tourists, leading to
congestion, overcrowding, pollution and the destruction of the
environment that formed the basis of the area's competitiveness.
Similar examples occur with ancient buildings, footpaths and
waterways. Private markets where there are private property
rights 'solve' such problems by charging a price that excludes
those who are unwilling to pay and using some of the income
to maintain the market value of assets. In tourism, there are
examples of the private ownership of stately homes and of parts
of the countryside (e.g. the National Trust as a non-profit agency
or water companies owning parts of Wales and the Lake District). However, substantial parts of the tourist market are based
on 'common property' in such forms as scenery, coastlines and
mountains. Such assets are regarded as 'natural' and not in need
of maintenance, and hence as 'free goods'. Beautiful views are
often available to all and my consumption of such a view does not
exclude you. In other words, parts of the tourist market are characterized by property rights that are ill-defined, unenforceable or
not worth policing and enforcing. Often in such situations,
societies might require some kind of correction to unregulated
outcomes, with collective action by central or local governments
an obvious and popular option. At the same time, though, the
form of collective action can be controversial. Efforts by governments to establish property rights and to restrict access (e.g. by
charging) are likely to be vigorously opposed. Those who benefit
from obtaining *access* (which involves resources) to views to 'consume free scenery' are often reluctant to pay!

Once again, externalities and public goods are a feature of
many parts of the UK economy and are not confined to tourist

markets. On this basis, environmental policy might be a more appropriate general policy solution for 'correcting' such market failures. It could, of course, be argued that tourist policy 'protects our heritage' for future generations. But, in principle, this should be a decision made by *UK citizens* and not by foreign tourists. Indeed, the case for a specific tourist policy raises fundamental questions about the definition of a tourist and the 'rights' of local residents and UK citizens. A York resident visiting York Minster adds to traffic congestion, pollution and wear and tear on the Minster in the same way as a tourist from Lancashire, London or the United States. Local residents might attempt to protect their 'community's property' by discouraging visitors from other areas and nations through, for example, parking restrictions and differential admission charges.

Inevitably tourism creates debates and controversy about 'rights', particularly the rights of locals or nationals versus 'outsiders', and such controversies are often resolved through the political process and political markets. In this context, there are dangers that market failure will be used to justify and rationalize any form of state intervention at the national or local levels, and that tourism policy will reflect the lobbying and influence of vested interests. Which groups are likely to gain and which are likely to lose from a tourist policy? The gainers include workers, local shops, restaurants, hotels and leisure activities; the losers might be local residents who suffer a loss of amenity through reduced access to their community's facilities.

There is considerable scope for critically assessing the form and extent of state intervention in tourist markets. For example, intervention to correct for some market failures can take the form of either *public provision* or *public finance*.[1] Is it a 'proper' role for local government to be involved in the *public provision* of, say, conference centres (as for example in Harrogate) and leisure complexes? After all, the private sector provides conference facilities and a local authority seeking to expand such facilities could always offer to subsidize additional capacity. There is a prior policy problem: how should central and local governments assess proposals for tourists projects submitted by private developers or by politicians?

2.4 PROJECT APPRAISAL: THE ECONOMIST'S APPROACH

Tourist projects are privately and/or publicly funded and they can be assessed from the perspective of the firm or the community at the local, regional, national or EC level. A firm will consider only *private* costs and benefits, as reflected in outlays, revenues and the expected profitability of its investment. In principle, policy-makers and economists are interested in the wider economic and social aspects shown by the costs and benefits for the community; hence the appropriateness of a cost–benefit approach for assessing public sector projects. For example, on this basis private developers might be taxed, with the revenue used to enhance the local environment.

Ideally, a project evaluation framework is required, to identify, evaluate and integrate all the positive and negative impacts of a proposed venture. This exercise, based on programme budgeting, is also valuable in highlighting the limitations and deficiencies of traditional approaches to appraisal. Applied to tourism, a proper and systematic project appraisal would focus on six elements of a proposed development:

1 *Its objectives* What are the aims of the scheme? What do the aims mean, and are there conflicts between the various objectives?

2 *A proper costing of the scheme*, which needs to consider both direct and indirect project costs. For example, access to a new conference centre might require road improvements and additional car parking facilities.

3 *An appraisal of benefits*, comprising both direct and indirect project benefits (including the multiplier effects of visitor spending extending throughout the regions).

4 *Life cycle impacts* The costs of operating, marketing, maintaining and repairing the facility must be taken into account, along with the initial construction costs. Similarly, the benefits will extend over the life of the facility. For example, to continue attracting visitors, a new museum will need to be maintained, repaired and modernized, and new collections will be needed, all of which involve costs.

5 *The reliability of the estimates* of costs and benefits must be considered by policy-makers when reaching their decision. For informed decisions, policy-makers need to know whether the estimates are highly reliable or highly uncertain!

6 *An appraisal of alternatives* Consideration needs to be given to alternative ways of achieving policy objectives. A comparison should be made with alternative tourist projects and with other private and public sector projects outside

tourism, which might be more cost-effective methods of achieving policy objectives.

This approach has to be adapted further for the appraisal of public sector projects. In considering public sector support for tourism developments, a city, region or nation has initially to determine the type of tourism appropriate to the area. This involves asking whether it has a resource base that gives it an actual or potential comparative advantage in attracting visitors (e.g. scenery, climate, built environment). If so, in which types of tourism is it most competitive and what are the likely future market prospects for such tourists? In answering these questions it has to be remembered that the future is uncertain: today's market leaders might be tomorrow's declining sectors. Nor is it at all clear that politicians and officials have the competence and the incentives to make such decisions. Entrepreneurs have a greater motivation than politicians and bureaucrats to take risks to meet new and unexpected consumer demands, namely their desire for profits. Decisions by politicians are more likely to be influenced by votes. As a result, politicians and officials might invest in prestige projects, which are then 'justified' by reference to their 'substantial' economic and social benefits – and the costs of such ventures are borne by the tax-payers!

A programme budgeting approach to project appraisal is not without its problems. Difficulties arise over policy objectives, the valuation of costs and benefits, the availability of data and the use of performance indicators.

Public sector policy objectives that may be sought from tourism include: the creation of income and wealth; job creation; maintaining and improving the image of an area, its environment and the quality of life; maintaining and improving links both within and between nations; and contributing to the nation's balance of payments position. These objectives have to be specified clearly and, in principle, they have to be accepted by, and reflect the wishes of, the electorate. But what do some of the objectives actually mean? Are all jobs equally valuable to policy-makers regardless of whether they are for young people, men or women, part-time or full-time, skilled or unskilled, temporary or permanent? Conflicts can also arise between some of these policy objectives. Job creation might destroy the environment and the image of an area. And how does society express its preferences for maintaining the environment and 'protecting its heritage'? Here, difficulties arise since local and national elections are usually fought on a range of issues, with tourism only one (perhaps minor) element in a complex voting situation (e.g. local taxation and services, defence, the EC, income tax, etc.), giving politicians considerable opportunities to interpret the 'public interest'.

It might be argued that the environmental improvements necessary to attract tourists also help to retain or attract industrial investment (as in Bradford). Indeed, investments in environmental, leisure, recreation, conference and hotel facilities have all been justified as creating an infrastructure necessary for industrial success. But these investment projects should be assessed against alternative forms of infrastructure investment, such as roads and education, and the full costs and benefits taken into account. There are also questions about who should pay. Should it be the private or public sector? If the state, should it be central or local government? And which budget should it be: tourism, industry, environment, etc.? The danger is that loosely defined and unquantified industrial benefits will be used to justify grandiose schemes for political purposes.

Further problems arise in valuing some of the costs and benefits in project appraisal, especially the intangible and environmental impacts. What valuations should be placed upon 'protecting our heritage for future generations', and who decides such valuations? Politicians and other interest groups seeking to justify a particular project have every incentive to ensure that the cost–benefit exercise supports their decision! Difficulties also arise because relevant data are not always available. For example, a project appraisal might require estimates of the likely number of visitors, their spending and its impact on the local economy and neighbouring regions (multiplier effects). Even for existing tourist attractions, such visitor surveys are fraught with problems (e.g. ensuring a representative sample, unreliable responses, distinguishing between local residents, UK citizens and foreign visitors). It is also necessary to separate out the impact of a tourist project from what would have happened otherwise: it is tempting to attribute *all* beneficial impacts to the project! Finally, data collection needs to be related to the selection of performance indicators relevant to the objectives of public policy. For example, visitor *spending* is a more appropriate indicator than the *number* of visitors for the objective of income creation. Similarly, full-time equivalent jobs on an annual basis and their market value might be more appropriate than simply the total number of jobs created, which will include part-time and temporary employment.

2.5 A PUBLIC CHOICE ANALYSIS

Programme budgeting assumes a decision making framework operated by selfless individuals pursuing something called the 'public interest' and the will of the people. Public choice analysis recognizes that programme budgeting, cost–benefit analysis and project appraisal will be implemented by self-interested politicians, bureaucrats and other interest groups, all operating in the political market (Hartley and Hooper, 1990). Often actual public policies depart from the economist's ideal model, such departures reflecting the political process, with rivalry between pressure groups whose income depends on tourism and opposing interest groups seeking to protect the local environment, each competing for the support of vote-sensitive governments. While private markets can fail, public choice analysis suggests that governments can also fail.

Public choice analysis applies economic concepts of self-interest and exchange to the political market of voters, parties, bureaucracies and interest groups. Each group is assumed to be a maximizing agent, with voters seeking benefits from rival policies, political parties pursuing votes, bureaucracies seeking budgets and pressure groups pursuing their own self-interest by trying to influence policy in their favour. A simple framework for identifying the various groups seeking to influence local and national UK tourist policy is shown in Figure 2.1. For simplicity, the focus is on local and national government but a more realistic representation would show a further series of linkages between the different groups (e.g. industry lobbying rival political parties).

Elections are usually general, ranging over a variety of issues, with tourism more often an element in local elections. Once elected, the local and national governing parties will implement their policies through bureaucracies. Economic models assume that bureaucracies are budget-maximizers and, as such, will exaggerate the demand for their preferred policies and underestimate their costs (Niskanen, 1971; Mueller, 1979). Departments will use information to their advantage. Consider the case that might be presented for a new publicly financed building, such as a conference or leisure centre. It will be argued that the project is 'vital' to prevent the city 'sliding down the league table' and that 'we must go ahead with the scheme because our rivals have done so'. Stress will be placed on its wider economic and social benefits in the form of increased spending in the city, job creation and an

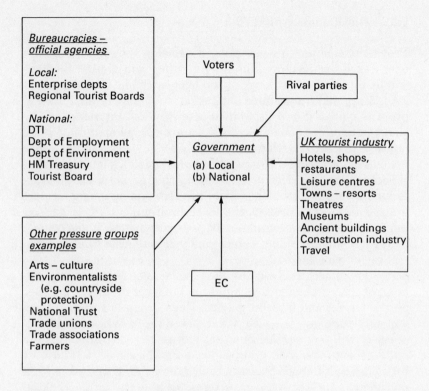

Figure 2.1 Tourism and the political market.

improved environment. It will, of course, be argued that the social benefits are difficult to quantify but none the less are 'substantial'. On the cost side, estimates might not be presented on a consistent price basis with, say, 1980 expenditures added to 1990 outlays. This, plus the neglect of indirect, life cycle and external costs (e.g. traffic congestion) will make the project appear relatively cheap. And, in the last resort, it can always be argued that vulgar notions of cost–benefit analysis and quantification are not appropriate for assessing projects vital to a nation's culture, its heritage and future generations!

Pressure or interest groups will also try to influence government policy in their favour through such means as lobbying, advertising, consultancy reports and public meetings. The various interest groups will represent the potential gainers and losers from different policies. For example, the construction industry will seek government and council contracts for new building projects, while hotels will seek subsidies and will lobby to prevent the opening of rival ventures. Indeed, public choice analysis predicts that the policies of democratic governments will tend to favour producers more than consumers (Downs, 1957).

2.6 CONCLUSION: A RESEARCH AGENDA

Public choice analysis shows that the form and extent of state intervention reflected in tourism policy can be explained by the behaviour of agents in the political market. While many of the arguments used by these agents appear persuasive, they are often emotional and lacking in both economic analysis and supporting evidence. However, efforts at reform need to recognize that individuals and groups have a tremendous capacity for ingenuity and the ability to thwart new reforms. For example, efforts by outsiders (e.g. politicians) to measure a bureaucracy's performance against its objectives will lead to the inevitable response that output is complex and cannot be measured, certainly not by any single performance indicator; that time is required to study the proposed changes; and that pursuit of the performance indicator approach will require politicians to make difficult and electorally unpopular choices!

Public choice analysis offers valuable insights into policy formulation, an area that economists have regarded as a 'black box'. It has a sound theoretical basis and is attractive for its descriptive reality. But descriptive reality and casual empiricism are no substitute for the critical evaluation and rigorous testing of its hypotheses and predictions.

For tourism policy, public choice analysis provides a new research agenda that needs operationalizing. Two examples illustrate the possibilities for further research. Firstly, consideration might be given to whether central and local governments award building contracts, grants and subsidies to activities located in marginal constituencies. Secondly, a public choice approach shows the 'distortions' that can be introduced into the economist's ideal approach to project appraisal. It identifies the arguments used by politicians and other groups to justify tourist projects; and these arguments need to be critically assessed.

27

Notes

Parts of this paper resulted from a research project undertaken by the Joint Programme for Tourism Policy Research of the University of York and Leeds Polytechnic involving Professor D.H. Green and Dr C. Hunter of Leeds Polytechnic.

1 Other forms of state intervention include laws changing property rights, together with specific and general regulatory arrangements (e.g. planning controls, competition policy).

References

Cmnd 288-II (1988) *The Government's Expenditure Plans 1988-89 to 1990-91*. London: HM Treasury, HMSO.

Department of Employment (1991) *Gazette*, February. London: HMSO.

Downs, A. (1957) *An Economic Theory of Democracy*. New York: Harper & Row.

Hartley, K. and Hooper, N. (1990) Industry and policy. In Curwen, P. (ed.) *Understanding the UK Economy*, pp. 266-305. London: Macmillan.

Mueller, D. (1979) *Public Choice*, Cambridge Surveys of Economic Literature. Cambridge: Cambridge University Press.

Niskanen, W.A. Jr (1971) *Bureaucracy and Representative Government*. Chicago: Aldine-Atherton.

3 The Environmental Impact Assessment of Tourism Development

Howard Green and Colin Hunter

3.1 INTRODUCTION

Tourism has become a high-profile activity in a number of economies. Increasingly, policy-makers and planners are turning to tourism development as a mechanism to restructure economies or to generate jobs. Such policies are found worldwide and are variable in their achievement of objectives. Tourism developments are accompanied by positive and negative effects, both economic and environmental. While the procedures for assessing economic costs and benefits are relatively well known, the potential environmental costs and benefits of tourism developments have tended to be left out of the appraisal of tourism projects, policies and programmes.

This chapter reviews the previous research concerned with tourism and the environment, particularly that relating to environmental impacts. It emphasizes the importance of the environment as a tourism resource before going on to discuss the importance of, and methodological issues raised by, the assessment of environmental impacts. The chapter concludes with a discussion of the application of the Delphi technique to environmental impact assessment.

3.1.1 Tourism and the Environment - The Literature on Impacts

The growing volume of literature on the environmental impacts of tourism emphasizes the importance of the environment to the encouragement and development of tourist activity (Latimer, 1985). Equally it expresses concern about the potential adverse effects of tourism on the environment (Edington and Edington, 1986). The environment is a key tourism resource and consequently its conservation and management are vital both to the future of the tourism industry and to society as a whole.

Generally, research in this area is still relatively immature. The subject area concerned with the assessment of the environmental effects of development is characterized by a potentially extremely complex set of impact interactions. Mainly because of this complexity and the relative immaturity of the discipline, the research literature is fragmentary. Work has tended to concentrate on the classification of impacts, taking the form of either detailed studies of selected impacts or more general broadly based work (see, for example, Bodowski, 1976; Cohen, 1978; Krol, 1986). Case studies are a common feature of the literature, in which island ecosystems and new tourist areas are the centre of interest (Camhis, 1980; Pluss, 1987). Contributions have originated from a number of disciplinary perspectives, including ecological, geographic and socio-environmental, but there has been little evidence of the emergence of a true multi-disciplinary perspective.

The literature has concentrated largely on the negative impacts of tourism development and the potentially destructive force which poorly managed tourism developments can create. The improvements and environmental benefits that tourism can bring have largely been ignored (Hall, 1974; Haulot, 1985). This focus on negative impacts is closely linked to the environments that have received the most attention. Studies of environmental impact have been almost exclusively concerned with rural areas and in particular natural or semi-natural ecosystems (Hall, 1974; Cook and Wells, 1983; Dupuy, 1987).

This concern may reflect the fact that the impacts of tourist activity on the natural environment – footpath erosion and fire damage, for example – are often easily seen, and specific impacts are more easily measured. It may also reflect the greater importance placed on the natural environment, its vulnerability and need for protection (Pivert, 1987). Where discussion is directed to urban areas, it is often superficial and descriptive in nature and frequently avoids the issue of assessment. The urban literature does, however, recognize the potential benefits of tourism (Beioley, 1981; McNulty, 1985). The urban environment, its improvement and maintenance, has been the concern of recent work. Tiard (1987), for example, describes the positive impacts of tourism on buildings in Norway.

It is only in the consideration of adverse impacts of tourism in rural areas that serious attention has been given to the methodological issues of conceptualization and measurement. Much of the work, however, has consisted of detailed measurement of very specific impacts, with little attempt to orientate the results in a form useful to policy-makers (Green *et al.*, 1990).

More recently, there has been explicit discussion of the importance of the environment as a tourism resource and the need to consider the sustainability of that resource (Papadopoulas, 1987). These issues have been developed by Romeril (1989), who argues that it is imperative to reconcile the need for an enduring and sustainable environmental tourism resource with a continuing pursuit of social and economic goals. As the tourist becomes more discriminating and has a greater awareness of the impact of tourism in the physical and aesthetic environment, environmental management and careful design will be key attributes of successful projects (McNeely and Thorsell, 1989).

In a discussion of the importance of maintaining a high-quality environment in sustaining tourism activity it is appropriate to consider 'thresholds' of tourism activity. A given environmental impact (or combination of impacts) can be tolerated up to a point beyond which the environmental resource (e.g. clean bathing water) ceases to be a positive attraction and the tourism activity that relies on it has to substitute other resources or decline. Tourism development on the North Sea coast in the UK, for example, places great pressure on sewage treatment infrastructure, with the result that, in some cases, raw (or only slightly treated) sewage is discharged directly into the sea. However, the sea is a significant tourism resource, being used for swimming, paddling, boating and as a source of aesthetic pleasure. Increasing sewage pollution progressively decreases the attraction of the sea to tourists, either through a decline in the sea's aesthetic attraction or through the public's perception of an increased health risk. Ultimately, pollution levels may reach a threshold of acceptability (e.g. by contravening water quality standards), access to the sea is withdrawn and the resource is no longer available.

3.1.2 What Is Meant by Environment?

As noted earlier, recent work on the environmental impact of tourism has been relatively unstructured and unquantitative. It does, however, provide a typology for the 'classification' of environment, which is a necessary precursor for a more systematic and comprehensive assessment of potential impacts. If the maintenance or enhancement of environment quality is to become a major element of tourism impact assessments, such a typology and structure is vital.

The literature suggests that a holistic approach to the definition of environment is necessary for a full appreciation of the complete range of potential impacts that may result from development projects or policies (e.g. OECD, 1991). However, for the sake of convenience, and to aid the discussion and understanding of potential impacts, the environment is often conceptualized as being composed of three components: natural, built and cultural environments (OECD, 1981). Although here defined as three discrete elements, the three components are interrelated and there will be cross-component effects associated with tourism developments.

The natural environment is perhaps the best documented and the component on which tourism impact research has concentrated. The natural environment may be seen to include air, land, clear light, climate, flora and fauna. The built environment encompasses the urban fabric, infrastructure, open space and elements of townscape. The cultural environment forms the third element of the typology. It is an area that has received increasing research attention during the 1980s, as the importance of culture as a tourism resource and the impact of tourism developments on culture become recognized (Meyer, 1988; Garrison, 1989). The cultural environment includes the values, beliefs, behaviours, morals, arts, law and history of communities. The cultural environment will include 'high' culture, such as opera and ballet, and popular culture, including elements such as folk, popular, contemporary and native expression, including folk music and craft work (OECD, 1981).

Although this typology is a useful starting point for a structured approach to recognizing and assessing potential tourism impacts, it is only a rudimentary initial framework. A more refined basis, or reference system, from which potential tourism impacts can be identified and assessed is presented in Table 3.1. It is limited to the consideration of potential impacts on the natural and built environments. However, it must be emphasized that the notion of environmental impact is of equal relevance in the cultural environment. Although it is possibly more difficult

Table 3.1 Potential impacts of tourism on the environment

The natural environment
A   Changes in floral and faunal species composition
    1   Disruption of breeding habits
    2   Killing of animals through hunting
    3   Killing of animals in order to supply goods for the souvenirs trade
    4   Inward or outward migration of animals
    5   Destruction of vegetation through the gathering of wood or plants
    6   Change in extent and/or nature of vegetation cover through clearance or planting to accommodate tourist facilities
    7   Creation of a wildlife reserve/sanctuary
B   Pollution
    1   Water pollution through discharges of sewage, spillages of oil/petrol
    2   Air pollution from vehicle emissions
    3   Noise pollution from tourist transportation and activities
C   Erosion
    1   Compaction of soils causing increased surface run-off and erosion
    2   Change in risk of occurrence of land slips/slides
    3   Change in risk of avalanche occurrence
    4   Damage to geological features (e.g. tors, caves)
    5   Damage to river banks
D   Natural resources
    1   Depletion of ground and surface water supplies
    2   Depletion of fossil fuels to generate energy for tourist activity
    3   Change in risk of occurrence of fire
E   Visual impact
    1   Facilities (e.g. buildings, chairlift, car park)
    2   Litter

The built environment
A   Urban environment
    1   Land taken out of primary production
    2   Change of hydrological patterns
B   Visual impact
    1   Growth of the built up area
    2   New architectural styles
    3   People and belongings
C   Infrastructure
    1   Overload of infrastructure (roads, railways, car parking, electricity grid, communications systems, waste disposal, and water supply)
    2   Provision of new infrastructure
    3   Environmental management to adapt areas for tourist use (e.g. sea walls, land reclamation)
D   Urban form
    1   Changes in residential, retail or industrial land uses (e.g. move from houses to hotels/boarding houses)
    2   Changes to the urban fabric (e.g. roads, pavements)
    3   Emergence of contrasts between urban areas developed for the tourist population and those for the host population
E   Restoration
    1   Reuse of disused buildings

Table 3.1 *continued*

	2	Restoration and preservation of historic buildings and sites
	3	Restoration of derelict buildings as second homes
F	Competition	
	1	Possible decline of tourist attractions or regions because of the opening of other attractions or a change in tourist habits and preferences

Source: Green *et al.* (1990).

to isolate in causal terms because of more general influences, such as mass communications, it is important to realize the potential that exists for tourism developments to impact both positively and negatively on the resource of the cultural environment.

3.2 ASSESSING ENVIRONMENTAL IMPACTS

Having introduced the importance of taking environmental considerations into account in the development of tourism projects and policies, we can raise an intriguing question: how can the potential environmental impacts of tourism be assessed and included in a project 'balance sheet', in order to prevent unacceptable environmental degradation and, indeed, to maximize the potential benefits of tourism? The short, and partial, answer to this question is that some form of environmental impact assessment (EIA) should be carried out before the commencement of a tourism project. It should be noted that the great majority of work on the assessment of environmental impacts of development has generally been concentrated at the level of the individual project, whether for tourism or other types of development (Wathern, 1988). However, an EIA can be applied to the assessment of different, area-based policies, plans or strategies (Wood, 1988).

3.2.1 What Is EIA?

EIA has been described as the embodiment of the preventive or precautionary approach to environmental management (Haigh, 1984), and is one manifestation of the much quoted and lauded 'prevention is better than cure' principle so prevalent in environmental policy documents (see, for example, Haigh, 1984; OECD, 1991). Recently, EIA has been defined as:

A process for identifying the likely consequences for the bio-geophysical environment and for man's health and welfare of implementing particular activities and for conveying this information, at a stage when it can materially affect their decision, to those responsible for sanctioning the proposals. (Wathern, 1988, p. 17)

It is apparent from this widely accepted definition that the primary concern of EIA is with potential impacts on the bio-logical and physical components of the *natural* environment. Although some researchers argue for the extension of this defini-tion to encompass potential socio-economic impacts (e.g. Davies and Muller, 1983), it is clear that EIA, as implemented, has largely remained 'loyal to its roots'. EIA has its origins in the USA, where it formed (initially a very small) part of the cost–benefit analysis procedures of the early 1960s. Its primary func-tion then, as now, was to indicate the impacts whose significance could not be measured in monetary terms. While some socio-economic impact data are usually included in EIA, as developers are often very keen to stress aspects such as job creation and the possible upgrading of infrastructure under the guise of human welfare, and the more comprehensive cost–benefit analyses often include some information on environmental 'unquantifiables' (Wathern, 1988), the approach is still very far from the situation where environmental and socio-economic analyses are fully inte-grated into project appraisal. In this respect, the work of Nijkamp (1980) may provide the basis for much-needed research.

3.2.2 Potential Benefits of EIA for the Developer

Apart from indirect potential benefits associated with being seen to be 'environment friendly' by an increasingly sophisticated and environmentally aware public, there are a number of direct benefits that may accrue from the full integration of EIA into the project formulation process. It has been suggested that the inclu-sion of EIA at the earliest possible stage in project formulation results in a number of potential benefits, including: more effec-tive compliance with environmental standards; improvements in the design and siting of plant; savings in capital and operating costs; speedier approval of development applications; and the avoidance of costly adaptations to plants once in operation (Cook, 1979; Dean, 1979; Canter, 1983; Lee, 1988). Htun (1988, p. 225) suggests that:

The concept that the environment and development can be mutually enhancing and do not inherently conflict is beginning to gain ground. In this context, the EIA process is seen as a means not only of identifying potential impacts, but also of enabling the integration of the environment and development.

3.2.3 Tourism Projects and EIA

A high quality environment is often the key tourism resource. Tourism projects are almost unique in their unusually close relationship with, and dependency on, the quality of the environment. EIA, if used properly, could help to avoid a situation of unfulfilled potential, or even collapse, of a tourism development owing to unforeseen environmental degradation. The remainder of this chapter is devoted to the description and discussion of the Delphi technique, which, if used properly, offers a progressive and very cost-effective way of assessing and anticipating environmental change resulting from tourism investment.

3.2.4 The Delphi Technique

THE TECHNIQUE ITSELF

If the use of EIA is to be encouraged for tourism projects, an environmental impact assessment technique that fulfils a number of criteria must be found. Although many tourism projects have the potential to generate significant and wide-ranging environmental impacts, they are often relatively small scale and lack the financial resources of large infrastructure or industrial developments. It is critical, therefore, that a cost-effective and efficient EIA technique is used to assess potential environmental impacts. Much of the cost of an EIA is normally taken up with the collection and analysis of large quantities of 'hard' environmental data. A technique should be used which rapidly identifies the potential impacts that are going to be significant before the collection of 'hard' environmental data begins. The resources available for the EIA can then be better targeted on the potential impacts causing the greatest concern. The early identification of significant potential impacts is known as 'scoping', and the Delphi technique is well suited to this process. Additionally, the EIA technique should be capable of assessing both positive and negative potential environmental impacts, across both the built and natural environments. Furthermore, in order to ensure that the findings of the EIA are of maximum benefit to policy-makers and decision-takers, the EIA technique should include an element of subjective assessment of potential impacts by the local community.

The above requirements suggest the use of judgemental techniques. These techniques avoid the collection of 'hard' environmental data, can be tailored to indicate the relative importance of potential impacts using a dimensionless measure of significance (a score which can be either positive or negative) and are flexible in terms of the range and type of opinion sought on a particular matter (e.g. judgements can be sought from local residents, as well as from recognized environmental specialists). The Delphi technique is a well established judgemental technique used as a means of collecting expert or informed opinion and of working towards consensus between experts on a given issue. Linstone and Turoff (1975, p. 3) have defined Delphi as: 'A method of structuring a group communication process so that the process is effective in allowing a group of individuals as a whole to deal with a complex problem.'

The Delphi technique achieves this goal by allowing a group of individuals to approach a consensus of opinion on the problem under consideration, without actually meeting face to face. This gives the Delphi technique two major advantages over other means of obtaining expert opinion. Firstly, the expert opinion expressed stems from the individual, not from a group of individuals in constant contact with each other, where peer pressure and the desire to conform may greatly alter any views expressed. Secondly, because the Delphi technique provides anonymity, more candid responses can be expected from the experts involved (a less personal, more corporate opinion may be given if responses are publicly attributed to the individual, as is often the case in a conference situation).

Any Delphi study falls into three distinct stages:

1 The preliminary questionnaire asks the experts to identify what they feel to be the most important considerations associated with the issue in question.
2 A second questionnaire is compiled based on the issues identified by the preliminary stage. This is the first-round questionnaire, which is circulated to the experts, who are asked to indicate which issues identified in the preliminary stage they feel to be most important. It may be necessary to enlarge this questionnaire, basing additions on information gained from the literature or other sources.

3 The second-round questionnaire is essentially the same as the first-round, except that it includes a feedback element in which experts are asked to modify their opinion if they so wish in the light of the overall expert response to the first round. The feedback element is designed to move the experts towards consensus.

Questionnaire rounds can be repeated as many times as is thought necessary until a sufficient level of consensus is reached. Each new questionnaire round will include the overall expert response to the previous round. The remainder of this chapter reports the findings of a Delphi study, the objective of which was to identify the potential major environmental impacts associated with the redevelopment of Salts Mill, in Saltaire near Bradford, for tourism. This is not the first time that Delphi has made a contribution to EIA (see, for example, Richey *et al.*, 1985), but this is the first time that Delphi has been used to identify environmental impact in both the natural and built environments.

THE SALTS MILL REDEVELOPMENT PROJECT
The mill complex is situated on the north-east side of Bradford Metropolitan District's built-up area, half a mile from Shipley town centre. Illingworth Morris plc ceased all operations in the mill complex in 1986, after 130 years of textile manufacturing on the site. The mill was purchased in 1987 by Salts Estates Limited, a private concern which proposed to redevelop and reorientate the mill towards a visitor market. The Salts Mill site is being turned into a major tourist attraction, potentially generating identifiable environmental impacts, both positive and negative. A gallery has already been opened and is currently attracting 3000 visitors per week, on average (Green *et al.*, 1990). This seems a good indication of the potential overall economic success of the project.

PANEL SELECTION
Panel size is a key issue in any Delphi study. Successful Delphi studies have been carried out in the past using only 20 initial respondents (Masser and Foley, 1987). In this case, it was decided to use 40 panel members to compensate for some expected initial non-response to the first-round Delphi questionnaire and for panel members dropping out between rounds. For the preliminary stage of the study a panel of 40 was seen as sufficient to obtain a balanced and broad cross-section of opinion on the environmental implications of the Salts Mill redevelopment proposals.

Table 3.2 The composition of the Delphi panel

Panel member	Preliminary stage	First round	Second round
Planner	3	3	2
Tourism officer	1	1	1
Economic development officer	1	1	1
Land evaluation officer	1	1	1
Environmental health officer	2	2	1
Conservation officer	1	1	1
Civil engineer	2	2	1
Councillor	3	2	2
Waterways Board representative	1	1	1
Employees of project	3	1	1
Academic	2	1	0
Resident	10	7	5
Trader	10	8	4
Total	40	31	21

It was seen as important that the Delphi panel should include people with a working knowledge of the project, such as planners, tourism officers and economic development unit personnel. However, to achieve a better balance, the definition of expert was broadened to include residents and traders (local experts) living and operating in Saltaire Village. This ensured that all interested parties could be involved and a wide range of opinion incorporated into the study.

IMPLEMENTATION

The panel was assembled following door-to-door visits in the case of residents and traders, and as a result of telephone calls to targeted individuals. Many of the latter group were employees of Bradford City Council. The composition of the panel assembled for the study is shown in Table 3.2. It consisted of three local planners, working out of both Shipley Town Hall and Jacobs Well in Bradford city centre, and personnel working within Bradford's Economic Development Unit, including an economic development officer, a land evaluation officer and a tourism officer. Other employees of the City Council were the conservation officer, two local civil engineers and two environmental health officers. The panel also included three local councillors, the political representatives for the Saltaire area. An employee from the British Waterways Board was included on the panel because of the proximity of Salts Mill to the Leeds–Liverpool Canal. Two academics (both environmental scientists), and three individuals directly involved with the Salts Mill redevelopment scheme were also included. The remaining 20 places on the panel were shared equally between residents and traders in the Saltaire area.

As already mentioned, the preliminary stage of the study involved the use of a general questionnaire, which introduced the study, and asked each panel member simply to state what he or she felt to be the main impacts, both positive and negative, of the Salts Mill redevelopment project. The use of this general questionnaire ensured that any potential environmental impacts which had not already been envisaged by the team could be incorporated into the first-round questionnaire.

After completion of the preliminary stage the first-round postal questionnaire was drawn up. The basis for this questionnaire was the extensive checklist of potential impacts stemming from tourism (shown in Table 3.1), supplemented by new impacts identified from the preliminary stage. The latter, however, identified only a small number of the more obvious potential impacts in this case and did not bring to light any information that had not already been considered as a result of the literature search.

The first-round questionnaire thus consisted of a comprehensive list of potential impacts on the natural and built environments. For each aspect of the environment panel members were asked to:

1 Indicate whether or not they felt that the redevelopment of Salts Mill would have a significant impact on the environmental aspect under consideration. If the panel member decided that the impact was not significant, then he or she could proceed to the next potential impact. A score of zero was recorded against each such response when questionnaires were analysed.
2 State whether the nature of this impact was positive or negative (i.e. beneficial or detrimental to the environment).
3 Rate the significance of the impact on a scale of one to seven.

Once the first round had been completed and the questionnaires analysed, the second-round questionnaires were despatched. The aim of the second round was to encourage the panel towards a greater degree of consensus. A feedback element was included next to each potential impact. Each panel member received a second-round questionnaire which showed the overall mean score found for each potential impact after the first round, alongside

Table 3.3 A summary of the Delphi results

| Aspects of the environment | Rank | n | Nature of impact | | |
			No. +	No. −	Mean
Reuse of disused buildings	1	21	20	0	6.48
Restoration/preservation	2	21	20	0	5.89
Infrastructure – roads	3	21	11	7	4.81
Land use – retail	4	21	18	1	4.43
Infrastructure – car parking	5	21	13	4	4.24
Visual – litter	6	21	0	20	4.19
Noise – vehicles and occupants	7	21	0	20	3.71
Visual – facilities	8	21	11	9	3.52
Infrastructure – railways	9	21	19	0	3.24
Restoration – second homes	9	21	13	2	3.24

No. +, number of panel members identifying a positive impact. No. −, number of panel members indicating a negative impact.

the score that he or she gave in the first round. Panel members were then asked if they would like to modify their initial response in the light of this information.

RESULTS AND DISCUSSION OF THE CASE STUDY

Of the 40 first-round questionnaires, 28 were returned fully completed, with a further three returned only partially answered. At the end of the second round, 21 questionnaires had been returned, giving an overall drop-out rate of nearly 50 per cent (Table 3.2). A detailed breakdown of the results after the second round is given in Table 3.3. This shows the aggregate responses to each of the individual environmental impacts listed on the Delphi questionnaire sent out to the panel members. For the sake of brevity, only the ten most significant impacts identified by the Delphi study have been placed in rank order in Table 3.3. The decision to give an analysis and comment on only the ten most significant impacts is arbitary, but also reflected the very low overall scores for the remaining aspects of the environment of Saltaire.

The impacts identified by the study showed a marked tendency towards the built environment. In both rounds, the reuse of disused buildings and the restoration and preservation of historic sites and buildings were identified as the most significant potential impacts. Roads and car parking were identified as being important issues (ranked 3 and 5 respectively in the final results). There was some degree of disagreement between panel members as to the nature of the impact on infrastructure. It is probable that those panel members who thought that the redevelopment of the mill would have a negative impact on infrastructure (as a result of traffic congestion), were unaware of the proposed improvements, which included a new access road linking the mill to Otley Road, a new bridge over the canal and the development of vacant land to provide car parking for 1180 cars. This issue of information levels among panel members should be addressed in future Delphi studies.

An increase in retailing within the area (ranked 4 in the final results) was identified as major potential impact of the mill redevelopment, as traders take advantage of the influx of tourists into the Saltaire area. The fact that retailing was seen to be such a significant positive impact may have been a reflection of the number of retailers included on the panel. If slightly fewer retailers had been included, opinion may have been more evenly split as to the nature of the impact. It could be argued that an increase in the number and size of retail outlets is not always a positive impact as the new shops may be oriented towards the visitor and not the local market. The question of panel composition is an area that should be addressed by future work on the application of Delphi to EIA.

The panel felt that the redevelopment of Salts Mill would generally cause beneficial environmental effects within its surrounding area. However, two negative potential impacts were identified, the first being litter and the second being noise generated by the visitors and their vehicles (ranked 6 and 7 respectively in the final results). Identifying these two negative impacts early on in the life cycle of the project eases the implementation of counter measures. As a condition of allowing the development to proceed the policy-maker could ensure that the problem of litter was partly or entirely met out of profits generated by the facility.

Identifying the potential negative impact of litter gives the policy-maker a clear indication of an area that may have to be subject to detailed monitoring in the future to ensure that the impact stays below acceptable levels. Similarly, the Delphi study indicated that noise pollution should be a topic for scientific, quantitative analysis and evaluation in the subsequent stages of any EIA investigation.

REVIEW OF THE DELPHI TECHNIQUE

The results above indicate that the Delphi technique, as applied in the Salts Mill study, offers a relatively quick and cost-effective means of identifying potentially significant impacts associated with tourism development projects. It is capable of identifying potential impacts across the natural and built environments, whether these are positive or negative, and provides for local community involvement and the qualitative assessment of impact magnitude. The results are in a form that is useful to policy-makers interested in weighing up the environmental costs and benefits of a tourism project alongside economic costs and benefits. The results would also enable the developer to concentrate resources efficiently on only those potential impacts identified as being significant, in subsequent stages of the EIA process. Furthermore, the information provided by a Delphi study can be used, at a very early stage, by the developer and policy-maker to minimize adverse environmental impacts and thus to achieve a tourism development that is sustainable in the long term.

Future research on the application of the Delphi technique should investigate the influence of panel composition and size on results, particularly the balance between experts with a working knowledge of the project and those with good knowledge of the area in which the project is located. It should also be possible to provide each panel member with a more detailed description of the project and associated attributes (e.g. changes to infrastructure provisions in the local area) to enable more informed judgements to be made concerning the environmental implications of the project. There is also the possibility of widening the Delphi questionnaire to include the explicit consideration of potential cultural and economic impacts, thus allowing all aspects of the effect of a project on 'quality of life' to be recognized and assessed.

Although this discussion has concentrated on the application of EIA generally and the Delphi technique specifically at the level of the individual tourism project, there is great scope for the use of EIA in the assessment of area-based tourism programmes and policies. An approach based on the Delphi technique for such assessments would appear to be of particular potential benefit, given Delphi's ability to assess alternatives without large inputs of 'hard' environmental data. Finally, it should be stressed that community involvement in the EIA process should not begin and end with a Delphi study. The results of the Delphi stage, and the subsequent stages of the EIA process, should be made public via, for example, a mediated public meeting. In this respect, significant advances are being made in the USA, Canada and the Netherlands, and continued research is needed in the UK to allow for a greater involvement of the local community in EIA.

3.3 CONCLUSIONS

The quality of the environment is a key tourism resource. No matter what the short- or medium-term economic benefits of tourism development appear to be, tourism cannot be sustained at the optimal level if the environmental resource base is degraded beyond a threshold capacity. An understanding of the potentially very complex relationship between tourism development and the maintenance of environmental quality (itself a multi-faceted concept) is crucial to the success of tourism projects, programmes and policies.

It must be recognized that tourism can have profound impacts (both positive and negative) on many aspects of the environment and future research should address the need for a more holistic and systematic approach to the identification and assessment of potential environmental and economic impacts. Tourism projects should be subject to EIA in order to ensure that, in the interests of their long-term success, they do not cause unforeseen and unacceptable environmental degradation.

It is very important that EIA procedures and methods are made as efficient as possible, and as useful as possible to policy-makers. This will involve continued research into 'scoping' techniques for rapid critical appraisal, the use of qualitative judgements by the local community and the integration of economic and environmental considerations, among other issues. The Delphi technique has much to offer in overcoming some of the problems currently associated with EIA, whether at the scale of the individual project or in the appraisal of area-based tourism policies.

References

Beioley, G. (1981) *Tourism and Urban Regeneration: Some Lessons from American Cities*. London: English Tourist Board.

Bodowski, G. (1976) Tourism and environmental conservation. Conflict, co-existence or symbiosis? *Environmental Conservation*, **3**, 27–31.

Camhis, M. (1980) Environment and tourism in island regions. *Planning and Administration*, **10**, 16–23.

Canter, L. W. (1983) A review of recent research on the utility of environmental impact assessment. Paper to Symposium on Environmental Impact Assessment, April, Chania, Crete.

Cohen, E. (1978) Impact of tourism on the physical environment. *Annals of Tourism Research*, **5**, 248–54.

Cook, M. and Wells, J.G. (1983) Environmental planning for tourism in the East Midlands. In Latimer, H. (ed.) *The Impact of Tourism and Recreation on the Environment. A Miscellany of Readings*. Selected papers from a seminar at the University of Bradford. University of Bradford Occasional Paper, pp. 59–64.

Cook, P.L. (1979) Costs of environmental impact statements and the benefits they yield to improvements to projects and opportunities for public involvement. Paper to the Economic Commission for Europe Seminar on Environmental Impact Assessment, Villach, Austria.

Davies, G.S. and Muller, F.G. (1983) A handbook on environmental impact assessment for use in developing countries. Report submitted to United Nations Environment Programme, Nairobi.

Dean, F.E. (1979) The use of environmental impact analysis by the British gas industry. Paper to the symposium on Practices in Environmental Impact Assessment, European Commission, Brussels.

Dupuy, A.R. (1987) Ressources naturelles et tourisme africain. *Espaces*, **87**, 22–5.

Edington, J. and Edington, M. (1986) *Ecology Recreation and Tourism*. Cambridge: Cambridge University Press.

Garrison, L. (1989) Tourism: wave of the future. *World Development*, **2**, 4–21.

Green, D.H., Hunter, C.J. and Moore, B. (1990) Application of the Delphi technique in tourism. *Annals of Tourism Research*, **17**, 270–9.

Haigh, N. (1984) *EEC Environmental Policy and Britain*. London: Environmental Data Services.

Hall, J. (1974) The capacity to absorb tourists. *Built Environment*, **8**, 247–57.

Haulot, A. (1985) The environment and social value of tourism. *International Journal of Environmental Studies*, **28**, 219–25.

Htun, N. (1988) The EIA process in Asia and the Pacific region. In Wathern, P. (ed.) *Environmental Impact Assessment: Theory and Practice*. London: Unwin Hyman.

Krol, B. (1986) Mass tourism and the natural environment: problems, conclusions, attempted counteractions. *Problemy Turystyki*, **34**, 24–36.

Latimer, H. (ed.) (1985) *The Impact of Tourism and Recreation on the Environment. A Miscellany of Readings*. Selected papers from a seminar at the University of Bradford. University of Bradford Occasional Paper.

Lee, N. (1988) Training requirements for environmental impact assessment. In Wathern, P. (ed.) *Environmental Impact Assessment: Theory and Practice*. London: Unwin Hyman.

Linstone, A.H. and Turoff, M. (eds) (1975) *The Delphi Method: Techniques and Applications*. Reading, MA: Addison-Wesley.

McNeely, J.A. and Thorsell, J.W. (1989) Jungles, mountains and islands. How tourism can help conserve the natural environment. In D'Amore, L.J. and Jafari, J. (eds) *Tourism: A Vital Force for Peace*. Montreal: D'Amore and Associates.

McNulty, R.W. (1985) Revitalising industrial cities through cultural tourism. *International Journal of Environmental Studies*, **25**, 225–9.

Masser, I. and Foley, P. (1987) Delphi revisited: expert opinion in urban analysis. *Urban Studies*, **24**, 217–25.

Meyer, W. (1988) Beyond the mask: towards a transdisciplinary approach of selected social problems related to the evolution and context of international tourism in Thailand. *Sozialwissenschaftliche Studien zu internationalen Problemen*. Saarbrucken: Verlag Saarbrucken.

Nijkamp, P. (1980) *Environmental Policy Analysis: Operational Methods and Models*. Chichester: Wiley.

OECD (1981) *The Impact of Tourism on the Environment*. Paris: OECD.

OECD (1991) *Urban Environment: Into the 1990s*. Paris: OECD.

Papadopoulas, S.I. (1987) World tourism: an economic analysis. *Revue de tourisme*, **42**, 2–13.

Pivert, M. (1987) Les gorges de l'Ardèche: reserve naturelle au parc de loisirs. *Courrier de la Nature*, **108**, 24–31.

Pluss, C. (1987) Tourism in the Maldives. *Problemy Turystyki*, **10**, 76–82.

Richey, J.S., Mar, B.W. and Horner, R. (1985) The Delphi technique in environmental assessment. *Journal of Environmental Management*, **21**, 135–46.

Romeril, M. (1989) Tourism and the environment – accord or discord. *Tourism Management*, **10**, 204–8.

Tiard, M. (1987) Le Parc Naturel de Brontonne. *Espace*, **85**, 27–32.

Wathern, P. (1988) An introductory guide to EIA. In Wathern, P. (ed.) *Environmental Impact Assessment: Theory And Practice.* London: Unwin Hyman.

Wood, C. (1988) EIA in plan making. In Wathern, P. (ed.) *Environmental Impact Assessment: Theory and Practice.* London: Unwin Hyman.

4 Tourism Employment and Policy Choices for Local Government

Ray Hudson and Alan Townsend

4.1 INTRODUCTION

In the 1980s, high levels of unemployment led to a focus on tourism as a source of jobs. Not least, as a part of local economic development strategies tourism attracted the interest of many local politicians and local government officers. This presupposed that local authorities could discover or create appropriate tourist attractions in their areas. Urry (1990, pp. 11–12) has recently stressed that the key point about what can become an object of the 'tourist gaze' is that it is literally seen as 'extra-ordinary', outside the range of everyday and mundane experience. What is defined as 'extra-ordinary' is, of course, a relative notion, especially in the context of the growing internationalization of tourism. This cuts two ways in terms of its implications for what can become the bases of tourism developments within the UK. Some places may cease to be seen as extra-ordinary (for instance, many traditional seaside resorts: Pickvance, 1990) while others come to be seen in this light, by UK residents and international visitors alike. This implies that there is a wide but shifting range of characteristics of places that can become tourist attractions (Townsend, 1992). Seemingly almost anything can be commodified, from the countryside (Cosgrove, 1984), to industrial heritage (Hewison, 1987), to post-modern theme parks. There are definite relationships here between the changing definitions of the extra-ordinary, the changing class structure of the UK population and the UK's place in the international division of labour, both in general and more specifically with respect to tourism.

In assessing the recent growing interest in tourism as a basis for local economic development and employment growth, it is important to remember that, in traditional spas or seaside resorts, a substantial dependence upon tourism as a source of jobs and income is not new. Nor is it a recent innovation that local authorities are promoting the virtues of their places as tourism resorts via policies to underpin tourism. What is distinctive, however, is the growing generalization of such involvement: more and more places are trying to sell their attractions to tourists on a widening range of dimensions in an increasingly global place market for tourists. Thus tourism has been seen as a tool for local economic development for the first time outside seaside resorts and spa towns, and has generated a sometimes uncritical bandwagon of interest while adding to the range and functions of local authority departments. Nevertheless, there are many merits in harnessing the long-term growth of leisure spending, which has a high income elasticity and attained a 13.4 per cent share of national household expenditure in 1989 (even when transport, food, tobacco and alcohol are excluded). The growth of leisure and tourism employment has inspired optimistic speculation, not least for depressed cities and regions.

The principal tenet of this chapter is that such optimism owes much to a policy climate that has been uncritical over a range of issues. The environmental and social disbenefits of traditional resorts were clearly outlined as long ago as 1973 by Young. There remain many conflicting interests in contemporary developments, such as the use of Birmingham streets for a one-day weekend motor race, or the pros and cons of timeshare developments in areas of landscape beauty. There remain moral and political issues in the artificial creation of 'heritage' work-sites, home interiors and spectacles (Harvey, 1989). Here the focus is on economic and, in particular, employment aspects, and it is argued that local policy-makers have had insufficient economic information on which to base decisions. A survey of all local authorities in Great Britain is reported, which shows that a large proportion of respondents openly admit that they lack an adequate information base on the economic impact and employment potential of tourism.

4.2 TOURISM EMPLOYMENT: DEFINITIONS, TRENDS, PROBLEMS

It is no justification of the situation outlined above to reiterate that the definition and measurement of tourism are intrinsically difficult. Data in Williams and Shaw (1988) indicate that, nationally, employment in tourism in Europe varies between 4 and 14 per cent, partly as a matter of definition and data availability. Thus, the production of even a baseline figure for UK or GB tourism employment is a matter of debate; there are different ways of attempting to isolate it from other kinds of employment. Johnson and Thomas (1990) demonstrate a range of estimates for 1985, from 1.1 million to 2.4 million. The high figure, including the whole of the 'main enabling activities' to tourism, such as passenger transport and the theatre industry, can be dismissed. The most frequently quoted series, standing at 1.6 million (including self-employed) in June 1991, covers certain 'tourism-related industries', i.e. the *whole* of hotels and catering (apart from canteens) and of museums and recreation.

It appears eminently more reasonable, if seeking a single national figure, to abstract different proportions of these various sectors, as determined by tourism's share of their overall activity. For example, Medlik's (1988) formulation incorporates 42 per cent of hotels and catering jobs and 25 per cent of recreation employment, and would produce an estimate for Great Britain of 1.1 million in 1989, a reduction of 30 per cent. An entirely different method is to find estimates of tourist expenditure in an area and apply ratios of sales-per-job. In general, such methods rely on the uncritical application of standard ratios in various conditions of the labour market. To direct employment can of course be added estimates of induced and indirect employment, on which there is a large literature (Archer, 1982; Sinclair and Sutcliffe, 1982; Vaughan, 1986; Wanhill, 1988). Nine national estimates reported by Johnson and Thomas (1990) are inflated, on average, by 64 per cent to allow for non-direct jobs. However, it is rarely commented that multipliers are infrequently included in the study of other industries!

It is possible that most kinds of estimates will yield similar trends. Although the use of the government definition of 'tourism-related industries' has been criticized, it provides a known starting point in comparing broad trends in different areas.

4.2.1 Trends in Tourism Employment

In the 1980s, both central and local government perceived tourism as a growth industry, particularly in terms of employment. Some indication of this priority was that the monthly government journal the *Employment Gazette* featured tourism for its coloured picture cover no less than a dozen times in the years 1986 to 1988. Some local authorities saw tourism as their principal, or even their only, prospect for job growth. The perception of employment growth in tourism was *strengthened* by the conventional view of the restricted scope for productivity gains in the industry, a topic little charted until the work of Medlik (1988, pp. 15–16). He showed that its net growth in productivity between 1979 and 1985 was slightly below that of all service industries and only about half of that of the whole economy; in 1985–90, the tourism sector was expected to show a continued growth in productivity of 1.5–2.0 per cent per annum. Has expenditure growth outweighed that of productivity?

Whatever the rate of employment growth in tourism, it cannot be isolated from more general patterns of employment change. For many local authorities, therefore, questions arise as to the relationships between policies to promote different types of economic activity. The tendency towards a blurring of the boundaries between tourism and other activities suggests that there is now potentially less conflict than previously; considerable scope for conflict nevertheless remains. While a romanticized image of the countryside may be a tourist attraction, how compatible is tourist activity with agriculture and mining? Is open-cast coal-mining incompatible with tourism development, as some local authorities have suggested in opposing open-cast coal-mining proposals (see Beynon *et al.*, 1990)? Might it not become the basis of a sort of tourism, as at Hambach in Germany, where the lunar landscape of the massive lignite pits has become a tourist attraction? If this sounds implausible, is it any more so than the Sellafield nuclear reprocessing plant becoming a major tourist attraction? To what extent are there complementarities between at least some forms of tourism and the attraction and promotion of certain forms of 'high tech' manufacturing, or research and development, which rely on an appeal to environmental quality?

Non-tourist activities that are incompatible with one type of tourism may be perfectly compatible with another. Thus, the broader question of the relations between tourism and other economic activities could be related to segmentation of the tourist market and to policy choices to develop one sort of tourism rather than another. Exploring possible combinations of activities, relative to the specific attributes of particular places, could identify windows of opportunity to which local authority policies might respond in formulating an overall programme for local economic development and employment.

4.2.2 Revisions of a Government Statistical Series

The growth of employment in the 1980s was subject to contradictory reports, but appeared to be confirmed by the issuing of the 1989 Census of Employment (*Employment Gazette*, 1981, 4, 209–26). The net growth of tourist employment turned out to be somewhat smaller than many extant estimates and statements, e.g.

> We really must throw off the image of tourism as a second class industry which is not part of the real economy. The fact is that tourism in Britain has a turnover of £15 billion a year. It earns massive amounts of foreign currency. It employs about 1½ million people and *at present 50 000 new jobs are created each year*. (Secretary of State for Employment in *Employment Gazette*, 1987, p. 36, emphasis added)

This not only illustrates the unqualified use of the crude total of 'tourism-related industries', but also falls foul of an inherent weakness of the government's estimated series of employees in employment, its major retrospective revisions (Townsend, 1991).

In all, the latest figures show that this category of employment grew by 327 000 from 1981 to 1989, an average rate of *40 900 per annum*. Even including many non-tourist jobs, the average rate over eight years was substantially lower than that quoted by the minister then responsible for the industry. Why is this? At the time he wrote, there indeed *appeared* to be an average increase of 54 200 per annum between 1984 and 1987. In fact, most public figures from this series are from monthly estimates of the *Employment Gazette*, which, like statistics for other industries, are superseded every three years by the only precise and systematic data, those of the Censuses of Employment. The series had as usual been projected forward by estimation, from

Table 4.1 Changes in employment in tourism-related industries by type, Great Britain, thousands, 1981–1989 (September)

	1989		Change 1981–1989	
	No.	%	No.	%
Male full-time	351.0	21.3	+ 48.6	+16.1
Male part-time	217.9	13.2	+ 75.2	+52.7
Total males	568.9	34.6	+123.8	+27.8
Female full-time	282.1	17.1	+ 48.9	+21.0
Female part-time	603.7	36.7	+126.3	+26.5
Total females	885.7	53.8	+175.2	+24.7
Total full-time	633.1	38.5	+ 97.5	+18.2
Total part-time	821.5	49.9	+201.5	+32.5
Total employees	1 454.6	88.4	+299.1	+25.9
Self-employed	191.0	11.6	+ 28.0	+14.7
Total	1 645.6	100.1	+327.0	+19.9
Full-time equivalent	1 234.8	–	+310.0	+25.1

Source: National Online Manpower Information System for Census of Employment data; *Employment Gazette*, March 1991, Table 8.1.

the revised 1984 figure right through until October 1989, when it was realigned with reference to the September 1987 Census benchmark.

We can be reasonably sure from the 1989 Census that there was a growth in this broad category of 327 000 from 1981 to 1989, or 19.9 per cent in all (299 100 or 25.9 per cent before including the self-employed; see Table 4.1). This makes for a much more modest contribution to overall all-sector growth than from the finance industries, which grew by 973 000 (56.8 per cent) in the same period.

The contribution is of course numerically smaller still if an attempt is made to eliminate non-tourist jobs, applying methods such as those used by Medlik and cited above. It is not readily possible to allow for variations over time in the proportions of different sectors' sales and employment that are attributable to tourism. However, applying the same ratios as before, direct employees in tourism in Great Britain are seen to increase from 864 600 in 1981 to 1 072 700 in 1989, an increase of 24.1 per cent.

This more refined statistic falls slightly below the level of 25.9 per cent for all employees in tourism-related industries principally because of the inclusion of relevant transport industries, which all declined in their employment levels. Moreover, within 'hotels and catering' it is important, for instance when considering prospects for different places, to note that a large part of the net growth in (finalized) employment data occurred in restaurants, cafes, pubs, and bars rather than in hotels, accommodation and clubs. Many forecasts for the 1990s continue to project tourism and recreation as a leading growth sector. However, few of these pay attention to the quality as well as the quantity of jobs generated.

4.2.3 Quality of Jobs

Many public calculations fail to mention tourism's element of female, part-time, low pay, non-union and seasonal work, even in calculations of productivity ratios. The low levels and growth of productivity in tourism mean that earnings and training are undoubtedly among the lowest of British industries. Bagguley (1987, p. 3) argues that

> the hotel and catering sector has specific economic and social characteristics which have meant that 'flexibility', both functional and numerical, is much more highly developed than elsewhere in the economy, and furthermore, that this labour flexibility cannot be properly understood or explained without a systematic consideration of gender relations in the workforce.[1]

Thus 'core' jobs, available all year for full-time males, are comparatively rare in the industry. However, the pattern is changing, even if this is not necessarily in the manner claimed by the industry. The seasonal element is still put as high as 70 per cent in some resorts, and Ball (1989) has revealed how many resort workers are seasonal migrants; none the less, there does appear to be agreement from a variety of sources that seasonality in hotel and catering has been reduced to a low level, although career structures are virtually absent and employment is precarious, with 25 per cent of staff in hotels and catering losing or leaving their job each year.

The Census of Employment records employees as at September, distinguishing those working less than 30 hours per week as 'part-time'. There should be little doubt that this distinction is less meaningful in this sector than others, because of the amount of informal work and double-jobbing in the season. The Censuses of 1981 and 1987 differ only by the introduction of sampling. Data for 1989 (Table 4.1) again utilize data for the crude total of tourism-related industries (including estimates of self-employed).

Table 4.1 amply confirms that female part-time workers provide the largest single group: 36.7 per cent of the labour force. Again, as expected, employment growth has been greater among the part-timers than among full-time workers. However, self-employment ceased to grow after 1986, and a little known feature is that it is male part-time staff employment that has been growing most rapidly. This results from the overall mix of growth, which is biased towards restaurants and public houses, followed by museums and hotels, although technological change has also affected women's jobs more than men's. It is likely that both the character and the scale of the growth of jobs vary geographically according to supply constraints. In producing data here for 'full-time equivalents', the method used is that endorsed by Medlik (1988, p. 60; similar to Townsend, 1986): part-time employees are counted as half units, but all the self-employed as whole units. The net effect of the calculation is to reduce the 1989 total by 401 800 (25 per cent).

As implied earlier, it was the collapse of industrial employment in the UK that led many local authorities to become more involved in formulating local economic development policies. Many of them came to see tourism as a source of new jobs, both directly and indirectly via a more general promotion of their areas. To some extent, their employment creating objectives were met, although, as shown above, questions remain about the aggregate numbers and, more crucially, the type of jobs. These characteristics of tourism employment have led several more perceptive local authorities to see it as complementary to more central industries in their economy rather than as a substitute for them.

What are the implications of this sort of employment growth for the local labour market? Are such jobs an *unavoidable* corollary of reliance upon tourism? While some undesirable aspects can be ameliorated (for instance, by developing complementary summer and winter activities to avoid the problems of seasonality), others pose more intractable problems, as job characteristics are closely tied to the organization and character of the tourism industries. Indeed, given the intensely competitive character of these highly labour-intensive industries, there are very powerful pressures to increase competitiveness by cutting labour costs.

This is not a straightforward process. For cutting labour costs may reduce competitiveness if standards of service are lowered. It could tarnish or wholly undermine the extra-ordinary character of the consumers' 'tourist gaze', since 'service' is part of what is purchased (Urry, 1990, pp. 40–1). This may have drastic implications both for the competitive position of individual enterprises and for the economic well-being of whole localities, and suggests that there are particularly acute problems of labour management to be negotiated in tourism industries.

One managerial response may be to distinguish between workers who have minimal contact with tourists and those who have high contact. The former can be subject to the impacts of technical change and an extensive Taylorized rationalization of labour, while the latter are managed very differently, recruited and trained on the basis of interpersonal and public relations skills. For such workers are participants in those 'moments of truth', face-to-face encounters between employee and customer, that determine the success or otherwise of any commercial organization (Carlzon, 1987, cited in Urry, 1990). These front-line workers are, therefore, to be more highly valued and rewarded and this implies potentially better wages and working conditions for *some* tourism workers if such a managerial strategy were followed. Their gains, however, might well be at the expense of other workers, producing greater differentiation within the tourism labour force. Such a strategy also raises questions as to who would pay for the enhanced training of the front-line workers: is there a role here for local authority involvement in training policies? What relationship might there be between this policy, tourism market segmentation and the sorts of tourism that a local authority seeks to promote?

4.2.4 Other Problems: Monetary Flows and Income Leakages

Of course, problems of employment itself are only one among a set of potential problems which affect the stability and growth of the industry in any one area. By definition, tourism relies upon residents of one place choosing to spend leisure time in another place. Consequently, the economic welfare of the destination must partly depend on the continuing prosperity of the origin *and* upon decisions by its residents on how, and where, to spend their leisure time and money. This sort of dependency relationship is unavoidable, but there are potentially great benefits to be gained if places can successfully project themselves in

Table 4.2 Tourism expenditure (current prices, £ billion), 1983–1990

	Domestic tourist trips of 1+ nights British residents	Visits abroad by UK residents	Overseas visitors to the UK	Price index 1985 = 100
1983	5 350	4 090	4 003	87
1987	6 775	7 280	6 260	114
1988	7 850	8 216	6 184	123
1989	n.a.	9 357	6 945	132
1990	n.a.	9 916	7 785	140

Source: *Employment Gazette*, various dates.

the increasingly global market for tourist sites.

The overall growth of leisure relative to other forms of consumer expenditure is well-known. However, the growth of foreign holidays by UK residents takes significant spending away. Overall, then, domestic tourism stagnated in the mid-1980s; tourist trips of one night or more had already levelled off at around 130 million from 1983 to 1988 (*Employment Gazette*, 1989, p. 437; a statistical discontinuity prevents comparison with 1989). There was, however, strong growth in visits by overseas residents, which increased from a low point of 11.5 million in 1981 to 18.0 million in 1990 (see Table 2.1), when they contributed 31.0 per cent of total tourist spending in the UK. The third element, that of estimated spending by UK residents on day trips, had meanwhile attained 13.4 per cent of the total (Baty, 1990, pp. 439–40) and largely contributed to the 183.3 million visits to attractions in 1989 (listed in BTA/ETB Research Services, 1990).

The scale of the potential rewards of success in the tourist place market is easily demonstrated. UK tourism spending rose from £13.5 billion in 1983 to £22.2 billion in 1987 (Table 4.2).[2] It further rose to £25.2 billion in 1989, of which £7.8 billion was spending by overseas visitors to the UK, £1.9 billion was payments by overseas residents to UK carriers, £10.5 billion was spent by UK residents on overnight stays and £5.0 billion was spent by UK residents on day trips. However, a key issue is whether money spent by tourists remains in the area in which it is spent.

Analyses of the effects of tourism in developing countries reveal that, on average, less than 25 per cent of the retail price of a holiday remains in the host country. This reflects the domination of the industry by vertically integrated multinationals (de Kadt, 1979). While it is dangerous to infer from one context to another, this suggests that leakage from local economies within the UK, especially in those areas where major multi-nationals are prominent actors, could be considerable. Williams and Shaw (1988, p. 88) suggest that about 50 per cent of the tourism expenditure remains in a locality, net of both direct and indirect effects.

More generally, though, it is problematic to assess the economic impact of any particular tourism initiative, and of tourism more generally, especially in view of the progressive 'de-differentiation' of tourism from other activities such as shopping or education (Urry, 1990). There are difficulties in tracing flows of wages and profits; inter-firm linkages are often complex; and definition of either 'a tourist' or ' a local economy' is problematic. This, of course, makes it particularly difficult to state whether the objectives of tourism development policies, themselves often vaguely specified, have been met, and what has been the cost of implementing tourism development policies, especially in terms of cost per job. Cynics might argue that it is precisely for such reasons that local authorities are attracted to tourism development! Certainly, when data on cost per job created are available, they often suggest that tourism is anything but a low-cost panacea to the problems of unemployment (see Department of Environment, 1990).

On the other hand, there may be considerable scope for local authority policy initiatives. If the needs of tourists are met by importing goods and services, is there scope to develop local 'import substitution', for example through networks for information exchange between companies, or through training policies? The following section now brings together some of the results of economic trends and policy in different regions and types of local authority area.

4.2.5 Geographical Disaggregation of a Government Statistical Series

Quite apart from the limited knowledge of means to disaggregate 'tourism-related' employment by gender and length of working week, published statements are on the national plane and are rarely accompanied even by a regional breakdown of total employees. It is argued here that spatial disaggregation will immediately destroy government confidence in tourism-related industries; i.e. the series is not congruent with commonsense versions of 'tourism'. However, the outstanding feature of Table

Table 4.3 Regional changes in employees in tourism-related industries, Great Britain, thousands, 1981–1989

	No.	%
London	+25.7	+14.2
Rest of South-East	+70.5	+41.0
East Anglia	+17.2	+53.4
South-West	+37.6	+34.9
East Midlands	+24.1	+38.0
West Midlands	+23.9	+26.0
Yorks. and Humberside	+30.2	+30.9
North-West	+25.3	+17.6
North	+10.3	+13.7
Wales	+15.0	+26.5
Scotland	+19.4	+14.3
GB (total)	+299.1	+25.9

Source: *National Online Manpower Information System*, Census of Employment.

4.3 is a contrast in growth between the South-East, East Anglia and the East Midlands and most other regions. This would, for example, suggest maximum growth in the Tourist Board areas of Thames and Chilterns, and East Anglia, when in fact they together receive only 17 per cent of 'nights spent' by British residents in England, and are far more notable for the growth of residential population (Champion and Townsend, 1990). If an attempt were made to reduce Table 4.3 to the core of 'genuine tourism', it would be necessary to apply ratios for the mix of component industries specific to areas of rapid population and income growth: such regionally variable ratios are simply beyond the scope of the present methodology.

Bagguley (1987, p. 16) wrote about the shift of hotel investment 'from traditional seaside holiday areas to the countryside and especially medium sized service centres where business, short stay and a little tourist demand can be maximally captured.' This type of change is better captured in Table 4.4.

This categorization indicates that the growth of tourism-related employment is as variable between types of local authority district as it is between 'North' and 'South'. The expected difficulties of 'resort and retirement' areas are reflected in employment increases at little more than half the national rate. Claims for the growth of inland tourism in 'principal cities', such as Liverpool and Manchester, are on average offset by the effects of declining population in these areas. Even the high level of activity in Inner London, with a high dependence on non-UK staff,

Table 4.4 Changes in employees in tourism-related industries by type of district, Great Britain, 1981–1989 (September), per cent

Groups of local authority districts	Hotels and other accommodation (665, 667)	Museum and recreation (977, 979)	All 'tourism-related employment' (661–3, 665, 667, 977, 979)
Inner London	− 0.2	− 3.1	+ 8.9
Outer London	+ 25.2	+ 5.3	+ 24.5
Principal cities	+ 25.1	− 7.5	+ 6.3
Other metropolitan	+ 9.3	+ 8.5	+ 17.0
Other cities	+ 7.0	+ 9.1	+ 20.7
Industrial areas	+ 54.5	+ 14.8	+ 30.3
Mixed incl. new towns	+ 33.1	+ 44.3	+ 50.1
Resort and seaside retirement	− 3.1	+ 10.3	+ 13.2
Remoter, mainly rural	+ 20.6	+ 44.1	+ 43.9
Total, Great Britain	+ 16.1	+ 14.2	+ 25.9

Allocation of local authority districts follows OPCS (1988) for England and Wales, extended to Scotland by Champion and Townsend (1990).

Source: National Online Manpower Information System.

produces only a modest recorded growth of jobs. The opening of the Birmingham International Exhibition Centre in 1991 may eclipse the growth of business and conference tourism in other cities.

Previously little known, Outer London is an area of near-average rates of growth, albeit from a low level, in hotel employment. This is partly explained by the performance of the Heathrow travel-to-work area. The 'mixed' urban–rural areas are largely coincident with the prosperous outer parts of the South-East, where exceptionally high rates of growth were recorded in the 1980s, especially in 1987–9. However, the widespread growth of employment in 'industrial areas' deserves more comment. These are areas, such as Chesterfield, Crewe, Kettering and Luton, lying beyond the metropolitan counties. It is likely that increased spending within the boundaries of these authorities arises from secular increases of local income, the growth of visitor attractions and day trips from adjoining conurbations. There is no great weight of evidence that attractions in industrial archaeology are particularly dominant (Townsend, 1992); indeed, the latest data indicate a marked urban–rural shift in museum and recreation jobs.

4.3 LOCAL AUTHORITY POLICY RESPONSES

Data such as those in Table 4.4 have been almost inaccessible to local authorities even though employment generation was the initial policy objective of most of those that entered the field of promoting tourism in the 1980s. In order to evaluate their basis of decision making we undertook a postal survey of all local authorities in Great Britain in May 1990. In all 103 replies were received from the 518 local authorities, with a further eight from territorially based tourist authorities, such as those for Northern Ireland and Wales. Replies came most frequently from departments of planning and, secondly, from those of economic development. Clearly, there was an element of self-selection in the replies, in that 70 had an explicit policy for tourism, larger than the usually credited proportion of one-half, and several more were considering such a policy.

Just over half of all counties (i.e. 31) replied. Among groups of district authorities as listed in Table 4.4, the strongest feature was the interest from the Outer London boroughs, nine of which replied out of a possible total of 19. They were stimulated by a joint endeavour to prepare visitor strategies as part of their development plans, and in several areas by prospects of hotel development (compare Table 4.4). By contrast, a few outer boroughs, and many of the responding new town and mixed urban–rural areas of the greater South-East, stressed that there was little need or scope for tourist development in their buoyant employment conditions, although tourism was often helped by leisure and recreation development for residents. Oxford, Cambridge and Kensington and Chelsea wished to restrict or divert tourism, and other authorities were aware of its disbenefits. The rest of the country, notably areas of industrial history, illustrated some very thorough and energetic approaches, for example in The Wrekin, Dudley, Stoke-on-Trent and Hamilton, although fewer generalizations are possible.

What is clear from the spread of comments by respondents, and from reports that they were able to furnish, is that the most substantial research base lies in the counties, in regions of Scotland and in larger urban areas (as opposed to larger tourist districts). In terms of commissioning special surveys and consultants' reports and securing estimates of visitor numbers and tourist-based employment, the counties, cities, metropolitan and industrial areas show the greatest commitment (although there are exceptions on the coast). Only about a quarter of respondents supplied reports that gave visitor numbers to their area, only half of these showing a trend between two or more dates. Two methods were used to estimate tourism-based employment (Vaughan, 1986). One depends on applying (usually national) employee-to-sales ratios and therefore on having estimates of expenditure by visitors. In view of what has been said, it is not surprising that direct use of data for employees in employment is more common.

Some 20 respondents cited otherwise unpublished Census of Employment data for tourism-related industries (usually acquired through the National Online Manpower Information System, and distinguishing part-time staff). Because of delays in Census availability and the fact that no series on local authority boundaries was established until 1987, only a minority of users demonstrated comparisons over time. Where both methods were used, as in Somerset, discrepancies were reported. Use of Regional Tourist Board estimates produced figures typically one-third lower than the Census figures, but this difference varied between resorts (where the Tourist Board estimates could be substantially *higher*) and cities (where they were much lower). Several authorities themselves made estimates that were substantially lower still for full-time equivalent workers: for instance, estimates for Hamilton, Tendring (including Clacton) and Vale of Glamorgan stood at 350, 500 and 200 respectively, whereas the tourism-related totals are 1800, 2600 and 3200. This is not to say that the generally accepted fuller method of considering direct, indirect, induced and diverted jobs is not in use at all. Notable examples, drawing the important distinction between local and regional multipliers, are worked by PA Cambridge Economic Consultants (1988) and in economic impact statements for the Rainham Marshes project. The point is, however, that even the 'non-survey' techniques are beyond local authorities' normal practice. Several made desperate pleas for help with data in their replies to the survey. Several stressed that they had no resources or staff for relevant research. One claimed that the 'lack of credibility' in tourism statistics leads to 'lack of investment'. Another said 'the data situation is woeful and there have been no improvements in the last 15 years'. It appears that detailed advisory notes for local authorities (English Tourist Board, 1981) have had less impact than shorter national statements. So there is just constant recitation of a few national figures in local plans; this is itself a kind of marketing which can seduce councils' thoughts when framing attitudes to the range of issues raised by tourism.

Thus, in summary, many places in the UK have a considerable, and some of them a still growing, dependence upon employment from tourism. There is also a growing involvement of local authorities in policies to sustain existing tourist developments and encourage new ones, although often the actual impacts of tourism on local employment and the economy are imperfectly understood. The direction of causality between growing employment and increasing policy involvement is often obscure and in any case is variable.

4.4 CONCLUSIONS: TOURISM DEVELOPMENT AND THE POLITICS OF DESPAIR?

There seems little doubt that many local authorities have turned to tourism as a last resort, in the face of falling employment in agriculture and industry and a failure to attract, say, 'high-tech' business services. In this sense, it seems fair to say that turning to tourism is often seen as part of a 'natural' progression towards a tertiarized economy. Indeed, without seeing it in any sense as 'natural', it is hard to deny that the turn to tourism is one expression of a structural shift in capitalist economies that emphasizes the production of services, rather than goods, as commodities. Thus the growing tourism and leisure market can be related to structural shifts in capitalist economies, to a move in the regime of accumulation towards more service-based activities and, in the broadest sense, cultural production (Harvey, 1989). If this interpretation is correct, the change may well be long-lasting. Clearly, for places able to promote themselves as attractive destinations and, crucially, able to continue to do so, the potential financial benefits are great. Conversely, to develop a local economic structure reliant upon tourism, and then to lose out in the battle between places for tourism, would be disastrous. How, then, can local authority policies be formulated to maximize the gains and minimize the risks?

Accepting that such a structural shift is under way is rather different from specifying the conditions under which tourism can provide the basis for a sustainable local economy (see also Hudson and Plum, 1986). In tourism, as in other activities, the active production of places with special qualities, places that can hold the tourist gaze, has become an important element in competition between areas at all spatial scales. As the market has become more differentiated, places have been forced to develop coherent strategies to sell themselves. It is reasonable to suppose that, initially at least, heightened competition will lead to the production of more variegated places within a global economy. But in practice what seems to be happening is the production of 'recursive' and 'serial' monotony, as places are cast in existing moulds to produce virtually identical attractions in different locations. The issue this development raises is the extent to which places will be able to sell themselves, if not as unique, then at least within a not too crowded segment of the market. Will imitative behaviour undercut every place's competitive positions as the initial edge conferred by 'uniqueness' is replaced by serial monotony?

Moreover, if places do successfully sell themselves in this way, it raises linked questions about the possible internal effects (for example, in terms of class structure) and about the extent to which they can exercise effective control over their own trajectories of change. The character of that part of the working class employed in tourism, the extent to which it is internally differentiated by occupation, wages and working conditions, and the relationships between types of job, gender and race have important ramifications for the places in which it is found. This in turn may have implications for the attractiveness of these locations to other economic activities and for the demands that its workforce may make on local authority services (such as housing and social services). But this itself is only one part of a broader issue, to do with class relations and control of tourist activities. At the risk of some over-simplification, is tourism to be based around wage labour employed by big (externally controlled, multinational) companies (involved in big projects) or is it to be based around local small firms (and much smaller projects), with a much greater involvement of local entrepreneurs, helping recreate an old middle class to meet the tourist demands of the affluent fraction of the working class and of a new middle class? Such differences have considerable implications for income distribution as well as class relations. There is no doubt that small capital continues to be of enduring significance, especially in some parts of the tourist sector, although there are important distinctions here between the self-employed, small employers and owner-directors (Hudson and Williams, 1989, 35–40). Without doubt, the intersection of growing local authority interest in tourism and growing national government interest in promoting small firms as part of an enterprise culture led to a proliferation of births (and deaths) of new small firms in tourism in the 1980s.

Equally, there is no doubt that in sectors such as hotels there is a growing dominance by very large and typically internationalized groups (e.g. THF, Ladbroke), to which some small owners are responding by joining consortia (such as Best Western) in search of scale economies, while preserving an element of local autonomy and control. This question of control is closely linked to that of income flows and multiplier effects: how should local authorities take account of this in their economic development policies?

If there are definite limits to tourism as the basis of local economic development strategies, it is difficult to avoid the question of whether, realistically, there is an alternative. The answer to this question will be place- and time-specific but, undoubtedly, there are local authorities and communities which, as of now, can see little alternative to a heavy, if not sole, reliance on tourism for work and incomes. What does the future hold for them?

Notes

1 These are long-established tendencies and long pre-date recent debates about the emergence of a flexible labour force (Hudson, 1989). Rather, the point is that particular forms of flexibility, closely tied to specific gender divisions within the workforce, and in the context of generalized non-unionization, have long been endemic in the tourism industries.

2 For comparison, it has been estimated that total UK leisure spending rose from £22.9 billion in 1983 to £37.4 billion in 1987. Within this, expenditure on foreign holidays by UK citizens rose from £5.0 billion to £10.3 billion over this period, spending by foreign visitors to the UK rose from £4.0 billion to £6.8 billion and that on holidays in the UK by its citizens from £2.6 billion to £4.1 billion (Henley Centre for Forecasting, cited in *Financial Times*, 12 May 1990).

References

Archer, B.H. (1982) The value of multipliers and their policy implications. *Tourism Management*, **3**, 236–41.

Bagguley, P. (1987) Flexibility, restructuring and gender: changing employment in Britain's hotels. Lancaster Regionalism Group, Working Paper 24. Lancaster Regionalism Group, University of Lancaster.

Ball, R.M. (1989) Some aspects of tourism, seasonality and local labour markets. *Area*, **21**, 13–26.

Baty, B. (1990) Tourism and the tourist industry. *Employment Gazette*, **98**, 438–48.

BTA/ETB Research Services (1990) *Visits to Tourist Attractions, 1989*. London: BTA/ETB Research Services.

Beynon, H., Cox, A. and Hudson, R. (eds) (1990) *British Coal and Opencast Mining: Digging out the Issues*. Durham: Department of Geography, University of Durham.

Carlzon, J. (1987) *Moments of Truth*. Cambridge: Ballinger.

Champion, A.G. and Townsend, A.R. (1990) *Contemporary Britain*. London: Edward Arnold.

Cosgrove, D. (1984) *Social Formation and Symbolic Language*. London: Croom Helm.

de Kadt, E. (1979) *Tourism: Passport to Development*. Oxford: Oxford University Press.

Department of the Environment (1990) *Tourism and the Inner City*. London: HMSO.

English Tourist Board (1981) *Planning for Tourism in England, Planning Advisory Note: 1*. London: English Tourist Board.

Harvey, D. (1989) *The Condition of Postmodernity*. Oxford: Blackwell.

Hewison, R. (1987) *The Heritage Industry*. London: Methuen.

Hudson, R. (1989) Labour market changes and new forms of work in old industrial regions: maybe flexibility for some but not flexible accumulation. *Society and Space*, **7**, 5–30.

Hudson, R. and Plum, V. (1986) Deconcentration or decentralisation? Local government and the possibilities for local control of local economies. In Goldsmith, M. and Villadsen, S. (eds) *Urban Political Theory and the Management of Fiscal Stress*, pp. 137–60. Aldershot: Gower.

Hudson, R. and Williams, A. (1989) *Divided Britain*. London: Belhaven.

Johnson, P. and Thomas, B. (1990) Employment in tourism: a review. *Industrial Relations Journal*, **21**, 36–48.

Medlik, S. (1988) *Tourism and Productivity*. London: BTA/ETB Research Services.

OPCS (1988) *Key Population and Vital Statistics, 1986*. London: HMSO.

PA Cambridge Economic Consultants Ltd (1988) *A Study of Rural Tourism*. London: Rural Development Commission and English Tourism Board.

Pickvance, C. (1990) Council intervention and political conflict in a declining resort. In Harloe, M., Pickvance, C. and Urry, J. (eds) *Place, Policy and Politics: Do Localities Matter?*, pp. 165–86. London: Unwin Hyman.

Sinclair, T. and Sutcliffe, C. (1982) Keynesian income multipliers with first and second round effects: an application to tourist expenditure. *Oxford Bulletin of Economics and Statistics*, **44**, 321–38.

Townsend, A.R. (1986) Spatial aspects of the growth of part-time employment in Britain. *Regional Studies*, **20**, 313–30.

Townsend, A.R. (1991) Employment. In Healey, M.J. (ed.) *Economic Activity and Land Use: The Changing Information Base for Local and Regional Studies*, pp. 27–42. Harlow: Longman.

Townsend, A.R. (1992) The attractions of urban areas. *Tourism Recreation Research*, **2**.

Urry, J. (1990) *The Tourist Gaze*. London: Sage.

Vaughan, R. (1986) *Estimating the Level of Tourism-related Employment: An Assessment of Two Non-survey Techniques*. London: BTA/ETB Research Services.

Wanhill, S.R.C. (1988) Tourism multipliers under capacity constraints. *Service Industries Journal*, **8**, 136–42.

Williams, A.M. and Shaw, G. (1988) *Tourism and Economic Development*. London: Belhaven.

Young, G. (1973) *Tourism: Blessing or Blight?* Harmondsworth: Penguin.

5 Tourism Multipliers in the Maltese Economy

Lino Briguglio

5.1 INTRODUCTION

This chapter estimates tourism multiplier effects in the Maltese economy using a Keynesian expenditure macro-model and an input–output model. The basic difference between the two models is that the latter contains disaggregated information about inter-sectoral relations, whereas the former does not. At an aggregate level, however, they should produce similar results.

A review of the literature on tourism multipliers is given in Archer (1977) for work published before 1977. A more recent review is given in Fletcher (1989). Some individual country tourism multiplier studies are Archer and Wanhill (1981) for Mauritius; Norton (1982) for Ireland; Lin and Sung (1983) for Hong Kong; Fletcher (1985) for Jamaica; Curry (1986) for Tanzania; and Liu (1986) for Hawaii. The aim of the present chapter is to extend the discussion by providing multiplier estimates for the Maltese economy.

This is not the first time that tourism multipliers have been estimated for the Maltese economy. Waldorf (1969) provided estimates through a simple Keynesian expenditure model. The estimates produced were very crude in that domestic consumption and tourist consumption were assigned a single import propensity and the tourism multipliers so derived were the same as those for autonomous domestic consumption. Moreover, transportation expenditure by tourists was not considered in the computation of the tourism multipliers.

A more recent study is that by Howarth & Howarth (1989). This study had a number of shortcomings. In particular, it produced a 'hybrid' input–output model where the non-tourist sectors were represented in a single row and column. Moreover, because of data limitations, Howarth & Howarth had to base their results on tourism data that did not pertain to the Maltese economy, but were collected from other European and Mediterranean countries (Howarth & Howarth, 1989, p. 139).

A very useful study is the report by PA Cambridge Consultants, written by Tarling and Rhodes (1990). The report presents survey data on the Maltese value-added content of tourist expenditures, including transportation. These results will be referred to in the present study in connection with the creation of a tourism row and column in the Maltese input–output tables. To compute tourism multipliers, Tarling and Rhodes first utilized a step by step method for calculating the inter-industry impact of tourist expenditure. They then constructed an aggregate expenditure model to calculate the induced income effect. This method is somewhat unorthodox in that it produces tourist income multiplier magnitudes that are not estimated simultaneously with the inter-industry effects.

The input–output model presented in this chapter is based on the widely used Leontief inversion method. This method combines, and simultaneously estimates, the direct, indirect and induced income effects of tourist expenditure. An expenditure macro-model has also been used to estimate tourism income multipliers, for two reasons. Firstly, this method yields rough aggregate estimates, which may be compared to the more disaggregated results of the input–output model. Secondly, it helps the reader to understand the multiplier relationships that underlie the induced effects of the input–output model.

This chapter is divided into six parts. Following this introductory section, a brief summary of the tourist industry in Malta is given in Section 5.2. In Section 5.3, the results obtained from the expenditure macro-model are presented. The fourth section gives multiplier estimates derived from the input–output model. Section 5.5 discusses some implications and shortcomings of multiplier models, while Section 5.6 gives a summary of the main conclusions.

5.2 THE MALTESE TOURIST INDUSTRY

Malta is a small Mediterranean island with a population of 350 000 and a land area of 316 square kilometres. The Maltese GDP amounted to approximately US$2000 million in 1989. About 27 per cent of the Maltese GDP is contributed by the manufacturing sector, about 33 per cent by the services sector and 23 per cent by the public sector. The remaining 17 per cent is contributed by the agriculture, fishing, construction and quarrying sectors, and by domestic property income.

The tourist industry is not very large when considered in isolation. During the 1980s, it contributed around 7 per cent to the Maltese GDP. However, as shown in this study, the industry has considerable direct, indirect and induced effects on the economy. During the same period, tourist expenditures (including transportation) accounted for over 70 per cent of total foreign exchange receipts from trade in services, and over 30 per cent of foreign exchange receipts from trade in goods and services.[1]

During the second half of the 1980s, the number of tourists averaged about three-quarters of a million per annum. Around 60 per cent of tourists came from the UK, 6 per cent from Germany and 7 per cent from Italy. Most of the tourists come to Malta during the summer months to enjoy the sea and the sun. The average duration of stay per tourist was 12 days.

5.3 THE MULTIPLIER PROCESS - AN EXPENDITURE MACRO-MODEL

The tourism multiplier process takes place because a proportion of tourist expenditure is received as income by Maltese residents, who then spend the non-taxed and non-saved portion of this income on consumption. The part of consumption expenditure that is not spent on imports is received by residents and this gives rise to new rounds of spending and re-spending, and therefore to yet further increases in the income of Maltese residents.

Multiplier models of this type often utilize marginal propensities, since the multiplier effect arises from changes in expenditure. Sometimes, however, average propensities are employed. In this study average propensities are used, since the object of the exercise is to compare the results obtained from an expenditure model with those obtained from an input–output model, which is based on inter-industry ratios and primary input ratios.[2] The

Table 5.1 The macro-model

Consumption

1 Residents' consumption $\quad CS + CG = cr\,(YP - TP - GG)$

Taxation

2 Personal tax $\qquad\qquad\; TP = tp(YP)$

3 Expenditure tax $\qquad\; TE = te(CS + CG + XC)$

4 Corporate tax $\qquad\quad\; TC = tc(SC + RP)$

Imports

5 Resident consumer imports $\quad MR = mr(CG)$

6 Tourist consumer imports $\quad\; MC = mc(XC)$

7 Tourist transport imports $\quad\;\; MT = mt\,(XT)$

8 Investment goods imports $\quad\;\; MI = mi\,(IM)$

9 Industrial imports $\qquad\qquad MM = mm(XG + CG)$

Corporate income and savings

10 Corporate savings $\qquad\quad\; SC = sc(PC - TC)$

11 Private corporate profits $\quad\; PC = pc(YF)$

12 Public corporate profits $\quad\;\; PG = pg(YF)$

Identities

13 GDP at market prices $\qquad YM = CS + CG + IM + IC + ST + GV + XC$
$\qquad\qquad\qquad\qquad\qquad\qquad\quad\;\; + XG + XS + XT - MC - MR - MT$
$\qquad\qquad\qquad\qquad\qquad\qquad\qquad\;\; - MI - MM - MS$

14 GDP at factor cost $\qquad\;\; YF = YM - (TE + TI)$

15 Personal incomes $\qquad\quad\; YP = YF - DP + PA - SC - TC - PG - RG$
$\qquad\qquad\qquad\qquad\qquad\qquad\qquad\;\; - GT + TA$

Definition of the variables

$\;\,CG$ = Consumer expenditure on goods by residents

$\;\,CS$ = Consumer expenditure on services by residents

$*DP$ = Depreciation

$*GG$ = Transfers to the government

$*GT$ = Transfers from the government

$*GV$ = Government current expenditure

$\;*IM$ = Investment in machinery

$\;*IC$ = Investment in construction

$\;MC$ = Imports induced by tourism consumer expenditure

$\;\;MI$ = Imports induced by investment goods

MM = Imports induced by industrial production

MR = Imports induced by residents' consumer expenditure

$*MS$ = Imports of other services

MT = Imports induced by tourism air/sea transport

$*PA$ = Property income from abroad

$\;PC$ = Profits (gross) of corporations in the private sector

$\;PG$ = Profits (gross) of corporations in the public sector

$*RG$ = Rents and interests received by the government

$*RP$ = Repatriated corporate profits

$\;SC$ = Corporate savings in the private sector

$*ST$ = Changes in stocks

$*TA$ = Transfers from abroad

$\;TC$ = Corporate taxes

$\;TE$ = Expenditure taxes

Table 5.1 *continued*

$*TI$ = Taxes on capital formation
TP = Personal taxes
$*XC$ = Exports of tourist-related goods and services
$*XG$ = Exports of goods, other than tourist-related ones
$*XS$ = Exports of services other than tourist-related ones
$*XT$ = Exports of tourist-related air/sea transport services
YF = Gross domestic product at factor cost
YM = Gross domestic product at market prices
YP = Personal income

* Indicates that the variable is treated as exogenous. All other variables are treated as endogenous.

expenditure model presented here has been specified in such a way as to enable a comparison of the results produced by the two models.

The expenditure model is a very simple one, but it contains the most important ingredients for computing tourism multipliers. It is not very different from the model proposed by Metwally (1977) and Briguglio (1987), except that it disaggregates imports into five components, whereas the previous models treated imports as an aggregate.[3] The model has 12 equations with average propensities (denoted by lower-case letters) and three identities as shown in Table 5.1.

Briefly, the model states that an exogenous increase in tourist expenditure $(XC + XT)$ gives rise to an increase in GDP, as shown in equation (13), in imports as shown in equations (6) and (7), and in expenditure tax as shown in equation (3). These initial changes further affect GDP, personal income, consumption and other induced variables. Because of the leakages associated with savings, taxation and imports, each round of spending is smaller than the previous one. The ultimate impact of the original tourist injections on personal income, consumption and GDP constitutes the multiplier effect of tourist expenditure on GDP.

The magnitude of tourism multiplier effects can be computed by solving the simultaneous system of equations and deriving reduced form equations for each of the 16 endogenous variables in the model. This requires the estimation of the propensities of equations (1)–(12). The solution of the system, and therefore the reduced form equations, can then be readily derived using matrix algebra.

The propensities of the model, with the exception of those in equations (6) and (7), were computed on the basis of 1985 data

Table 5.2 Tourism multipliers using 1985 Maltese data derived from a Keynesian macro-model

Injection	Tourist consumption	Air / sea transport	Weighted average
Multiplier effects on			
GDP at market prices (*YM*)	1.039	0.436	0.872
Disposable personal income (*YP*)	0.673	0.329	0.574
Retained income (*SC* + *PG*)	0.061	0.030	0.052
Taxes (*TP* + *TE* + *TC*)	0.298	0.010	0.215
Imports (*MR* + *MC* + *MT* + *MI* + *MM*)	0.572	0.521	0.561

available from the National Accounts of the Maltese islands.[4] The average propensities in equations (6) and (7) were calculated on the basis of secondary data reported in the Maltese Exit Passenger Survey and in Tarling and Rhodes (1990). The procedure used to calculate the propensities of the model is explained in detail in Briguglio (1990) and is available from the author on request.

The total multiplier impacts of tourism expenditure on consumer goods and air/sea transport, via equations (3), (6), (7) and (13), are numerous, since there is an impact on every endogenous variable in the system. The main results of interest here are given in Table 5.2.

Table 5.2 shows that the multiplier effect on GDP associated with consumer expenditure is much higher than the multiplier effect associated with transport – the reason being that tourist transport expenditure has a much higher import content than tourist consumption expenditure. The tourist weighted multiplier (i.e. consumption and transport taken together) indicates that for every Lm100 spent by tourists, the Maltese GDP grows by Lm87.2, corporate retained income increases by Lm5.2, disposable personal income by Lm57.4, taxes by Lm21.5 and imports by Lm56.1.

It should be noted that these results are based on the assumption that government expenditure is independently determined. It can be argued that government expenditure is not strictly exogenous, because it depends on taxation, which is induced within the system. If government expenditure were endogenized, the multiplier impact would be somewhat greater.

The multiplier estimates for taxation indicate that for Lm100 expenditure on tourism, government tax revenue increased by Lm21.5. Assuming that this revenue is re-spent and assuming further that the multiplier associated with government expenditure is 1.11,[5] the impact on GDP is about Lm23.9. The multiplier effect of tourist expenditure on GDP, allowing for induced government expenditure, is in the region of 1.07.

Investment is also assumed to be exogenous. This is a plausible assumption for the short run. However, a given increase in GDP (giving rise, in particular, to an increase in retained profits) in any one year may generate investment expenditure in following years. The above computation does not take into account this lagged induced investment effect, since the model is a static one, and assumes that the multiplier process is completed in one year.

5.4 AN INPUT-OUTPUT MODEL

5.4.1 The Basic Approach

The main advantage of an input–output model over a Keynesian expenditure macro-model for computing multipliers is that with the former the effect of an exogenous change can be decomposed at industrial or sectoral level. For example, it is possible to follow through the way in which an increase in tourist expenditure gives rise to a direct increase in the output of the tourist industry itself, and then to an increase in indirect demand for products from other industries which are used as inputs by the tourist industry.

These direct plus indirect effects in turn give rise to direct and indirect increases in demand for primary inputs (imports, employment income and gross profits), which normally include a fairly large component received in the form of income by households. There is therefore a simultaneous induced effect, which arises from additional rounds of spending by the households whose income has increased. The direct and indirect plus the induced effects lead to a multiplied effect on personal income, and on other endogenous variables such as GDP, consumption, savings and so on.

The analysis of sectoral multipliers is usually carried out by calculating the inverse of a matrix of input–output coefficients. As is well known, the input–output table breaks the economy into industries or sectors. It is generally expressed in rows, representing sales, and columns, representing purchases. A given row – say row i – shows the amount of sales by industry i to other industries and to the final buyers. A given column – say column j – shows the purchases of industry j from other industries, and the primary inputs purchased by the same industry.

The approach often used to solve the system is known as the Leontief inversion. It is based on the following equation:

$$Ax + y = x$$

where **x** is a vector of total sales of each industry; A is a matrix of technical coefficients; and **y** is a vector of final demand. Each cell in the A matrix can be derived from the original input–output matrix, and represents the ratio of sales by one industry to a second industry. In general, element $a(i,j)$ of matrix A shows the sales of industry i to industry j expressed as a ratio of total output of industry j.

The equation just presented states that total sales of the ith industry are equal to inter-industry sales of that industry (Ax) plus final sales (**y**) of that industry. Final sales cover consumption, exports, investment and government expenditure. The equation can be arranged as follows:

$$x = (I - A)^{-1} y$$

where the matrix $(I - A)^{-1}$ shows the direct and indirect output increases in response to a one unit increase in final demand. If consumption expenditure and personal income are considered as part of the transaction matrix, the solution also yields information about the induced effects arising from personal consumption expenditure.[6]

As stated, input–output tables include information about primary inputs, covering imports, income from employment and trading profits. A matrix of primary input coefficients, expressing these inputs as a ratio of total output of each industry, can be computed from the original data. The information given in the $(I - A)^{-1}$ matrix can be multiplied by the primary input ratios, say the ratio of corporate savings or of imports to final sales, to calculate the increases in sectoral savings and imports for the production of the direct, indirect and induced output increase arising from an increase in final demand.

5.4.2 Adjusting the Maltese Input-Output Data

The inter-industry transaction matrix of the Maltese input–output tables, as published in the National Accounts of the

Maltese Islands, contains 23×23 entries. The matrix is not suitable for computing tourism multipliers, since all the services are aggregated into one large sector called 'other production and trade'.[7]

Moreover, the Maltese input–output tables do not permit the computation of the induced effects arising from household expenditure, since the primary input matrix does not contain a separate row for disposable personal income. A component of such income appears under the heading 'income from employment', while another component (self-employment income, dividends, rent and interest) appears under the heading 'gross profit and other trading income'.

For this reason, a great deal of computational work had to be undertaken by the present author to construct (a) a separate row and a separate column representing the inter-industry sales and inter-industry purchases associated with tourism and (b) a row for personal disposable income. The procedure used to construct these rows and columns is explained in detail in Briguglio (1990) and can be obtained form the author on request. The following is a brief description of the procedure used.

The construction of the foreign travel row was relatively straightforward. Since all the output is exported, and nothing is sold as input to other industries, total tourist expenditure (on consumer goods and services and on air/sea travel) was entered in the final demand section of the input–output table, and these exports were deducted from the exports of the other production and trade sector, of which foreign travel originally formed a part.

The construction of a foreign travel column was more complicated, because this required data on purchases from other industries, imports and value added. The information was derived from the Exit Passenger Survey and from Tarling and Rhodes (1990, Chapter 4). The newly constructed column shows value added, imports and inter-industry purchases of tourism inputs from other industries. The data pertaining to the new foreign travel column were deducted from those in the original other production and trade column.

As stated above in the primary input section, the Maltese input–output tables contain two rows representing income, namely (1) income from employment and (2) gross profit and other trading income. To construct a separate row for disposable personal income it was necessary to estimate: (a) sectoral self-employment income;[8] (b) sectoral distributed corporate income;[9] and (c) sectoral personal income tax.[10] The disposable income row was created by adding the sectoral estimates of self-employment income and distributed corporate income to the original income from employment, and deducting personal income tax. The gross trading profits row was then adjusted to cover disposable retained profits only. A total tax row was also constructed by adding estimates of sectoral income tax and estimates of corporate tax[11] to the original sectoral expenditure tax. To compute the induced effect of final expenditures, the household sector was included as one of the productive sectors, and the matrix of coefficients was augmented to include the personal disposable income row and the consumption column.

In this way, the original 23 × 23 Maltese transaction matrix was first enlarged to 24 × 24 entries to create a separate row and a separate column for foreign travel, where row 24 and column 24 represented foreign travel. The matrix was enlarged again to 25 × 25 entries to allow for the induced effects of household consumption, where row 25 represented household disposable income and column 25 represented consumption.

5.4.3 Computing Input-Output Multipliers Using Maltese Data

The multipliers for disposable household income given by the Maltese input–output tables, modified as just described, can be derived from the equation $x = (I - A)^{-1} y$, where in this case, the $(I - A)^{-1}$ is a 25 × 25 inverse matrix. It can be shown that the elements of the disposable income row of the inverse matrix measure the multiplier effects on disposable household income arising from an increase in exogenous final demand. Thus, in the case of the modified Maltese inverse matrix, element j in row 25 contains the direct, indirect and induced effects on disposable personal income arising from an increase in demand for the final product of sector j.

Using the 1985 Maltese inverse matrix (see note 4) it was found that a Lm100 increase in tourist final expenditure gave rise to a direct, indirect and induced increase of Lm55.7 in personal disposable income. This is given in column 24, row 25, which correspond to tourism inputs and disposable personal income respectively.

The impact of changes in the final demand of the other sectors on disposable personal income can be read off the other elements in row 25 of the inverse matrix. The results show that tourism income multipliers are relatively high, but not the highest when compared to the other industries in the Maltese economy. Final demand for public services, construction, agriculture and furniture had higher multiplier impacts on personal income than tourism. However, when compared to the two other principal export-oriented Maltese industries, namely clothing and electrical machinery, tourist expenditure had the highest income multiplier impact. In fact, the income multiplier associated with tourism was approximately one and a half times that associated with clothing and two times as much as that associated with machinery.

Column 24 of the inverse matrix shows the impact of tourist expenditure on the output of other sectors. The results obtained show that tourism has the highest impact on personal services, public services, food, agriculture, electricity, beverages, tobacco and clothing in that order.

From the inverse matrix and the primary input coefficients, multipliers for aggregate corporate savings, taxation and imports arising from tourist expenditure can also be derived. The Keynesian-type sectoral savings multipliers for tourism can be computed by multiplying cells 1 to 24 of column 24 (representing tourism sectoral inputs) by the elements of row 26 of the matrix of coefficients, where row 26 shows the ratios of sectoral savings to total sectoral output. The sum of these sectoral savings multipliers would give an aggregate corporate savings multiplier, measuring the increase in aggregate savings arising from an increase in tourist spending. In the present study the aggregate increase in corporate savings associated with a Lm100 increase in tourist spending is Lm10.1.

Keynesian-type sectoral taxation and imports multipliers for tourism can be constructed in a similar manner by multiplying the cells of column 24 by the taxation and imports ratios. When summed, these multipliers give the aggregate taxation and imports multipliers arising from an increase in tourist expenditure. The estimates show that for every Lm100 in tourist final expenditure, taxation increases by about Lm20.1 and imports increase by about Lm63.9.

Table 5.3 shows that a Lm100 increase in tourist expenditure is estimated to give rise to an increase of Lm85.9 in GDP at market prices (equivalent to about a Lm77.3 increase in GDP at factor cost).

As was the case with the expenditure model, the input–output model just described is based on the assumption that government expenditure and investment expenditure are exogenous. If

Table 5.3 Aggregate tourism multipliers on value added derived from the input–output model

1	Keynesian sectoral personal income multiplier	0.557
2	Keynesian sectoral corporate savings multiplier	0.101
3	Keynesian sectoral taxation multiplier	0.201
	Implied GDP multiplier (1 + 2 + 3)	0.859
4	Keynesian sectoral imports multiplier	0.639

these expenditures are endogenized, the multiplier is somewhat greater, as explained earlier.

5.5 SOME IMPLICATIONS

5.5.1 Preliminaries

The aggregate multiplier magnitudes computed through the input–output model did not differ much from those obtained from the expenditure model, as can be seen by comparing Tables 5.2 and 5.3.[12] The reason for this is that care was taken to specify the expenditure model in such a manner as to render it consistent with the input–output model.

As stated elsewhere in this chapter, the expenditure macro-model has the advantage of requiring less data than the input–output model, but it has the disadvantage of not being suited for analysing how the multiplier process works through the different sectors of the economy. The input–output model, on the other hand, requires vast amounts of data, but it yields important information on the production interrelationships within the economy. The input–output model can therefore be used to trace the multiplier process through the various parts of the economy.

The input–output multiplier magnitudes produced in this study have a variety of uses for policy making. They provide the government with an indication of the degree to which sectors depend on each other and of the extent of relevant linkages. This may in turn help the government to take action to strengthen weak interconnections. The results may also identify possible supply rigidities arising from an increase in tourist expenditure and other exogenous variables. For example, the inverse matrix, augmented as described above, indicates that tourism expenditure generates direct, indirect and induced demand for agriultural inputs, a sector that might suffer from supply rigidities. Agriculture in Malta is heavily protected, is dominated by an ageing farm population, and may not be dynamic enough to adjust to sudden increases in tourist spending.

The inverse matrix also indicates that tourism expenditure has the highest impact on personal income when compared with other export-oriented industries, as explained above. This has important implications regarding the effect of exports on the Maltese economy. It shows, for example, that an aggregate Maltese exports multiplier conceals important variations between goods and services in the economic impact of exports.

5.5.2 Shortcomings of Multiplier Models

The results presented in this study should be interpreted with some caution, since the models utilized suffer from a number of shortcomings, notably (a) data deficiencies and (b) restrictive assumptions.

DATA LIMITATIONS

The problems associated with the data required for computing the multipliers in the present study have been described above. The modification of the Maltese input–output table for this purpose has been particularly time-consuming, and there is still much work to be done (see note 4). Data deficiencies currently limit the usefulness of the approach. However, this should not be considered as an argument against the use of multiplier models, but as an indication that better data are required. In the absence of sectoral data, multiplier analysis might have to be confined to expenditure macro-models of the type presented in this chapter, which, although very aggregative, may be of use for estimating the possible overall gains or losses accompanying changes in tourist expenditures.

RESTRICTIVE ASSUMPTIONS

Both the expenditure model and the input–output model presented in this paper are based on assumptions that may be too restrictive. It is assumed that prices remain constant in response to changes in demand, that there are no supply constraints, that technical coefficients and expenditure propensities remain constant, that imports are not substitutes for domestic production and that there is no effect on, or feedback from, the monetary sector. These and other restrictive assumptions are discussed by Bryden (1971), Copeland and Henry (1975), Diamond (1976) and Archer (1977).

Some researchers have suggested ways to ease these assumptions. For example, Sadler *et al.* (1973) have allowed for the possibility that not all income earners have the same propensity to consume, O'Connor and Henry (1975) propose a framework for considering imports as substitutes to domestic production, and Wanhill (1988) has developed a method for relaxing the 'no supply constraints' assumption. In general, when these assumptions are relaxed, more data would be required, in the absence of which such an exercise may not always be possible unless further assumptions are made.

Even if absence of data prevents the researcher from abandoning certain restrictive assumptions, the results of multiplier models could still have a useful application in the real world. One can, for example, estimate the impact of changes in certain expenditures, given different scenarios. It is to be expected, for example, that the multiplier effect associated with a given stimulus would be larger in the absence of excess capacity than otherwise. To assess this effect, the researcher can examine the sensitivity of results to different assumptions about capacity constraints.

It needs to be emphasized, in this regard, that all models make assumptions, and that it is of vital importance that the estimates produced from any model are interpreted in the light of the assumptions made.

5.6 CONCLUSION

This study has attempted to estimate the impact of tourism expenditure on the Maltese economy using two multiplier models, one based on expenditure and withdrawals propensities and the other on inter-industry relations. The results, although not identical, suggest that a Lm100 increase in tourist expenditure would give rise to an increase of between Lm80 and Lm90 in GNP, owing to direct, indirect and induced effects.

Because of the deficiencies in the Maltese input–output data, it was not possible to analyse the sectoral impact of tourism as thoroughly as would have been desirable. The Maltese National Accounts input–output table represents the services sector as one row and one column, and combines it with ship building and repair. Furthermore, there are no separate sectoral data for disposable personal income. Because of these limitations, it was necessary to carry out a disaggregation exercise based on secondary data and on assumed, though plausible, relationships in order to create the necessary rows and columns.

In spite of its limitations, the study has served three purposes. Firstly, it contains an attempt (perhaps the first of its kind for the Maltese economy) to organize and modify the Maltese input–output tables to render them suitable for simultaneously estimating the direct, indirect and induced effects of tourist expenditure on the inter-industry sales and primary inputs.

Secondly, the results produced from the two models yield useful information for policy making. In particular, the input–output multipliers may be used as guidance regarding the extent to which the different sectors respond to a change in tourism demand. In turn this may be helpful in identifying possible bottlenecks and supply rigidities.

Thirdly, the study may have served to make a case for improving the quality of input–output data in Malta. With such an improvement, the computation of input–output multipliers would be more reliable and the economic effects of tourism in Malta would be better evaluated.

Notes

1 Tourist expenditures as reported in the Maltese National Accounts statistics may be somewhat understated owing to the presence of unrecorded transactions (see Tarling and Rhodes, 1990).

2 Copeland and Henry (1975) have utilized marginal analyses in the context of an input–output model. Here average values for inter-industry relations and for primary input ratios are utilized.

3 Metwally (1977) and Briguglio (1987) based their multiplier estimates on marginal propensities using ordinary least squares. It should be noted that they did not consider tourist expenditure as a separate injection, and they did not therefore produce a tourism multiplier.

4 Similar macro-multiplier models have been estimated for 1986–8, with results very similar to the ones reported in this study, since the average propensities did not change in a significant manner. The 1985 results are reported here because they can be compared with the sectoral multipliers, which are based on the Maltese input–output table for 1985.

5 The GDP multiplier of 1.11 with respect to total government expenditure was estimated on the basis of the expenditure

macro-model, as a weighted average of current expenditure, with a multiplier of 1.39, and capital expenditure, with a multiplier of 0.85.

6 A discussion on the different multiplier concepts associated with input–output tables is given in Copeland and Henry (1975) and Archer (1977).

7 All the inter-industry purchases of 'foreign travel' come from the 'other production and trade' sector. When foreign travel was removed from this sector, there still remained a number of different industries, including retail and wholesale trades, transport services, and shipbuilding and repair. Clearly, there remains much work to be done to construct a properly disaggregated input–output table for Malta.

8 Sectoral self-employment income was estimated by decomposing aggregate self-employment income, as published in the National Accounts, on the basis of sectoral weights derived from the ratio of sectoral self-employment to sectoral hired-employment.

9 Sectoral personal income in the form of interest, rents and dividends was estimated by allocating fractions of the total, as published in the National Accounts of the Maltese Islands, on the basis of sectoral output shares, with some adjustments made for the banking sector.

10 Sectoral personal income tax was estimated by allocating total personal income tax, as published in the National Accounts, on the basis of sectoral personal income weights.

11 Sectoral corporate income tax was estimated by allocating total personal income tax, as published in the National Accounts, on the basis of weights represented by sectoral corporate income.

12 Howarth & Howarth (1989) and Tarling and Rhodes (1990) also produced multiplier estimates for the Maltese economy. The Howarth and Howarth tourist multipliers appear to be somewhat lower and Tarling and Rhodes's approximately equal to the ones produced in the present study. However, the methods used in these three studies differ from each other, and the results are therefore not strictly comparable.

References

Archer, B.H. (1977) *Tourism Multipliers: The State of the Art.* Cardiff: University of Wales Press.

Archer, B.H. and Wanhill, S.R.C. (1981) *The Economic Impact of Tourism on Mauritius.* Washington, DC: World Bank.

Briguglio, L. (1987) *Multiplier Effects in the Maltese Economy*. Malta: David Moore Publishing.

Briguglio, L. (1990) Technical appendix accompanying the paper Tourism Multipliers in the Maltese Economy, presented during the conference Tourism Research into the 1990s, Department of Economics, Durham University, December.

Bryden, J.M. (1971) Multiplying the tourist multiplier. *Social and Economic Studies*, **20**, 61-82.

Copeland, J.R. and Henry, E.W. (1975) *Irish Input-Output Income Multipliers, 1964 and 1968*. Dublin: Economic and Social Research Institute.

Curry, S. (1986) The economic impact of the tourist industry in the United Republic of Tanzania: an input-output analysis. *Industry and Development*, **19**, 55-75.

Diamond, J. (1976) Tourism development policy: a quantitative appraisal. *Bulletin of Economic and Social Research*, **28**, 36-50.

Fletcher, J.E. (1985) *The Economic Impact of International Tourism on the National Economy of Jamaica*. A report to the Government of Jamaica, WTO/UNDP RAS/83/007.

Fletcher, J.E. (1989) Input-output analysis and tourism impact studies. *Annals of Tourism Research*, **16**, 514-29.

Howarth & Howarth (1989) *The Economic Impact of Tourism. The Maltese Islands Tourism Development Plan*. Reproduced in *Economic Survey '89*, pp. 139-48. Malta: Office of the Prime Minister.

Lin, T. and Sung, Y. (1983) Hong Kong. In Lin, T. and Pye, E.A. (eds) *Tourism in Asia: The Economic Impact*. Singapore: Singapore University Press.

Liu, J.C. (1986) Relative economic contributions of visitor groups in Hawaii. *Journal of Travel Research*, Summer, 2-9.

Metwally, M.M. (1977) *The Structure and Performance of the Maltese Economy*. Malta: A.C. Aquilina & Co.

Norton, D.A.G. (1982) Export tourism input-output multipliers for Ireland. In *Quarterly Economic Commentary*. Dublin: Economic and Social Research Council.

O'Connor, E. and Henry, E.W. (1975) *Input Output Analysis and Its Applications*. London: Charles Griffin & Co.

Sadler, P.G. Archer, B.H. and Owen, C.B. (1973) *Regional Income Multipliers - The Anglesey Study*. Cardiff: University of Wales Press.

Tarling, R.J. and Rhodes, J. (1990) *A Study of the Economic Impact of Tourism on the Economy of Malta.* Malta: PA Cambridge Consultants for the Ministry of Tourism.

Waldorf, W.H. (1969) *An Econometric Model of the Maltese Economy.* Malta: Office of the Prime Minister.

Wanhill, S.R.C. (1988) Tourism multipliers under capacity constraints. *Service Industries Journal,* 8, 136–42.

6 Tourism Manpower Planning: The Case of Nepal

Stephen Wanhill

6.1 MANPOWER PLANNING

6.1.1 Basic Principles

At the micro level, manpower planning is a system that tries to match recruitment and wastage so that at any one time the staffing levels in an organization are consistent with the policies of that organization. Thus any analysis or quantification has to consider three principal aspects:

- future manpower needs;
- losses through retirement and other forms of wastage;
- replacement policies.

Within the economy at large, the availability of manpower is inextricably bound up with population trends and the education system. This is based on the reasonable notion that a well-educated labour force is essential for the creation of wealth in a modern economy. Sainsbury (1989) argues that to maintain a high standard of living a country must add value to its resources. In the past limited access to capital and technology enabled some countries to maintain a high standard of living, but increasingly all factors of production other than labour are freely mobile around the world, and so more than ever countries must fall back on the skills and cumulative learning of their workforce to maintain their standard of living. As a positive example of this doctrine, Sainsbury cites Japan as a country that has become a leading economic power with few natural endowments, but with an extremely well-educated population. On the downside, he cites the United States of America, whose declining economic strength can to some extent be attributed to failures in its education and training systems.

Manpower planning is a strategic matter involving long-term considerations of human resource development. Too often, however, manpower is the subject of short-term tactical adjustments. Organizations react to fluctuations in profitability by cutting out staff training, recruitment bans, early retirements, voluntary and compulsory redundancy, and so on, in the hope that these changes will solve their problems, when the task is for managers at a senior level to analyse what business they are in, what the objectives are and how they are going to adjust the business to meet changing conditions.

Imposing tactical adjustments on the staff may only deepen the problem: in this respect, the tourism industry, particularly hotels and restaurants, has gained itself a poor image in many countries. Excessive concentration on short-term profitability has acted as a disincentive for good personnel policies and staff development. Managers frequently hold the notion that labour supply can be found in competing organizations and this in turn engenders in employees the view that they have sole responsibility for their own careers, which they develop by changing companies as opposed to jobs within a company.

Maintenance of a good workforce depends on effective recruitment and retention: the opposite is defective recruitment and high labour turnover, which can cause a downward spiral. Placing the burden of adjustment on employees can open managers to hasty recruitment when the upturn comes. Poor choices may discourage promising recruits, and inadequate training and the lack of career prospects will lead to high wastage. Staff leave, spreading unfavourable impressions, and this leads managers, who are desperate to fill vacancies, to lower standards and engage ill-trained staff who take out their experiences on the customers. The firm then finds itself being pushed into further difficulties that could have been avoided if manpower had been properly considered from the beginning. The cost in human terms and the misallocations of resources that ensue are the fundamental justifications for having strategic manpower policies at both government and private sector levels.

6.1.2 Education

The link between education and the skills base of the labour force is in reality somewhat loosely geared. This is because skills are produced in formal and informal ways, and the education system has wider objectives than employment for national prosperity. In many countries the majority of the labour force have acquired their skills outside any formal system of education or training, merely by informal learning on-the-job. Vocational education and training is a way to tighten the link between education and the skills base in the labour force and thereby speed up the acquisition of those same skills. However, even here the curriculum has to be generalized because the output is not tied to the demands of a particular employer.

The tightest of all possible relationships only takes place within in-service training because the course structure is intimately connected to the employer's own establishment. A failure to understand this on the part of employers is an ongoing source of disputes between practitioners and teachers in vocational education schools. There is also a distinction to be made between education and training. Principally, education is for life skills while training is for immediate use in a job. Precisely where the balance is struck depends on where the line is being drawn between developing an individual or an efficient employee, and on the capacity of that individual.

6.1.3 Manpower Modelling

Despite the inexactitude of mapping the education sector onto the labour force skills of the national economy, governments have placed very little reliance on the market mechanism to provide the necessary skills, but rather have intervened in the education sector on a massive scale. For example, primary education, which is considered a prelude to development, is almost universally provided by the state. This is because movements of wages and salaries in labour markets do not generally adjust at a speed and in a manner that would be effective at eliminating skill deficits and surpluses in the required time frame. Labour markets are hedged about by institutional, political, social and cultural factors that confound the logic of economic behaviour; society does not view favourably an employer who releases all his or her workers simply because a cheaper source can be found elsewhere. Thus, to secure a nation's economic future, governments have

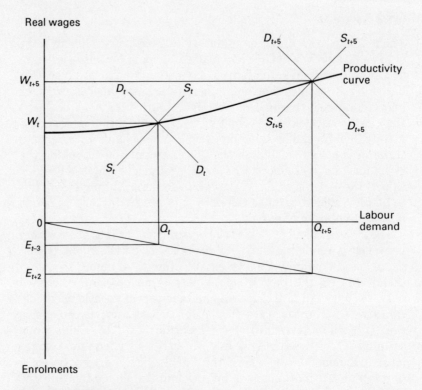

Figure 6.1 Manpower planning model.

become major suppliers of education and training and in so doing
have taken on the responsibility of maintaining a reasonable balance between the demand and supply of skills; however, because
of cost and the difficulties of manpower planning, under-provision
is more likely to be the norm than over-provision.

A diagrammatic exposition of manpower modelling is illustrated in Figure 6.1. The two demand curves D_t and D_{t+5} are
positioned by the output of the economy and the state of technology, which determines capital/labour ratios. W_t is the level
of real wages, and the supply curves for labour, S_t and S_{t+5}, are
only moderately sensitive to changes within the relevant range
of real wages, but shift in the longer run in response to the rate
of return to investment in education and training. The diagram
is expositional and the model looks at labour requirements rather
than the dynamics of short-run supply adjustment in the labour
market. In reality, short-run supply curves are somewhat more
complicated than shown because the individual is not solely
motivated by economic forces to change jobs when earnings

differentials exist for the same skills in different firms. The existing demand for labour, OQ_t, is maintained by annual enrolments in the education sector of OE_{t-3} (assuming a three-year output lag). At the end of a five-year planning period output is expected to rise sufficiently to justify the labour demand schedule D_{t+5} and the rewards are such to cause a shift in the supply curve to S_{t+5}. The supply and demand adjustment process is traced out along a curve of rising labour productivity, which may come about through new technology, through transferring functions to the customer as in self-service or through a rise in the qualification and experience profile of employees. The realized demand for labour is now OQ_{t+5} and the expectation of this has caused educational planners to increase enrolments to OE_{t+2}.

In common with other planning activities, the practical steps required to implement the model described in Figure 6.1 are broadly as follows:

- assessment of the current occupational distribution of the workforce, which is mapped on to the general educational level of each occupational group;
- the production of five-yearly and frequently ten-yearly manpower forecasts with respect to planned targets for the national output;
- projections of supply from existing trends in the education system;
- estimates of surpluses and deficits;
- the laying down of a strategy to implement projects in the education sector to bring demand and supply as close together as might be deemed practical.

It is important to note that at the company level few organizations would try to forecast and recruit exact job categories, save for key personnel in specialist areas, such as kitchen work in hotels. This is because people are often freely transferred from one department to another and an individual may have multiple skills. Organizations tend to recruit by general skill level and then allocate recruits to particular tasks after a period of induction in the company culture. This is not to say that, upon contemplating a period of expansion, it is not useful for a company to know what the manning levels should be for the departments so that areas with particular shortages may be easily identified.

If the above is true of organizations it is no less true at the macro forecasting level. Assessment of manpower needs at a

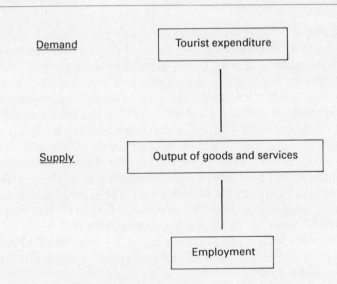

Figure 6.2 Impact of tourism.

national level can only be realistically accomplished at the broad level of the skills base, such as managerial, clerical and operative skill requirements, subdivided if necessary by functional area.

6.2 MANPOWER IN TOURISM

6.2.1 Nature of Tourism

Tourism is not an industry defined by any standard industrial classification. It is demand led; its influence pervades many sectors of the economy and so it is impossible to measure the employment created by tourism through examination of the supply side or tourism-related sectors. For example, a good deal of employment in the restaurant sector has little to do with tourism. Many restaurants exist mainly to serve local demand. This is also true, to varying degrees, for shopping, transport, entertainment and several other areas where tourists spend their money. Thus the only way to calculate the total employment effects of tourism is to trace through the impact of tourist expenditure on the economy in the manner illustrated in Figure 6.2.

The direction of economic causation runs from tourist expenditure through output to employment, the last relationship being characterized by the technology of the economy. Thus, in order to quantify manpower requirements for the tourist industry, it is necessary to have an integrated model that links the demands of tourists to the economy as a whole. Too often projections of manpower are made on forecasts of visitor numbers or the expected development of hotel rooms. These fail to examine linkages and feedback effects, leaving manpower planning only partial in nature. A much more complete scenario may be obtained by using an input–output table, which provides the required integrated system to model the effects of tourism demand.

The input–output table is a common planning tool and many countries that embark on national plans (usually of five years) use such a table to benchmark the planning process. It is well suited to tourism analysis because of the way it picks up inter-industry linkages and hence can be used to model manpower requirements generated by future tourist spending. Another alternative would be to use supply-side employment functions relating jobs to output as measured by value added. However, as before, these are likely to give incomplete coverage and while they may offer some advantage in construction by employing non-linear variables, they are normally linear in coefficients and include the Leontief assumption of constancy in the proportion of intermediate purchases to gross output. The latter enables output to be measured by value added and serves to reduce any superiority employment functions may have over the input–output table.

6.2.2 Model Structure

BASIC EQUATIONS

The structure of a tourism input–output table consists of a series of linear equations linking each sector of the economy to tourism expenditure at the destination. Lino Briguglio has outlined the fundamentals of the input–output approach in Chapter 5. Here a slightly different notation is employed, as follows:

$$\mathbf{X}_t + A\mathbf{X}_t + \mathbf{T}_t \qquad (6.1)$$

where $\mathbf{X}_t$ is an $n \times 1$ vector of gross output generated by tourism expenditure at time t; A is an $n \times n$ matrix of coefficients representing in column form purchases by the jth sector from all other sectors; $\mathbf{T}_t$ is an $n \times 1$ vector of tourist expenditure at time t – some cells may be blank, corresponding to sectors where tourists do not spend their money.

The system (6.1) may be solved for $\mathbf{X}_t$ in terms of tourist expenditure through the following relationship:

$$\mathbf{X}_t = (I - A)^{-1}\mathbf{T}_t \tag{6.2}$$

where the coefficients of $(I - A)^{-1}$ represent the amount of direct and indirect output needed to supply one unit of the jth product to meet tourists' demands. Further, let

$$\mathbf{L}_t = E\mathbf{X}_t \tag{6.3}$$

where $\mathbf{L}_t$ is an $n \times 1$ vector of labour requirements in each sector; E is an $n \times n$ diagonal matrix of employment coefficients per unit of gross output. Then, through substitution of system (6.2) into (6.3) it is possible to estimate the volume of direct and indirect employment created in each sector by total tourist expenditure:

$$\mathbf{L}_t = E(I - A)^{-1}\mathbf{T}_t \tag{6.4}$$

FORECASTING

Equation system (6.4) may be used to forecast manpower needs. Suppose in period $t + n$ the volume and pattern of tourist expenditure is predicted to be $\mathbf{T}_{t+n}$: then by substitution into (6.4) the future labour requirements in period $t + n$ are:

$$\mathbf{L}_{t+n} = E(I - A)^{-1}\mathbf{T}_{t+n} \tag{6.5}$$

However, system (6.5) supposes that there is no productivity growth in the labour force; but it may be that labour is becoming more efficient, so that, for a given size of labour force, output grows with time. Using system (6.3) we have the sequence:

$$\mathbf{X}_t = E^{-1}\mathbf{L}_t$$
$$\mathbf{X}_{t+1} = (I + p)\mathbf{X}_t = E^{-1}\mathbf{L}_t \tag{6.6}$$
$$\mathbf{X}_{t+n} = (I + p)^n\mathbf{X}_t = E^{-1}\mathbf{L}_t$$

where $I + p$ is an $n \times n$ diagonal matrix of productivity growth factors for each sector.

From this it follows that the amount of labour required in period $t + n$ to produce $\mathbf{X}_t$ is:

$$\mathbf{L}_{t+n} = (I + p)^{-n}\mathbf{L}_t = (I + p)^{-n}E\mathbf{X}_t = E(I + p)^{-n}\mathbf{X}_t \tag{6.7}$$

If output is also growing due to expanding tourist expenditure, then substituting $\mathbf{X}_{t+n}$ from (6.5) into (6.7) gives:

$$\mathbf{L}_{t+n} = E\,(I + p)^{-n}\,(I - A)^{-1}\mathbf{T}_{t+n} \qquad (6.8)$$

REPLACEMENT

System (6.8) merely determines the manpower needs of each sector. It does not allow for replacement. Every year there will be persons leaving the labour force through retirement and other processes of natural wastage. For a static labour force this will draw out a pattern over time as follows:

$$\mathbf{L}_t$$

$$\mathbf{L}_{t+1} = \mathbf{L}_t - r\mathbf{L}_t = (I - r)\mathbf{L}_t \qquad (6.9)$$

$$\mathbf{L}_{t+n} = \mathbf{L}_{t+n-1} - r\mathbf{L}_{t+n-1} = (I - r)^n\mathbf{L}_t$$

where $I - r$ is an $n \times n$ diagonal matrix of coefficients representing the fraction that remains of the labour force after retirements.

Suppose that after n periods it is required that the labour force available, say $\mathbf{L}_{t+n}^*$, should be as it was originally. This implies that the numbers retiring would have been compensated for by replacement. Thus:

$$\mathbf{L}_{t+n}^* = \mathbf{L}_t > \mathbf{L}_{t+n}$$

It therefore follows from (6.9) that:

$$\mathbf{L}_{t+n}^* = (I - r)^{-n}\mathbf{L}_{t+n} \qquad (6.10)$$

Substituting system (6.8) into (6.10) gives a complete tourism manpower model which allows for both productivity and retirements. That is:

$$\mathbf{L}_{t+n}^* = E\,(I - r)^{-n}\,(I + p)^{-n}\,(I - A)^{-1}\mathbf{T}_{t+n} \qquad (6.11)$$

If $\mathbf{R}_{t+n}$ represents a vector of accumulated replacements over n periods, then:

$$\mathbf{R}_{t+n} = \mathbf{L}_{t+n}^* - \mathbf{L}_{t+n} = E\,[\,(I - r)^{-n} - I\,]$$

$$(I + p)^{-n}(I - A)^{-1}\mathbf{T}_{t+n} \qquad (6.12)$$

UWCC LIBRARY

Table 6.1 Nepal tourism input–output sectors

Intermediate transactions sectors

1	Five-star hotels	14	Local traders
2	Four-star hotels	15	Handicrafts
3	Three-star hotels	16	Carpets
4	Two-star hotels	17	Garments
5	One-star hotels	18	Alcoholic beverages
6	Non-star hotels	19	Non-alcoholic beverages
7	Other accommodation	20	Printing, publicity, stationery
8	Restaurants	21	Textiles
9	Travel agencies	22	Food
10	Trekking agencies	23	Communications
11	Airlines	24	Repairs and maintenance
12	Cargo agencies	25	Utilities
13	Local transport		

Primary sectors

26	Income from employment	30	Profit/loss
27	Rent	31–33	Indirect taxes/subsidies
28	Depreciation	34–36	Imports

6.3 TOURISM MANPOWER IN NEPAL

6.3.1 Using the Model

To illustrate how the manpower model developed in Section 6.2 can be used for planning and forecasting, the example of Nepal is taken as a case study. The Nepal Rastra Bank (1989) has put together an input–output table which refers specifically to tourism. The sectors covered by the bank's model are shown in Table 6.1, the structure closely following that of Burger (1978). The data required to service the model were put together from a number of sources during a much larger study of tourism in Nepal commissioned by the Asian Development Bank (1990).

The emphasis was on employment generation from foreign tourist spending, so the manpower forecasts could only be undertaken once the future overseas marketing strategy for Nepal had been worked out. The basic model as shown by equation (6.4) was used to obtain a positional statement on the number of employees directly and indirectly attributable to foreign tourist spending for the year 1988, as presented in Table 6.2. These values were obtained after calibrating the model against known supply-side estimates derived from manpower surveys of the tourism related sectors carried out by New ERA (1988). The Nepal Rastra Bank model did not include the public sector, so separate estimates

Table 6.2 Estimated employment attributable directly and indirectly to foreign tourism expenditure, 1988

Category	Number
Five- to three-star hotels	3 055
Two- and one-star hotels	904
Non-star hotels, guest houses and lodges	3 041
Restaurants	3 917
Travel agencies	2 352
Trekking agencies	1 665
Handicrafts	2 276
Carpets	842
Garments	885
Other sectors	
Local transport	544
Local traders	768
Other suppliers to the tourist industry	2 420
Total	22 669

had to be obtained from the ministries concerned. It is estimated that 4044 people are employed in the public sector, although not all these employees were necessarily dependent on the volume of foreign tourism. This is not the end of the story: there is a considerable volume of seasonable employment generated for the hill people by mountaineering expeditions and trekking agencies. The numbers for 1988 were estimated to be 10 839 for mountaineering and 72 156 for trekking.

The values shown in Table 6.2 provided the basis for projecting net additional manpower requirements to service foreign tourism. The tourism expenditure forecasts resulting from the proposed marketing strategy were fed into the model structure given by equation (6.8). The essence of the strategy was repositioning the tourist product in favour of the high-spending groups who want quality hotels and the commensurate staffing ratios that go with them. To this were added productivity estimates obtained from interviews and the examination of trends in the relevant sectors. The following productivity factors were used:

Five- to three-star hotels: 2 per cent
All other accommodation: 1 per cent
Travel and trekking agencies: 2 per cent
Other suppliers to the tourist industry: 2.5 per cent
Remaining sectors: 0 per cent

Table 6.3 Target employment demands created by foreign tourist expenditure in Nepal to 2000

Category	1990	1995	2000	Growth 1990–1995	Growth 1995–2000
Tourism-related sectors					
Five- to three-star hotels	3 590	7 860	11 790	4 270	3 930
Two- and one-star hotels	980	1 850	2 380	870	530
Non-star hotels, guest houses and lodges	3 280	6 020	7 490	2 740	1 470
Restaurants	4 280	8 440	11 360	4 160	2 920
Travel agencies	2 680	5 350	7 390	2 670	2 040
Trekking agencies	1 890	3 770	5 160	1 880	1 390
Handicrafts	2 560	5 500	8 170	2 940	2 670
Carpets	950	2 050	3 050	1 100	1 000
Garments	970	2 040	2 930	1 070	890
Sub-total	21 180	42 880	59 720	21 700	16 840
Other sectors					
Local transport	600	1 270	1 850	670	580
Local traders	860	1 860	2 740	1 000	880
Other suppliers to the tourist industry	2 730	5 270	7 010	2 540	1 740
Totals	25 370	51 280	71 320	25 910	20 040

Values are rounded to the nearest ten units.

Productivity in service industries is normally low, in the order of 0–3 per cent, and may even be negative in labour-surplus economies where people create their own work. The first reason for low productivity rates is that customers demand labour services directly and not in an embodied form, as would occur with the production of a physical product. Secondly, in labour-surplus economies, as for example in Asia, labour is so cheap that having large numbers of staff in hotels to deal with guests does not add much to costs but can add greatly to perceived quality.

The results from using the model are shown in Table 6.3. Public sector requirements are not included since these were planned separately by reference to the appropriate departments.

Recruitment growth or total additional requirement for man-power has to make allowance for labour turnover. Survey evidence in Nepal revealed low wastage rates. The reasons for this appeared to be: (a) the tourist industry was comparatively young and so there were few retirements; (b) there was relative job security in an uncertain and over-supplied labour market, although over-supply did not apply to skilled labour, which accounted for a higher percentage of staff turnover in five- to three-star hotels. Employment security is enshrined in the Nepal Factory/Factory Workers' Act 1959, and subsequent amendments. This lays down: minimum wages for unskilled workers, currently RP 532 per month; hours of work, currently 48 per week; amounts of overtime, three hours per day; and procedures for dismissal.

Interviews with various organizations confirmed low labour turnover, normally 2–3 per cent, with the highest rates being recorded among the quality star-rated hotels, and the lowest rates, less than 1 per cent, in the wildlife resorts, the travel trade and small family businesses. At the time when the interviews were conducted, hoteliers were reporting rising labour turnover, up to 5 per cent, in response to recruitment overseas, particularly the Middle East. Such turnover rates include inter-industry movement, so replacement rates will be less. Clearly some allowance has to be made for replacement and so the following wastage rates have been used:

Five- to three-star hotels: 2.5 per cent until 1995, 2.0 per cent thereafter
Two- and one-star hotels: 2.0 per cent until 1995, 1.5 per cent thereafter
Non-star hotels, guest houses and lodges: 1 per cent
Restaurants: 1 per cent
All other sectors: 0.75 per cent

The results of applying such replacement rates to the model defined by equation (6.11) are shown in Table 6.4. These may be compared with the results shown in Table 6.3. The effects are to raise manpower recruitment in the tourism-related sectors by 12.6 per cent above net additional demand during the period 1990–5 and 20.4 per cent for the rest of the decade. Simple annual averages are shown in the last two columns of Table 6.4. These give an indication of the amount of recruitment that must take place each year to meet the demands of an expanding international tourist industry.

6.3.2 Model Reliability

All quantitative economic models are in effect statistical caricatures of the real world. They are usually linear in structure because the exact underlying processes are often unknown

Table 6.4 Target manpower requirements arising from foreign tourist expenditure in Nepal to 2000

Tourism-related sectors	Recruitment growth		Annual averages	
	1990–1995	1995–2000	1990–1995	1995–2000
Five to three star hotels	5 330	5 180	1 066	1 036
One and two star hotels	1 070	720	214	144
Non-star hotels, guest houses and lodges	3 050	1 860	610	372
Restaurants	4 600	3 510	920	702
Travel agencies	2 880	2 320	576	464
Trekking agencies	2 020	1 590	404	318
Handicrafts	3 150	2 980	630	596
Carpets	1 180	1 120	236	224
Garments	1 150	1 000	230	200
Totals	24 430	20 280	4 886	4 056

Values are rounded to the nearest ten units.

and because linear approximations make estimation easier. Most input–output models are based on an industrial census and therefore have a sound foundation in terms of data reliability. Their disadvantage is that they are taking a 'snapshot' of the economy at one time and so for planning purposes they must resort to the law of large numbers that fluctuations on average cancel each other out.

Any problems in quantifying manpower needs are usually outweighed by the inherent weakness of manpower forecasts used for educational purposes. This is the looseness of the relationship between the objectives of the education system and the manpower a nation needs to meet its economic objectives. The common-sense approach is to use the manpower forecasts to guide the direction of the education system in terms of skills provision and knowledge acquisition, but at the same time to ensure that government provision is on the low-risk side of the estimates. This can be achieved by under-provision of courses or ensuring that the courses themselves have a strong element of transferable skills.

6.3.3 Tourism Education and Training in Nepal

Although it may be deemed desirable, it was neither possible nor necessary for the education system in Nepal to train all the labour for the tourism industry. Five- and four-star hotels preferred, in most instances, to train their own operative staff provided they had a good basic education (the School Leaving Certificate) and were competent in English. What was important was training to supply the key skill areas of the tourist industry. These were employees who may be destined in time to become supervisors, middle managers and then senior managers or executives, and who will also have the task of training their subordinates.

There were three institutions that could be considered to provide vocational education and training in some form for the tourism industry: Tribhuvan University, the Hotel Management and Tourism Training Centre (HMTTC), and the technical schools of the Council for Technical Education and Vocational Training (CTEVT). Tribhuvan University had no courses in tourism, but provided graduates, mainly to the travel trade, from a variety of non-specialist backgrounds. However, the university was expanding at a rate that was far in excess of available resources, with the result that staff salaries were taking an increasing share of the budget, leaving little over for equipment, materials and development. It has to be remembered that vocational education is expensive and it is difficult to obtain recognition from the industry if the teaching facilities are inadequate, the equipment obsolete and the staff inexperienced. From this standpoint, it was quickly realized that the university could not resource vocational education courses for the tourist industry.

The provision made by the nine technical schools controlled by the CTEVT was at secondary level, none of which had any courses in tourism and hospitality. The council was proposing a further four schools, of which one was likely to have courses in lodge management, handicrafts and trekking and mountaineering. Thus the burden of any future educational initiatives for the tourist industry in Nepal would have to fall on the HMTTC, which was already providing a wide range of tertiary level courses. The centre had an output of over 1000 students, but more than half had been taking basic courses in their home location run by the centre's Mobile Training Unit. Running the manpower model up to the year 2000 would give an indication of the level of supervisory and management course provision that would be needed at the centre's headquarters in Kathmandu.

By linking the data on occupational status collected by the Nepal Rastra Bank with the survey results of New ERA (1988), it was possible to use the manpower model to forecast the skill requirements of the tourist industry that were likely to be generated by foreign tourist expenditure over the next decade. The

Table 6.5 Target skilled manpower requirements in the accommodation and restaurant sector

Category	Recruitment growth	
	1990–1995	1995–2000
Star-rated hotels		
Kitchen	505	464
Housekeeping	445	410
Food and beverage	411	378
Front office	293	269
Central administration	466	429
Totals	2 120	1 950
Non-star hotels, guest houses and lodges		
Kitchen and food and beverage	810	494
Housekeeping	337	206
Other areas	393	240
Totals	1 540	940
Restaurants		
Kitchen	963	734
Food and beverage	936	713
Other areas	411	313
Totals	2 310	1 760

Totals rounded to the nearest ten units.

results for the accommodation and restaurant sectors are shown in Table 6.5; the values do include an allowance for wastage.

For small properties and restaurants, the multi-function staffing that takes place in such businesses will blur the divisions that have been made and therefore they are to be regarded as indicative only. Even for star-rated properties, vocational education and training, with the exception of the kitchen, will be generalized to varying degrees because of possible movement within divisions and different company cultures. The kitchen in luxury hotels is a specialist activity and this has to be regarded as a prime skill area. Attracting good kitchen staff is and will continue to be a priority for the hotel sector in Nepal.

The likely skill requirements of the travel trade are given in Table 6.6. For travel agents key skill areas are guiding and tour operation, ticketing and the management of activities in central administration: accounts, sales, marketing and so on. Priorities for trekking and rafting agencies are guiding, provision of cooks and some growth in adventure tourism.

Table 6.6 Target skilled manpower requirements in the travel trade

Category	Recruitment growth	
	1990–1995	1995–2000
Travel agents		
Guiding and tour operation	585	470
Ticketing	387	311
Trekking	80	64
Cargo	194	156
Central administration	484	389
Totals	1 730	1 390
Trekking and rafting agents		
Guiding and tour operation	390	308
Ticketing	19	15
Trekking cooks	194	154
Adventure tourism[a]	9	7
Central administration	149	118
Totals	810	640

Totals rounded to the nearest ten units.
[a] Includes rafting, hang gliding and other such developments.

The results of the model shown in Tables 6.5 and 6.6 were used to formulate a strategy for hospitality and tourism education in Nepal. In outline this strategy was:

1 To give the HMTTC autonomous status so that it would be in the same position as the university with regard to controlling its curriculum and conducting examinations.
2 To develop the curriculum around the following core activities:
   • basic craft and skills training;
   • management development;
   • short course programme;
   • mobile training;
   • skills testing.
3 To expand and refurbish the physical plant.
4 Gradually to devolve some of the lower level activities to the CTEVT – for example, skills testing and basic craft work.
5 To provide an ongoing programme of staff development.
6 To provide technical assistance through appropriate aid agencies.

6.4 CONCLUSION

The use of an input–output model of the tourism sector permitted the construction of a complete manpower planning model for Nepal in which forecasts were dependent on:

- the market strategy in relation to the level of tourist spending and the pattern of that spending;
- the technical structure of the inter-industry matrix;
- productivity and wastage rates in the labour market.

By manipulating the above information the model can be calibrated to produce target manpower forecasts that are consistent with the overall scenario for the tourism sector and enable the formulation of an educational strategy for the sector.

Note

The author would like to acknowledge the contribution made by friends and colleagues at Touche Ross, particularly Oliver Bennett, who led the project mission, Peter Blok of the Asian Development Bank and the numerous officials of the Department of Tourism in Nepal, especially Dipendra Purush Dhakal, the Director General.

References

Asian Development Bank and Ministry of Tourism, Nepal (1990) *Nepal Tourism Development Programme*. Manila.

Burger, V. (1978) The economic impact of tourism in Nepal: an input–output analysis. PhD thesis, Cornell University.

Nepal Rastra Bank (1989) *Income and Employment Generation from Tourism in Nepal*. Kathmandu: Nepal Rastra Bank, Tourism Study Project Office.

New ERA (1988) *Manpower Projections for the Tourism Sector*. Kathmandu: HMTTC.

Sainsbury, D. (1989) *Education for Wealth Creation*. Sheffield: TSB Forum.

7 Monitoring and Evaluating a Tourism Development Programme: A Study of Chepstow

Marion Jackson and David Bruce

7.1 INTRODUCTION

This chapter reviews the issues and research methods involved in setting up a monitoring and evaluation programme for a five-year grant-aided project to develop tourism in Chepstow, a market town of some 11 000 people in south-east Wales. It is suggested that an appropriate framework is one that defines the aim of the project as the maximization of turnover due to tourism in Chepstow, within certain environmental and social constraints. The choice and application of appropriate methodologies, and the progress during the first year of the research, are detailed below.

In 1989 Monmouth Borough Council (MBC) successfully bid to the Wales Tourist Board (WTB) for funding under the board's Local Enterprise and Development (LEAD) initiatives to develop tourism in Chepstow. £1 million is being made available to the council over the five years 1990–4 for capital grant-aid to expand existing private sector tourist facilities and/or new enterprises and to improve infrastructure, traffic management schemes and pedestrianization, street furniture, tourist information centres and signposting. MBC claims that the LEAD funding will lever significant private sector funding and generate increased activity and tourism-related employment in the town.

Unusually, the borough council included a commitment to monitor the progress of the project, and to amend the scheme as necessary in the light of interim reports from a monitoring team, in its bid for funding. This work is being undertaken by a multi-disciplinary team from the Tourism and Leisure Research Unit at Bristol Polytechnic, including the authors of this chapter.

Chepstow, claimed by the borough council to be 'the first historic town in Wales', is situated near the mouth of the river Wye on the English–Welsh border. There is a well preserved eleventh-century Norman castle, a museum and a factory shop owned by Stuart Crystal. Up the hill from the castle, the old heart of the town is protected by the thirteenth-century Port Wall and contains other historic features that are little known to outsiders. Newer development has taken place beyond the wall and many residents commute to work in Newport, Bristol or Cardiff. At the foot of the Wye Valley, some 7 miles from Tintern Abbey and on the edge of the Forest of Dean, Chepstow could be the natural centre for the growth in tourism all round it. Twenty million people live within two hours' drive but Chepstow is described as probably the shortest-stay visitor destination in Wales.

The numbers visiting the castle have dropped since the 1987 opening of the A48 by-pass. Previously the Severn Bridge had a similar, probably more drastic, effect; in the 1990s the new Severn Crossing, if built, will take motorway traffic even further away. Chepstow tourism is in danger of fulfilling the dictum that 'all that is human must retrograde if it do not advance' (Gibbon, 1784). It is therefore supremely suitable for promotion under the LEAD initiative.

The monitoring and evaluation process must measure the results in terms that reflect the objectives of the funding body (WTB) and the commissioning authority (MBC). These are defined in terms of job generation, raising the level of turnover in the town, and stimulating investment in the extension and upgrading of existing tourist facilities and in the establishment of new ones (Section 7.2). The impact of tourism on any defined local area (discussed in Section 7.3) is conventionally seen in three dimensions: economic, physical/environmental and social/cultural (Mathieson and Wall, 1982, p. 3; Pearce, 1989, p. 183). All three are to be considered in the Chepstow study.

A five-year longitudinal study of this nature enables the research team to analyse changes in the visitor profile, the numbers coming to Chepstow, the length of stay and the volume and pattern of expenditure as well as the wider impacts of tourism. Such longitudinal studies are necessary to identify changes in visitor behaviour at the local level and could confer a marketing advantage on destinations that have access to this knowledge (Shaw and Williams, 1989, pp. 248, 250). Furthermore, they allow monitoring of the host community's attitudes to visitors in terms of Doxey's irritation index (Murphy, 1985, p. 124).

The agreed research consists of six elements:

1 Annual attitude surveys and pedestrian counts, among residents and visitors.
2 Annual surveys of the commercial effects of visitors on shops, hotels and other employers in the town and surrounding area.
3 Surveys of the cost effects of visitors on local authority and other agencies.
4 Economic and environmental analysis of costs, benefits and multiplier effects.
5 Analysis of market trends and perceptions of Chepstow as an attractor of tourists.
6 Annual recommendations for the scheme's amendment and development.

The requirement for annual recommendations allows the research team to influence the direction of the programme and outcome. The work is being extended to assess the wider impact on the local community and will be used to reflect community views and aspirations.

How far progress directed towards the achievement of fairly narrow economic objectives should be influenced by local community views therefore becomes a key issue but, in any case, positive community involvement is essential to the success of the whole LEAD project in Chepstow. Ideally progress should be controlled and directed to minimize conflict between the different interest groups that inevitably exist in such a situation. Section 7.2 discusses criteria for evaluating success in this context.

7.2 SUCCESS OF THE LEAD INITIATIVE: SOME CRITERIA

Evaluation of local economic initiatives, whether tourism-related or not, has not been widely undertaken. Coulson suggests that this may be partly because of a political desire to avoid possibly unfavourable judgements and partly because evaluation methodologies are uncertain and subjective (in Campbell, 1990, p. 174).

He contrasts a 'rational' model of evaluation, where the objectives of investment are clearly defined at the start of a programme and against which the outcome can be assessed, with 'action-research', where objectives are not fully defined at the start and are expected to change as the programme progresses.

The objectives of the LEAD initiative in Chepstow, as seen by the commissioning borough council, were to create extra jobs and to raise the level of turnover and investment in the town. But the wide range of the research they commissioned, and the requirement to modify the programme as interim results and recommendations are made known, suggests that the 'action-research' concept is appropriate here.

Although Coulson lists ten objectives for local economic development projects, he recognizes that recent discussion has concentrated on job creation (Campbell 1990, pp. 178–80). Tan *et al.* (1983) used this criterion in evaluating the impact of English Tourist Board (ETB) grant-aid and certainly it is an important aspect of tourist development policies, but it should not be the only indicator of success or failure. In one sense the problem is relatively simple in a small centre like Chepstow, with little prospect of major new local job alternatives (although a hoped-for supermarket could siphon off tourism labour). In a place the size of Bristol policy-makers face more options in job-generating policies in the inner city (Jackson and Bruce, 1988).

The WTB applies its normal Section 4 (Development of Tourism Act 1969) criteria to LEAD projects, including the jobs to be generated, the volume of private sector investment to be levered by the public-sector injection (aiming for a ratio of £3 to £1), the viability of the proposed project and evidence that public-sector pump priming is necessary for it to happen at all. In addition, under the LEAD initiative, the WTB was looking for partners from local authorities and the private sector in the area. Here again job generation is seen as one of the main criteria of success.

In fact, the initial employment and training survey undertaken in Chepstow with funding from the Training Agency suggested that a shortage of labour may hinder potential tourism development in the town as the LEAD programme develops. Unemployment is below the Welsh average and the image of the industry among job seekers in the town was poor (Chepstow LEAD Initiative Tourism Development Final Report, April 1990). The town is increasingly a dormitory for people working in Bristol, Newport and Cardiff, and simple employment maximization may therefore be an inadequate criterion for judging the success of the Chepstow LEAD project.

It is concluded that, for the purposes of this monitoring and evaluation programme, the aim of the LEAD project should be defined as:

the maximization of turnover in Chepstow, within constraints imposed by the varying objectives of the different elements in the Chepstow community.

A focus on levels of turnover and associated job creation may be thought to limit the criteria of success for LEAD but the identification and examination of constraints allow the team to assess the impact of tourist development in Chepstow on much broader terms. These constraints include satisfying social and environmental criteria for successful tourism in Chepstow.

The approach to policy evaluation in terms of a maximization problem within constraints derives from concepts associated with linear programming without, at this stage, any attempt to force the data into the rigid form of a computer model, as has been done elsewhere (Knijff and Oosterhaven, 1990). Estimating a ratio between job generation and the level of turnover (as suggested by Johnson and Thomas 1989, p. 6) for tourism in Chepstow allows the maximization of turnover, identified above as the key criterion for the success of LEAD, to be related to the more readily quantifiable number of jobs in tourism.

7.3 METHODOLOGY OF IMPACT STUDIES

Many studies have concentrated on the economic impacts of tourism (Mathieson and Wall, 1982, pp. 35-6), especially on the economic benefits to the exclusion of the economic costs (Flemming and Toepper, 1990, p. 36). The methodology typically yields estimates of turnover, income and employment due to tourism within a local economy.

Tourism services earn export income by bringing in an injection of spending from outside the area, which is called 'basic income' (Smith, 1989, p. 270, quoting Tiebout). This creates additional direct, indirect and induced local income and employment through the various multiplier effects. The direct effect is in the organizations that sell goods and services directly to the tourists, the indirect effects follow on in firms that supply the tourist-related enterprises and the induced effect is the result of the extra household income accruing to the local population through wages earned in the direct and indirect tourist-related firms (Witt, 1987, p. 306). These effects can be estimated if the flows of spending and income are traced through successive rounds of spending in the local economy, so that the proportion that stays within the local economy is identified. There are many such studies in the literature and several useful reviews of the approaches used (Archer, 1977, 1982; Jackson, 1986; Pearce, 1989). Chapters 8, 9 and 10 of this book provide some case studies.

The first, most accurate but also most expensive method involves the estimation of an input–output model of the local economy, within which all the direct and indirect effects of tourism are measured. (See Chapters 5 and 6 for applications of the input–output model.) The derivation of such a model with a separately defined tourism sector in order to estimate tourism impacts is relatively rare but theoretically ideal (Archer, 1973; Baster, 1980). The second method simply involves a desk exercise to estimate tourism multipliers from the secondary data available. The third method is known as the reduced form method (Archer, 1973) or proportional multiplier method (Vaughan, 1984). It achieves cost-effectiveness and reasonable accuracy by combining primary data collected in the tourism and closely related sectors with secondary data on other relevant coefficients. It involves fairly substantial fieldwork with tourists and with the business sectors that supply them.

No matter how well carried out, such studies can lead to an over-estimation of the benefits of tourism. They ignore both the opportunity cost of the tourist developments they are assessing (Jackson, 1986, p. 47) and the distribution of those benefits (Wanhill, 1983, p. 16). The indirect and induced effects will be slight in a small, open economy such as that of Chepstow and attempts to trace them may not be justified (Hughes, 1982, p. 169). The full effects of any increase in tourism spending are not instantaneous (Archer, 1977, p. 42) but take time to work through the economy. They are not easily picked up by a survey conducted at a particular time, although they could be traced in a longitudinal study.

There is also the issue of the costs of tourism and of the physical and environmental implications of expanding it. These are identified as constraints in this study (Section 7.2 above), an approach which assists integration of the results of the disparate research within the monitoring programme in progress in

Chepstow (Section 7.1 above). Linear programming in the context of land use planning for tourism within constraints has been reviewed in Knijff and Oosterhaven (1990). They claim it has two advantages: its consistency as a problem-solving technique and the information that it offers on the shadow prices of environmental and social constraints.

The most comprehensive way to carry out evaluation of the impact of tourism in Chepstow, including environmental and other unquantifiable effects, would be social cost–benefit analysis (Murphy, 1985, p. 102) but the demanding data requirements and assumptions (Jackson, 1986, p. 54) that have to be made in quantifying all the costs and benefits make its use within the constraints of this project impracticable, and explain why it has been little used in tourism impact studies (Mathieson and Wall, 1982, p. 182).

The linear programming framework proposed here achieves a structured method of identifying some of the wider costs and benefits, including those not immediately quantifiable, by treating them as constraints. It may be seen as an intermediate methodology between the multiplier approach, which focuses only on the benefits (income and employment generated) from tourism, and a full social cost–benefit analysis. It also fits the needs of action research as the identification of, and recommendations on, the critical constraints related to the marginal costs of relieving them will help to optimize the use of the public funds available through the LEAD programme.

7.4 THE FIRST YEAR OF THE PROGRAMME

7.4.1 Proposed Lead Schemes

The proposed public and private sector schemes under Chepstow's LEAD initiative are shown on Figure 7.1, which is drawn from an aerial photograph taken by the authors to give a 'visitor's eye view' of Chepstow; i.e. it is a 'perceptual map' (Pearce, 1982) helping visitors to relate elements to their initial mental map of the town (Gould and White, 1986).

The public sector schemes include (numbers refer to the map in Figure 7.1):

1 Floodlighting and restoration of the Iron Bridge.
2 A riverside walkway.

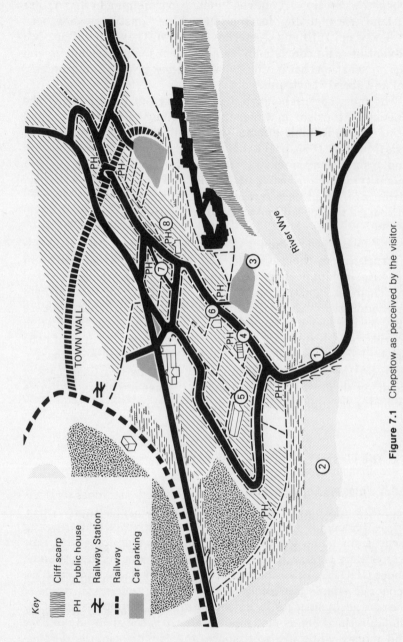

Figure 7.1 Chepstow as perceived by the visitor.
(See text for a description of the numbered locations).

Key

∕∕∕	Cliff scarp
PH	Public house
≢	Railway Station
┋	Railway
▨	Car parking

TOWN WALL

River Wye

3 Castle car park improvement and relocation to it of the tourist information centre.
4 Museum improvements.
5 An interpretation centre in a former drill hall.
6 Improving a gap site as a public garden.
7 Pedestrianizing St Mary's Street.
8 Redesigning Beaufort Square.

Private-sector plans included a new hotel on a development site just outside the town, the restoration of an eighteenth-century mansion near the racecourse and a leisure park on the site of the bridge construction yard below the railway. The first two have been delayed by the recession. The third is deferred while the yard is used by builders working on the Severn Bridge, and there are increasing doubts about whether a major leisure park would be suitable on this site.

Smaller-scale private-sector investment was also deterred in 1990–1 by the recession and by fears of the Uniform Business Rate. However, an active local body called CAATE (Chepstow Area Association for Tourism and Enterprise) was created to stimulate tourism marketing and development for the town and local area by merging the Chamber of Commerce with a tourist association, community festival committee, conservation/heritage society and other local interests. Co-operation with, and the development of, CAATE is part of the ongoing monitoring and evaluation programme (an example of action-research) and emphasizes the community basis for tourism development in Chepstow.

7.4.2 Defining Chepstow Tourists

The tourism research literature contains many attempts to define a tourist (Mathieson and Wall, 1982, pp. 10–12; Murphy, 1985, pp. 5–10), usually in terms of travel and activities while staying away from home for at least 24 hours. Excursionists or day-trippers are those who temporarily leave home for less than 24 hours (IUOTO, 1968). Since impacts include more than just the economic effects (see Section 7.3), defining tourism in terms of the tourist businesses in a destination, i.e. a supply-side definition (Smith, 1988), is also inadequate. It is the spending of time and money while utilizing space and facilities in the destination area (Murphy, 1985, p. 7) that determines the impact of tourism, so the crucial criterion should be whether the person has arrived from elsewhere, not how long he or she stays.

Amending the IUOTO general definition by substituting 'place' for 'country' (after Murphy, 1985, p. 5) yields:

> a visitor is any person visiting a place other than where he or she has his or her usual place of residence, for any reason other than following an occupation remunerated from within the place visited.

'Visitor' will be used in this sense to include overnight and day visitors to Chepstow.

7.4.3 The 1990 Surveys

ON-STREET VISITOR SURVEY

This was conducted on 32 days between April and September 1990, with a collection of 60 points of information from 760 people. This approach differed from recommendations that a recreation site should be saturated by many interviewers on a limited number of days per year (TRRU, 1983) because to attempt such comprehensive coverage of a town on one day would be very expensive. A sufficient sample can be achieved by fewer interviews over more days (English Tourist Board, 1979). The results provided the numerical control data which, taken with data for admissions to Chepstow Castle (visited only once per trip), enabled a grossed up estimate of total visitors to Chepstow to be derived (following English Tourist Board, 1979). Trends in Chepstow Castle admissions will be monitored against those at other CADW castles in Wales (CADW is the Welsh equivalent of English Heritage) to give national comparisons largely missing in previous work undertaken by Bristol Polytechnic researchers in Weston-super-Mare. The figures were weighted by length of stay to minimize the bias inherent in street sampling, where those staying longer are more likely to be interviewed (English Tourist Board, 1979). Repeating the survey annually for five years will permit comparisons over time.

Approximately 100 000 people visited Chepstow during 1990, of whom 70 per cent paid to visit the Castle. Fifty per cent of day visitors were under 45 with both sexes about equally represented while two-thirds of the over-45s were female. Fifty per cent of overnighters interviewed in the street had arrived on foot, bicycle or by public transport, emphasizing Chepstow's gains from the large numbers of young adults who take walking holidays on Offa's Dyke path and in the Forest of Dean.

Seventy per cent of interviewees were day visitors, of whom just under half confirmed the characteristically short visit by spending less than two hours in the town. Eighty per cent of over-nighters stayed for one night and only 1 per cent for over three nights. From the commercial survey it is clear that those involved in the tourism-related businesses in the town were well aware of the need to find ways of persuading visitors to stay longer and to encourage them to walk up into the town from the castle, yet there are no signposts and little tourist information to direct them.

The low level of spending was another feature: half the visitors interviewed on the street had spent nothing on accommodation, eating and drinking or shopping. For those who did spend, the amounts were relatively small at £12 per head on accommodation, £6 for food and drink and £25 for shopping; but even this resulted in an increase in local turnover of approximately £1.4 million annually in these three sectors of the Chepstow economy.

Although the on-street survey provides the main statistical base for monitoring the LEAD initiative, it has not obtained a statistically unbiased sample of visitors to Chepstow. It did not cover a representative number of the business visitors who were encountered in the hotels (qualitative survey) and who formed an important part of the trade in the accommodation sector. Many overnight visitors arrived in the town after 5 p.m. and left in the morning before the castle or museum opened, so they did not pass the survey points. In 1991 visitor interviewing will be extended in the accommodation sector, while the on-street survey will be continued in its original form in order to ensure a consistent basis for year-on-year comparisons.

OFF-STREET VISITOR SURVEY

In-depth qualitative interviews were carried out with randomly selected visitors in hotels and other accommodation and at the tourist information centre (TIC) to assess their attitudes and beliefs about Chepstow and its surroundings and to develop hypotheses about the nature of the town's appeal as a tourist destination and the markets that it serves (see Glaser and Strauss, 1967). This usefully complemented the structured on-street interviews, although such qualitative results cannot be subjected to tests of statistical probability.

There were many repeat visitors among the business tourists but, apart from being good customers for local pubs and restaurants, they rarely visited any attractions. Many staying holiday-makers had not made advance bookings and knew little about the town when they arrived; some did not even know about the castle. The image of Chepstow is obviously very weak among potential visitors. On the other hand, repeat visitors among holiday-makers liked the quiet of the town and were strongly of the opinion that it should not change. This is a potential source of conflict with those in the tourism business community who are anxious to see expansion and more activity. Several landladies said that there was a need for more for visitors to do.

BUSINESS SURVEY

A questionnaire was administered to a randomly selected sample of businesses in the four main tourism-related sectors of the Chepstow economy: accommodation; food and drink; attractions; craft and gift shops. The aims were to establish the percentage of turnover in these businesses derived from visitors, to estimate the local income and employment generated by visitors' expenditure within these businesses and to assess the volume of indirect and induced effects on other sectors of the local economy. The results confirmed that the main economic impact of tourism in the town is the employment generated. Wages (excluding the income of self-employed proprietors) constituted 10–30 per cent of the turnover of the responding businesses and almost all employees lived in the town or within five miles. Few businesses purchased supplies locally, except fresh food and small cleaning items. Any multiplier effect therefore depends almost entirely on the spending of the additional household income of the employees and proprietors. Detailed financial data were supplied by very few responding businesses and it proved impossible to estimate by how much turnover was raised elsewhere in the town within the resources of this project. The estimates of increased turnover in Chepstow due to tourism, quoted above, were the direct effects derived from the on-street survey expenditure data, i.e. from the demand side (Pearce, 1989, p. 194).

There were approximately 500 jobs (200 full-time and 300 part-time) in the four tourism-related sectors but, apart from the attractions and guest house sectors, few were solely dependent on tourism. There was very little seasonality of employment or trade in the pubs and restaurants or in the craft and gift shops, although attendance figures at the castle and museum did show a seasonal variation.

TRAFFIC, PEDESTRIAN AND ENVIRONMENTAL SURVEYS

Traffic, pedestrian and environmental surveys were conducted to identify traffic and environmental problems (Coombe *et al.*, 1990) and to support recommendations on pedestrianization, traffic calming and management, remodelling and landscaping. Traffic counts, photographs, video recordings and noise monitoring yielded a base set of data against which to assess developments as the LEAD initiative progresses, and specific recommendations were made to the council about areas where pedestrian safety could be improved. Increased tourism and associated commercial activity will create transport and parking problems and could worsen the environment for pedestrians, so problems of accessibility and environmental deterioration could slow down both tourism and economic growth. It will be part of the ongoing research programme to monitor this.

OTHER SURVEYS

Surveys of the costs of tourism to the local authorities and others were carried out during the winter of 1990–1. Fifteen hundred residents visited an exhibition about the LEAD initiative in Chepstow in September 1990, providing about 250 written comments and giving a preliminary indication of local attitudes. There was an overwhelmingly favourable response, suggesting that Doxey's state of 'euphoria' (Murphy, 1985, p. 124) exists among Chepstow's residents. Initial analysis of a recent residents' survey (conducted early in 1991) has confirmed this view and provides a base from which to evaluate any future changes in attitude. The latter aimed to test whether the majority of favourable attitudes to tourism in Wales found by the WTB at the beginning of the 1980s holds in Chepstow (Wales Tourist Board, 1981, p. iv). It also allows residents' views to be represented to the LEAD planning process, so improving the chances of success (Liu and Sheldon, 1987, p. 20), but the full results were not available in time for inclusion here.

7.4.4 Conclusions from the First Year's Fieldwork

The results have largely confirmed the initial hypotheses about tourism in Chepstow, where there is clearly substantial scope for the expansion of tourism-related activity, but such development should be sensitive to the atmosphere as it is now, and should not seek to change it. The general picture is of a town with potential but, as yet, with few facilities to secure the full benefits to local commerce and employment that 100 000 and more visitors could bring. Currently the largely day-trip trade to the castle generates remarkably little extra business in the town.

The research team has recommended to the borough council that growth in activity should stem from increasing the length of visitor stay by providing appropriate information and sign-posting, so that visitors move around the town more (as suggested for Caernarfon by Karski, 1990); using the linking factor of the medieval Port Wall has been suggested (Binks, 1990). This would increase the usage of the shops and other tourist facilities, although opening times would need to be extended (especially on Sundays) and increased length of stay could involve extra resources in terms of car parking and accommodation.

The prevalence of young adults and walking holiday-makers among Chepstow's visitors makes it important to have low-cost accommodation available, yet the Youth Hostel (providing over 7000 bed-nights in 1990) closed permanently at the end of the 1990 season owing to the high capital costs arising on the listed Georgian building that it occupied. LEAD money may be used to pump prime the provision of a more suitable replacement.

7.5 CONCLUSIONS ON METHODOLOGY

In Section 7.2 it was proposed that the aim of the LEAD project should be seen as the maximization of turnover in Chepstow within constraints imposed by the varying objectives of the different elements in the community. Satisfying the demands of the residents on the environmental and social implications of increasing tourism may become major constraints on the future maximization of tourism-related turnover, although there is little indication that these constraints are yet tight.

The analysis of the results on tourist patterns and behaviour, residents' objectives and attitudes, human and vehicle traffic in the town identified the following as constraints on tourism growth which should be accommodated if its development is to be judged a success. It should take place:

- without road traffic growth;

- without detriment to the lives of the citizens;
- without impairing pedestrian safety;
- without imposing costs on the local authorities greater than any resultant yield in Uniform Business Rate, Poll Tax or their successors;
- without damaging the fabric of the medieval and historic town and castle;
- without damaging the rural environment around the town;
- without inflating local wages in other sectors;
- within the budget of LEAD and generated private sector capital.

Meeting these constraints would establish a strategy for tourism growth that is 'green' in both of the often conflicting senses of the concept: not contributing further to global warming; community based and supported (Murphy, 1985) and therefore sustainable (Lane, 1991).

The methodology remains to be further developed and refined but it is our contention that, even without a formal mathematical model, linear programming is a useful conceptual tool in the analysis of tourism policy and that looking at the promotion of tourism in Chepstow in this way has helped to clarify the issues. One aim of the research project in future years will be to attempt to quantify the relationships so that an optimization programme can be applied.

References

Archer, B.H. (1973) *The Impact of Domestic Tourism*, Bangor Occasional Papers in Economics, No. 2. Cardiff: University of Wales Press.

Archer, B.H. (1977) *Tourism Multipliers: The State of the Art*, Bangor Occasional Papers in Economics, No. 11. Cardiff: University of Wales Press.

Archer, B.H. (1982) The value of multipliers and their policy implications. *Tourism Management*, **3**, 236–41.

Baster, J. (1980) Input–output analysis of tourism benefits: some lessons from Scotland. *International Journal of Tourism Management*, **1**, 99–108.

Binks, G. (1990) *Towns in View*. Manchester: Centre for Environmental Interpretation (CEI), Manchester Polytechnic.

Campbell, M. (ed.) (1990) *Local Economic Policy.* London: Cassell Educational.

Coombe, D., Goodwin, R., Turner, D. and Shaheed, A. (1990) Conservation and traffic in the historic town of Bury St Edmunds. *The Planner,* 4 May, 11–16.

English Tourist Board (1979) *Woodspring Tourism Study.* London: ETB.

Fleming, W. and Toepper, L. (1990) Economic impact studies: relating the positive and negative impacts to tourism development. *Journal of Travel Research,* **29,** 35–43.

Gibbon, E. (1784) *Decline and Fall of the Roman Empire,* 1801 edn, volume 12. London: Strachan.

Glaser, B.G. and Strauss, A.L. (1967) *The Discovery of Grounded Theory: Strategies for Qualitative Research.* New York: Aldine.

Gould, P. and White, R. (1986) *Mental Maps,* 2nd edn. Boston: Allen & Unwin.

Hughes, C.G. (1982) The employment and economic effects of tourism reappraised. *Tourism Management,* **3,** 167–76.

IUOTO (1968) *The Economic Review of World Tourism.* Geneva: IUOTO.

Jackson, M.J. (1986) *Economic Impact Studies: the Methodology Applied to Tourism.* Bristol: Bristol Polytechnic.

Jackson, M. and Bruce, D. (1988) The impact of various developments on the local economy. In *Watersite 2000 – Proceedings of an International Congress on Waterfront Development.* Bristol: Bristol City Council.

Johnson, P. and Thomas, B. (1989) *Measuring the Local Employment Impact of a Tourist Attraction: An Empirical Study.* Durham: University of Durham.

Karski, A. (1990) Urban tourism – a key to urban regeneration? *The Planner,* 6 April, 15–17.

Knijff, E. van der and Oosterhaven, J. (1990) Optimising tourist policy: a linear programming approach. *Regional Studies,* **24,** 55–64.

Lane, B. (1991) Will rural tourism succeed? In Hardy, S., Hart, T. and Shaw, T. (eds) *Tourism in the Urban and Regional Economy,* ch. 7, pp. 34–9. London: Regional Studies Association.

Liu, J.C. and Sheldon, P.J. (1987) Resident perception of the environmental impacts of tourism. *Annals of Tourism Research,* **14,** 17–37.

Mathieson, A. and Wall, G. (1982) *Tourism: Economic, Social and Physical Impacts.* Harlow: Longman.

Murphy, P.E. (1985) *Tourism: A Community Approach.* London: Methuen.

Pearce, D. (1989) *Tourism Development,* 2nd edn. Harlow: Longman.

Pearce, P.L. (1982) *Social Psychology of Tourism.* Oxford: Pergamon.

Shaw, G. and Williams, A. (1989) Case study: UK visitor survey. *Tourism Management,* **10,** 247–51.

Smith, S.L.J. (1988) Defining tourism: a supply-side view. *Annals of Tourism Research,* **15,** 179–90.

Smith, S.L.J. (1989) *Tourism Analysis: A Handbook.* Harlow: Longman.

Tan, T., Wanhill, S. and Westlake, J. (1983) Grant-aided tourism projects and employment creation – experiences of the English Tourist Board. *Tourism Management,* **4,** 107–17.

TRRU (Tourism Recreation Research Unit) (1983) *Recreation Site Survey Manual.* London: Spon.

Vaughan, D.R. (1984) The cultural heritage: an approach to analysing income and employment effects. *Journal of Cultural Economics,* **16,** 1–36.

Wales Tourist Board (1981) *Survey of Community Attitudes towards Tourism in Wales.* Cardiff: WTB.

Wanhill, S.R.C. (1983) Measuring the economic impact of tourism. *Service Industries Journal,* **3,** 9–20.

Witt, S.F. (1987) Economic impact of tourism on Wales. *Tourism Management,* **8,** 306–16.

8 The Economic Impact of College Football Games: A Case Study of the University of Alabama

Mary Fish

8.1 INTRODUCTION

On autumn Saturday afternoons in Alabama, the focus of the state is on university football games. This study estimates the economic impact on Tuscaloosa County, Alabama, of three football games held at Bryant-Denny Stadium on the University of Alabama campus situated in the county in the autumn of 1989. This study is part of a larger project which estimated the total impact of the university.[1]

The primary economic impact of the games played in Bryant-Denny Stadium is spending by out-of-county fans, which represented direct expenditures to county businesses that occurred because of the football games. The study measures both the direct and the indirect economic impacts of non-local fans who attended the games in 1989. Each of the three games attracted over 70 000 fans, with about 46 000 fans from outside the county. These non-local fans spent an estimated $1.8 million per game that went directly into the county economy.

In the rest of this section, a brief summary of the research on attendance at college football games establishes the factors affecting demand and provides several criteria for evaluating the attraction of the Alabama team. The stature of football at the university is also described. Several recent football impact studies are reviewed in Section 8.2. Section 8.3 describes the methodology used in this study and presents the results. Some comments are made in Section 8.4 concerning the value of this study to the university and the community. Section 8.5 concludes the study.

Researchers indicate that several factors determine attendance at a college football game: the team's current win–loss record (Conlin, 1986); the team's standing in conference and national football polls published by the Associated Press and the United Press; the competition between the two teams; the historical rivalry between the teams; the tradition or following of the college alumni (Pacey and Wickham, 1985); and whether the game is on television (Greenspan, 1988). The most competitive and potentially exciting games are televised by national networks or regional stations.

University of Alabama tradition is the factor that has the strongest positive affect on game attendance. The team is nationally recognized and avidly supported by its fans. Alabama's former coach, Paul W. (Bear) Bryant, is a legend, being the most successful coach in National Collegiate Athletic Association Division 1 football. Since the Bryant legacy of the 1970s, the university has employed three new coaches. In the 1980s, the record of the team was excellent, although less spectacular. Table 8.1 shows the win, loss and tie record for the school's team over the past three decades. Alabama won the national championship six times between 1960 and 1990, and won the Southeastern Conference championship 14 times.

Local spending after the games appears to be greater when Alabama wins. Restaurants and bars are more crowded; fans seem to hang around a longer time savouring the victory. Fortunately for Tuscaloosa County, Alabama wins regularly.

8.2 PREVIOUS STUDIES

Before the development of Alabama's football study, the general literature on the economic impact of college football games was surveyed. The football stadiums at universities with prestigious teams have capacities of up to 100 000 fans. Season tickets sell for between $16 and $25 each, or more. A team plays three to seven home games a season. Fans come from the university vicinity (between 25 and 35 per cent), throughout the state and outside the state. The direct expenditures generated by football fans per game to the local area varies from $1 to $3 million with a total economic impact varying from $2 to $6 million.

Table 8.1 The University of Alabama football team records

Year	Record	Coach	Championships	Polls AP	UPI
				AP	UPI
				(top 20 ranks)	
1960	8–1–2	Bryant		9	10
1961	11–0–0		National, SEC	1	1
1962	10–1–0			5	5
1963	9–2–0			8	9
1964	10–1–0		National, SEC	1	1
1965	9–1–1		AP-National, SEC	1	4
1966	11–0–0		SEC	3	3
1967	8–2–1			8	7
1968	8–3–0			16	–
1969	6–5–0			–	–
1970	6–5–1			–	–
1971	11–1–0		SEC	4	2
1972	10–2–0		SEC	7	4
1973	11–1–0		UPI-National, SEC	4	1
1974	11–1–0		SEC	5	2
1975	11–1–0		SEC	3	3
1976	9–3–0			11	9
1977	11–1–0		SEC	2	2
1978	11–1–0		AP-National, SEC	1	2
1979	12–0–0		National, SEC	1	1
1980	10–2–0			6	6
1981	9–2–1		SEC	7	6
1982	8–4–0			–	17
1983	8–4–0	Perkins		15	12
1984	5–6–0			–	–
1985	9–2–1			13	14
1986	10–3–0			9	9
1987	7–5–0	Curry		–	–
1988	9–3–0			17	17
1989	10–2–0		SEC	9	7
1990	7–5–0	Stallings		–	–

AP is Associated Press, UPI is United Press International, SEC is Southeastern Conference. Record is wins–losses–ties.

Source: Athletic Department, the University of Alabama (1990).

The methodologies used in previous studies were relatively similar. Most studies selected a random sample from the list of annual ticket-holders. The selected fans were surveyed and asked to recall their spending for each game. In the studies, expenditures were generally broken down by type; for example, stadium expenses, restaurants, lodging, private car costs and costs of other modes of travel, clothing and equipment for games, night clubs, food and beverages in retail stores, other retail shopping and miscellaneous expenses.

The three reviewed studies all collected data by using questionnaires sent to selected football fans at the end of the season. Respondents were thus faced with a lengthy time lapse between the game dates and the survey date. In addition, Pennsylvania State University researchers suggested that fans tend to underestimate their spending in surveys of this type (Erickson and Guadagnolo, 1988). The ideal method of gathering the spending information would be to send ticket-holders questionnaires in advance of the games and have them record all expenditures immediately after the events. Details can be recalled more clearly if they are requested as soon as feasible.

The direct expenditures of surveyed visitors were tabulated and applied to the entire population. Estimated multipliers based on the judgement of the researchers were used to estimate the total economic impact of football game visitors.

Relatively recent football studies are available from Pennsylvania State University (Erickson and Guadagnolo, 1988) and the University of Oklahoma (Dikeman, 1988). An earlier study was conducted at the University of Arkansas (Broyles and Hay, 1980). Summaries of the methodologies and findings of these three studies follow.

8.2.1 Pennsylvania State University

The Pennsylvania State University (PSU) study estimated a total economic impact of non-local football fan spending in the PSU area of $40.3 million in the 1986 season, an average of $5.8 million per game for that season's seven home games (Erickson and Guadagnolo, 1988). The direct expenditures totalled $20.5 million, $2.9 million per game. An expenditure multiplier of 1.97 was used to account for the ripple effect of the direct expenditures throughout the local economy. The PSU region studied had a population of 72 000, including 33 000 PSU students.

The researchers surveyed 1974 randomly selected out-of-town season ticket-holders, 86 per cent of whom responded. The study includes the expenditures of 54 000 fans, 41 500 of whom were season ticket-holders who lived 25 miles or more outside the state college area. An additional 32 100 fans who lived within 25 miles of the state college were not included in the survey (Erickson and Guadagnolo, 1988). Fans within the 25-mile range were regarded as residents, and the study was limited to non-resident spending.

The expenditure estimates also included the cost of game tickets, $14 each in 1986, and the returns made by the university on concessions and souvenirs.

8.2.2 University of Oklahoma

The University of Oklahoma's (OU) Center for Economic and Management Research estimated the total economic impact of football games on the Norman–Oklahoma City area, a large metropolitan area of 440 000 people including 19 000 OU students, to be $23.9 million in 1987 (Dikeman, 1988). This was an average total impact of $4.8 million per game for the five home games played that season. Direct expenditures totalled $14.0 million or $2.8 million per game. The total economic impact was derived using a multiplier of 1.71, whereas the multiplier used by PSU was 1.97. Both figures were considered to be conservative.

Approximately 75 700 fans attended each of OU's home football games. The researchers randomly selected 1500 season ticket-holders for the survey. At the end of the season, over 1000 of these reported their expenditures at the games. The study excluded spending by the 10 000 OU students who attended each game, but included expenditures by the remaining 65 700 fans regardless of whether they were local residents or not. Under the PSU methodology, the 9500 OU-area fans would have been excluded. The expenditure estimates excluded the $17 cost of game tickets, but included the returns made by the university on concessions and souvenirs.

8.2.3 University of Arkansas

The University of Arkansas (UA) study determined that the total economic impact of UA football spending on the north-west Arkansas area was $5.0 million in 1979 (Broyles and Hay, 1980). For the three home games in 1979, total economic impact and direct expenditures averaged $1.7 million and $1.1 million per game, respectively. The researchers used a multiplier of 1.5, the lowest of the three studies, to calculate the total economic impact. The UA region had a population of 48 000, including 16 000 UA students.

The study results were based on the responses of 266 non-student season ticket-holders out of the original 492 who were polled. Survey responses were used to estimate the spending of all 41 421 fans per game, including both local residents and students.

Table 8.2 The University of Alabama 1989 football season

Game	Location	Score	Television
Alabama v. Memphis State	Birmingham	35–7 win	–
Alabama v. Kentucky	Tuscaloosa[a]	15–3 win	WTBS
Alabama v. Vanderbilt	Nashville	20–14 win	WTBS
Alabama v. Ole Miss	Jackson	62–27 win	–
Alabama v. SW Louisiana	Tuscaloosa[a]	24–17 win	–
Alabama v. Tennessee	Birmingham	47–30 win	CBS
Alabama v. Penn State	State College	17–16 win	CBS
Alabama v. Mississippi State	Birmingham	23–10 win	WTBS
Alabama v. Louisiana State	Baton Rouge	32–16 win	ESPN
Alabama v. Southern Mississippi	Tuscaloosa[a]	37–14 win	–
Alabama v. Auburn	Auburn	20–30 loss	CBS
Alabama v. Miami	New Orleans[b]	25–33 loss	ABC

[a] A home game played in Bryant-Denny Stadium.
[b] The prestigious post-season Sugar Bowl game.

Source: Athletic Department, the University of Alabama (1990)

The expenditure estimates included the cost of game tickets, $8.50 in 1979, and university concessions and souvenirs.

8.3 UNIVERSITY OF ALABAMA METHODOLOGY

The purpose of this study was to estimate the direct and indirect impact of the University of Alabama football games on the economy of Tuscaloosa County for the calendar year 1989. The impact of football games in Tuscaloosa extends far beyond the county, whose population is 138 000, which includes the 19 000 University students. However, the study includes only Tuscaloosa County. Details of the University of Alabama's 1989 season are shown in Table 8.2.

8.3.1 Expenditure Estimates

Only the local spending of football fans from outside of Tuscaloosa County was considered in this study. It was assumed that local residents and students would have spent their money in the county regardless of the football games. Thus, of over 70 000 fans in attendance at each of the three home games, only the spending of about 46 000 fans per game was considered. The university athletic department was able to identify whether tickets were sold to people inside or outside of Tuscaloosa County. Of the three studies reviewed, only PSU used this methodology. In the University of Oklahoma study, only students were excluded, and no game attendees were excluded in the University of Arkansas study.

Expenditure estimates in the Alabama study excluded the $16 cost of game tickets and the university share of stadium concessions and souvenirs. This spending went into the university accounting system and may or may not have gone directly back into the community. Any inflow of this money into the community economy would have been the result of university expenditures, not those of visiting fans. Total university expenditures in the county were captured in a separate component of the overall university study. Of the three studies reviewed, only the University of Oklahoma study excluded ticket costs from the economic impact measurement. None of the studies omitted the university share of stadium revenue, but this was considerably less significant than ticket costs. Inclusion of the ticket costs and university stadium revenue in the study results would have enhanced the direct economic impact to the county by about $775 000 per game. Revenue from several other sources is not included. For example, hotel, restaurant and transportation expenses of visiting teams and television crews are omitted.[2]

A per person expenditure estimate of $39.79 per game was derived for the University of Alabama and was used to estimate total spending in Tuscaloosa County excluding payments to the university. This figure was obtained by adjusting the PSU survey results. The PSU results were selected because they appeared to be the most conservative and most representative of the University of Alabama's situation. Adjustments were made to account for the noted differences in assumptions between the two studies and to account for changes in price levels since the PSU study was conducted.

8.3.2 Tuscaloosa County Econometric Model

The direct expenditures of football visitors become income to local and non-local businesses and government; these entities, in turn, by purchasing local goods and services generate added income. Instead of an approximation of the multiplier for each sector as recommended by Caffrey and Isaacs (1971), a single income multiplier was determined which measured the total economic impact of the university on Tuscaloosa County.

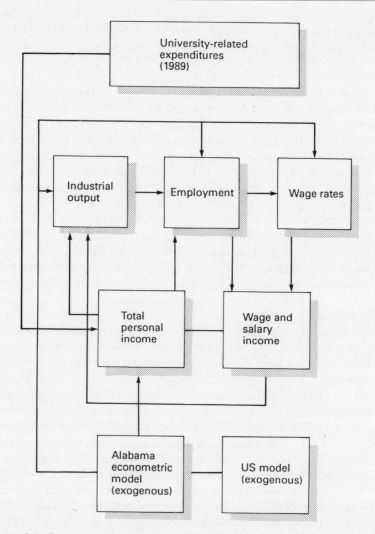

Figure 8.1 Tuscaloosa County econometric model.

Source: Center for Business and Economic Research, the University of Alabama (1990).

An econometric model of Tuscaloosa County was used to estimate the total economic impact of the university (Figure 8.1).[3] The increased use of econometric models in regional impact studies results from their ability to link direct expenditures to personal income (Fritz and Konecny, 1981).[4] The Tuscaloosa County econometric model was developed and is continuously updated by the Center for Business and Economic Research at the university.[5] The Tuscaloosa County econometric model comprises 91 equations and identities which are solved simultaneously. The Alabama econometric model estimates provide the exogenous assumptions for these solutions. Exogenous assumptions incorporated in the model include: the annual rate of increase in real gross national product, consumer expenditures, fixed business investment, consumer price inflation, total state employment, industrial output, total personal income and the estimated United States and Alabama unemployment rates. Data from the State of Alabama and the Bureau of Economic Analysis, United States Department of Commerce, are used to update the model.

In the Tuscaloosa County econometric model, industrial earnings determine total employment. Wage rates and employment establish wage and salary income. The personal income sector feeds back into the industrial output sector as a demand-side component. Industrial earnings are the dollar value of total goods and services produced in Tuscaloosa County. They are a proxy for the output figure, which is not available at the county level because of disclosure concerns. Changes in industrial earnings result from changes in income or increases in expenditures. Both increase the demand for goods and services in the region. It is at this juncture that the fan expenditures were incorporated. The model's basic structure and its linkages are pictured in Figure 8.1.

The 1989 economic impact generated by the direct expenditures at the three university football games was included in Tuscaloosa County's 1989 baseline estimates; then the County's 1989 total economic activity was estimated without these direct expenditures. The difference between the two estimates represented the total impact of the three football games played in Bryant-Denny Stadium in 1989.

8.3.3 Impact on Tuscaloosa County

Total direct expenditures by the Alabama fans were $5 675 000. The indirect impact, as calculated by the econometric model, was $4 821 000. The total impact on Tuscaloosa County of the three games was $10 496 000. Thus, a multiplier of 1.84 was obtained for this study. The multiplier estimates noted in the literature survey were 1.5, 1.71 and 1.97 for UA, OU and PSU, respectively.

Table 8.3 presents a breakdown of the 1989 personal income generated by type of income. Wages and salaries represent

Table 8.3 Income generated in Tuscaloosa County, 1989

Sector		Income ($)
Proprietor's and labour income		461 000
Dividends, rent and interest		272 000
Wage and salary		
Manufacturing	761 000	
Construction	1 239 000	
Wholesale and retail trade	836 000	
Government	432 000	
Other	820 000	4 088 000
Direct expenditures		5 675 000
Total		10 496 000

the income category that was the principal benefactor with $4 129 000. The structure of the model imputed $461 000 to proprietors' and labour income, and $272 000 to dividends, rent and interest.

The employment generated by the increase of personal income of $10 496 000 was 222 persons. Table 8.4 shows the classifications in which the indirect employment was added, based on the structure of the employment component in the Tuscaloosa County econometric model. Construction and wholesale and retail trade were estimated to be the primary benefactors.

8.4 THE VALUE OF THE STUDY

The results of this study are of interest to both the university administration and the Tuscaloosa County community. Football games are tourist attractions and the local community directly benefits as a result of the games played at Bryant-Denny Stadium located in Tuscaloosa. Although community members are aware that the games have a significant impact on Tuscaloosa County, they may be surprised at the magnitude of the contribution. Quantifying the impact will enable the university and the community to be better informed when making decisions regarding the stadium in which future games will be played. This study is especially timely, since three of the university's home games are played 50 miles outside of Tuscaloosa County because the distant stadium has a larger seating capacity. There is current discussion about expanding Bryant-Denny Stadium and playing all of the home games in Tuscaloosa County. The university needs

Table 8.4 Employment generated in Tuscaloosa County, 1989

Employment	Number employed
Manufacturing	29
Construction	75
Wholesale and retail trade	56
Government	21
Other	41
Total wage and salary employment	222

these data for negotiating the funding of stadium expansion with Tuscaloosa City and County officials.

This study would also be of interest to other comparable universities and communities facing decisions regarding football programmes. Stadium expansions, playing more or less games, and building new stadiums would all be scenarios applicable to a study of this nature. The results presented here may convince other university or community leaders of the usefulness of information of this type and lead to more collegiate impact studies.

A few comments about the scope of this study are in order. The estimates do not include the large expenditures by the university that are directly and indirectly related to the games, such as police personnel and stadium upkeep. Expenditures by Tuscaloosa County for extra police protection and traffic control are also not included. No attempt has been made to quantify the cost to residents of game-day inconveniences, such as traffic congestion and noise. The positive effects would certainly outweigh the negative on these three days a year.

The university is an institution of higher learning which offers huge tangible and intangible benefits to Tuscaloosa. This analysis does not address the intangible rewards, such as the state pride generated by the university football team, the endless conversation and analysis arising from its games and the excitement of the fans generated on game day.

8.5 CONCLUSIONS

The three home football games played by the University of Alabama team generated direct expenditures in Tuscaloosa County of $5 675 000 by fans from outside the county. The Tuscaloosa County econometric model assigned an income multiplier of 1.84. Thus, a total of $10 496 000 was generated by the three 1989 games. In addition, 222 people were employed in the county because of the games.

The quantification of the substantial impact of the three football games played at Bryant-Denny Stadium during the year provides valuable information to the university and the community. It is definitely information that the community should be made aware of and that will add to the positive image of the university. As previously mentioned, three home games are played outside Tuscaloosa County because of insufficient seating at Bryant-Denny Stadium and expansion of the stadium has been proposed as a solution. This study can serve as an estimate of the extra annual income the county would gain if those three games were also played in Tuscaloosa County.

Notes

Doug Waggle, PhD student in Finance, assisted in collecting and analysing the data and writing this project. The Tuscaloosa County econometric model was revised by Ahmad Ijaz, Econometric Analyst for the Center for Business and Economic Research at The University of Alabama. He provided the econometric data generated by the model. Deborah Hamilton, Assistant Director of the Center, participated in all stages of the project.

1 This study is a component of a University of Alabama economic impact study. Many studies are available on the economic impact of colleges and universities. The classic work by Caffrey and Isaacs (1971) on estimating the economic impact of colleges on local economies has been used as a guide for conducting most of these studies. The model estimates aggregate demand in the region 'resulting from expenditures by the institution itself and by persons associated with it' (Caffrey and Isaacs, 1971, pp. 5-6). Current university studies available include the University of Tennessee (Murray, 1987), the University of Montana (Polzin *et al.*, 1988), the University of Alabama at Birmingham (Lewis, 1988), the University of California at Berkeley (Hughes, 1989), and the University of Virginia (Knapp *et al.*, 1990).

2 In addition, profits from ticket touting are not estimated. They are probably not particularly large. Ticket touting is not illegal in the State of Alabama.

3 The Tuscaloosa County econometric model is based on the original Wharton econometric model, which became the Wharton Economic Forecasting Associates' model. They, in turn, merged with Chase Econometrics and became the Wharton Econometric Forecasting

Associates Group. Data from the State of Alabama and the Bureau of Economic Analysis, United States Department of Commerce, are used in the Tuscaloosa County econometric model.

4 In 1986 the Department of Economics at the University of Central Florida estimated the regional economic impact of enlarging the stadium in Orlando, Orange County, Florida, which had a seating capacity of approximately 52 000, to a seating capacity of 72 000. This expanded capacity was to be used for the Florida Citrus Bowl – a game of some stature – played at the end of the football season. Fan expenditures were collected from a visitor survey. A regionally based model was used to estimate the total impact. The model used was a modification of the Bureau of Economic analysis of the United States Department of Commerce (Fritz and McHone, 1986).

5 The use of econometric models in tourism impact studies is not new. The literature has discussed their general benefits and limitations (Fritz and Konecny, 1981). The increased use of econometric models in regional impact studies also stems from their ability to link tourist expenditures to government revenues and employment. Thus, detailed cost–benefit and planning data are accessed. However, the expertise and expense required to build, revise and continually update models such as the Tuscaloosa County econometric model are substantial.

References

Broyles, F.J. and Hay, R.D. (1980) The economic impact of a Razorback football game on northwest Arkansas business community. *Arkansas Business and Economic Review*, **13**, 5–8.

Caffrey, J. and Isaacs, H.H. (1971) *Estimating the Impact of a College or University on the Local Economy*. Washington, DC: American Council on Education.

Conlin, D.W. (1986) Intercollegiate football winning and finance. Doctoral dissertation, Brigham Young University.

Dikeman, N.J. Jr (1988) The economic impact of Sooner football. *Oklahoma Business Bulletin*, **56**, 15–17.

Erickson, R.A. and Guadagnolo, F.B. (1988) *Penn State Football Expenditure Survey*. Philadelphia, PA: Center for Travel and Tourism Research, Pennsylvania State University, University Park.

Fritz, R.G. and Konecny, M. (1981) A functional planning and policy-making tool: tourism impact model. *Journal of Urban Planning and Development*, **107**, 19–31.

Fritz, R.G. and McHone, W.W. (1986) *Estimating the Impact of Expanding the Capacity of the Florida Citrus Bowl*. Orlando, FL: University of Central Florida, University Park.

Greenspan, D. (1988) College football's biggest fumble: the economic impact of the supreme court's decision in National Collegiate Athletic Association v. Board of Regents of the University of Oklahoma. *Antitrust Bulletin*, **33**, 1–65.

Hughes, K.S. (1989) The economic importance of academic institutions in their communities. Presentation to Southern Association of College and University Business Officers, KPMG Peat Marwick.

Knapp, J.L., Fox, T.J., McGrath, R.D. and Cox, R.W. (1990) *The University of Virginia's Impact on the Charlottesville Metropolitan Area: A Study for 1989–90*. Charlottesville, VA: Center for Public Service, University of Virginia.

Lewis, D. (1988) *UAB's Impact on the Birmingham Economy: 1987*. Birmingham, AL: Business and Economic Data Service, Department of Economics, University of Alabama at Birmingham.

Murray, M. (1987) *An Evaluation of the Economic Impact of the Knoxville Metropolitan Statistical Area: 1985–1986*. Knoxville, TN: Center for Business and Economic Research, College of Business Administration, the University of Tennessee, Knoxville.

Pacey, P.L. and Wickham, E. (1985) College football telecasts: where are they going? *Economic Inquiry*, **23**, 93–113.

Polzin, P.E., Lenihan, M.L. and Haefele, C. (1988) The University of Montana and Missoula: economic interdependence. *Montana Business Quarterly*, **26**, 3–10.

9 Employment Effects of Irish Tourism Projects: A Microeconomic Approach

James Deegan and Donal Dineen

9.1 INTRODUCTION

Despite the improvement in its public finances from 1987 onwards the Irish economy still faces a major unemployment problem. The November 1991 figures for unemployment reflect this, with 259 833 unemployed (representing 19.5 per cent of the labour force). Numerous government initiatives have been, and continue to be, undertaken in an attempt to alleviate this problem. One of these initiatives puts heavy emphasis on the tourism sector. This to some extent reflects a change in policy as it is only over the past three or four years that tourism has received the same intense interest as other sectors of the economy.

One reason for the scant attention to tourism in the past may have been the highly diffuse nature of the industry. For example, Deane (1986) has suggested that 'the loose association of the different types of operation that contribute to tourism provides a poor basis for establishing the presence of a strong pressure group'. Other constraints, such as poor image, poor climate and the dearth of cultural attractions of the kind that cities such as Paris, London or Rome can offer, undoubtedly played a part. The changing nature of tourism in the 1980s, coupled with Edwards's (1985) forecasts for international tourism, has dramatically changed the scenario, with increasing emphasis now being placed on tourism in the Republic and elsewhere.

Ireland's National Development Plan (1989–93), submitted to

the European Commission in March 1989 (Stationery Office, 1989a), allocates substantial European Regional Development Fund (ERDF) monies to tourism. Over the five-year period 1989–93 it is proposed that total investment in tourism will be in the order of IR£300 million. It is proposed that £138 million of this will come from the ERDF, £152 million from the private sector and the remaining £10 million from the public sector. These increased structural funds represent the most important source of finance ever made available to the tourism sector and reflect the great expectation of positive results. The Irish government has set a target that requires both the number of visitors and expenditure by those visitors to double over the period 1988–92, i.e. an annual compound growth rate of 15 per cent.

The growth rate of Irish tourism in the decade up to 1987 was 1 per cent per annum. This performance (when projected forward) suggests that revenue from overseas visitors will reach £480 million by 1992 (1987 prices). The government target is for overseas tourism to generate £1008 million by 1992, a result that would require a compound growth rate of 15 per cent per annum. The government estimates that in order to fulfil this ambitious target the required number of visitors would be 4.2 million per annum by 1992, with an additional 25 000 new jobs in tourism (compared with 2.8 million visitors and 69 000 jobs in 1988).

In order to achieve these targets a policy that recognized the strengths and weaknesses of Irish tourism was formulated. A number of gaps in the market were identified and numerous projects have subsequently been put forward for funding. In fact, 600 schemes, which together would cost over IR£1.5 billion, are currently being considered by Bord Failte (the Irish Tourist Board). While a target for additional employment has been set, there is no explicit statement on where and what kind of jobs will be created. Table 9.1 illustrates the changes in the industry in recent years.

The growth rates set for 1988, 1989 and 1990 were achieved. However, the decline in North American tourists due to the Gulf War makes it virtually impossible that the 1991 targets will have been achieved. The management of Bord Failte accepted this inevitability although they did envisage that growth in the continental European market might alleviate some of the shortfall. Despite this situation the overall targets set for 1992 were not abandoned, but their attainment would seem a much greater task than it did previously. This guarded optimism is principally based on the continued growth of visitors from continental Europe.

Table 9.1 Employment and revenues generated in Irish tourism, 1985–1990

	Visitor numbers (thousands)		Total revenue[a] (IR£ million)		Employment	Revenue as % of GNP	Employment % of total at work
	Domestic[b]	Out of State	Domestic	Out of state[c]			
1985	3 820	2 536	269	685	*	6.2	*
1986	3 231	2 467	217	649	*	5.3	*
1987	4 489	2 664	291	731	63 000	5.7	5.8
1988	4 161	3 007	311	842	69 000	6.2	6.3
1989	5 060	3 484	331	991	64 000[d]	6.5	5.9
1990	5 065[e]	3 675[e]	413	1 139	n.a.	n.a.	n.a.

* Figures for employment in 1985–6 were calculated on a different basis from those for subsequent years. The figures for 1987 and 1988 are Bord Failte estimates.
[a] At current prices.
[b] Includes home holidays and other non-business domestic trips.
[c] Includes carrier receipts.
[d] *Source:* Henry (1991). These figures may be regarded as lower limits if one allows for some share of a further maximum 25 000 man-years and IR£361 million GNP owing to implied income and responding on a 'balanced budget' hypothesis.
[e] Estimates provided by Bord Failte and the Central Statistics Office.

Sources: Bord Failte, Annual Statistics, and the Central Statistics Office.

Visitor numbers from this market area increased from 390 000 in 1987 to 740 000 in 1990. The increase in 1990 over 1989 was 36 per cent.

The factors underlying the growth in visitors from Europe are varied. In the period 1977–87 visitor numbers from Europe were virtually stagnant. This was mainly because of the perception of Ireland as an expensive holiday destination and the effects of the 'troubles' in Northern Ireland (Williams and Shaw, 1988, p. 16). Lower inflation in Ireland in the latter half of the 1980s, lower VAT rates for tourists and liberalization of air fares have undoubtedly made Ireland a more attractive destination. In addition, the increased awareness of green issues throughout the world has been an advantage to a country generally regarded as being environmentally unspoilt.

Given the increased emphasis on employment in tourism and particularly on tourism projects, we thought it timely to attempt an estimate of the direct, indirect and induced employment outcomes from a selected number of tourism projects in Ireland. The structure of this chapter is as follows: Section 9.2 provides a brief résumé of the tourism projects; Section 9.3 reviews methodological issues and the debate on export tourism multipliers in the Republic of Ireland; Section 9.4 explains the methodology and data used; Section 9.5 presents the results and elaborates upon some theoretical and practical issues in employment measurement; finally, brief conclusions are offered.

Table 9.2 Tourism projects – principal characteristics, 1989

	House	Caves	Park	All
Location	Tourist area	Off main tourist route	On tourist/ commercial route	West of Ireland
Facilities	House, gardens	Underground caves	Nineteenth-century village	Tea-room shop
Admission charges[a]	21	43	47	
Shop sales[a]	55	33	45	
Tea-room sales[a]	24	24	8	
Visitor numbers	144 000	104 000	264 000	
(per cent foreign)	(52)	(53)	(70)	
Ownership	Public	Private	Public	
Season	All year	Mar.–Oct.	All year	

[a] Per cent of gross revenue

9.2 DESCRIPTION OF CASE STUDY ATTRACTIONS

Three case studies of well-known tourism projects with good visitor traffic and different product mixes are presented. One is a country or period 'manor' house and gardens located in a premier Irish tourist centre (Killarney); the second is an underground cave complex in the Burren district (County Clare); the third is a folk park at Bunratty (County Clare). These projects are representative of Ireland's well-established tourist attractions. A summary of the characteristics of the three facilities is presented in Table 9.2, which helps to categorize their similarities and differences.[1]

9.3 THE MEASUREMENT OF TOURISM EMPLOYMENT

9.3.1 Some Methodologies

There are four principal approaches to measuring tourism employment:

1 The survey method.
2 Input–output modelling.
3 The proportional method.
4 Macroeconometric modelling.

The *survey method* is extremely expensive, although it may give the best direct employment estimates. Surveys of employment at businesses associated with tourism are undertaken. The method suffers from the usual caveats relating to all questionnaires and it cannot capture secondary effects on employment relating to tourist expenditure.

Input–output modelling has the advantage of being able to calculate direct and secondary effects of tourist expenditure. The major problem in Ireland (as elsewhere) is the time taken to develop input–output (I–O) tables. The most recent I–O tables for Ireland relate to 1975, although an update to 1982 was undertaken by Henry and later repriced to 1989 values (Henry, 1990). The age of the tables and the changing structure of the economy cast doubts on the validity of estimates from I–O tables. A recent paper by Henry addresses some of these problems (Henry, 1991).

The *proportional method* estimates the proportion of total expenditure in each sector that is derived from tourism and then applies this proportion to total employment in the relevant sector. Although less satisfactory from a theoretical viewpoint it does have the major advantage of incorporating up-to-date information.

The *macroeconometric model* used by the Economic and Social Research Institute (ESRI) and Department of Finance is very useful for measuring the incremental effect of out-of-state tourist revenue on existing employment. The major problem with the model is that it does not include a separate tourism sector.[2]

While each method has certain benefits and deficiencies, we decided to adopt the proportional method because of the time constraints, the resources and data available, and the fact that it is the method which incorporates the most up-to-date information. (It should not be confused with the proportional multiplier method referred to on p. 110.)

9.3.2 Export Tourism Multipliers

The conventional Keynesian export tourism national income multiplier is usually defined as the coefficient linking the change in gross national product (GNP) (an endogenous or dependent variable) to a change in export tourism expenditure (an exogenous or independent variable), given the assumptions that government expenditure on goods and services and net investment are unaffected by changes in export tourism expenditure. The size of the multiplier is clearly relevant for estimating the employment effects of tourism.

Deane (1980) reports two unpublished studies on the size of the Keynesian multiplier arising from export tourism. However, as Norton (1982) correctly points out, Deane does not provide a precise definition of these multipliers. The first (unpublished) study, by the Economist Intelligence Unit (EIU), calculated that in 1964 the multiplier was 1.9, and the second study, by the Economist Advisory Group, obtained an estimate of 1.8 in their calculations for 1967. Neither of these studies used I–O methodology, (detailed I–O tables for Ireland were not available until 1970), but apart from this there is no information on the methodology used. A study by Bord Failte in 1974 reported by Deane did use I–O analysis and reported a multiplier of 2.08, later revised downwards, in view of the changing openness of the economy, to 1.8. Subsequent work by Byrne and Palmer (1981) concurs with Deane's estimates of 73 500 jobs attributed to export tourism in 1977.

A major contribution by Norton (1982) casts grave doubts on these studies and results. In particular, Norton's upper bound estimates based on his formal Keynesian model suggested an export tourism multiplier of only 1.09. He also suggests that a correction of the assumptions which biased his estimate would give a multiplier in the region of 0.8 for 1976. With respect to employment, his upper bound estimate for employment generation from export tourism was 47 656. He suggests that this again is an overestimate not only because his multiplier is an upper bound estimate but also because the export tourism sector, according to his calculations, is more capital-intensive than the economy-wide average. 'This is because, although export tourism expenditure by tourists in Ireland is of about average capital intensity the export tourism activity of the international carriers is well above average in capital intensity' (Norton, 1982).

A paper by Bradley *et al.* (1981) estimated an export tourism multiplier of 0.5 for 1977. Norton suggests that this work was probably a little too pessimistic in relation to the marginal propensity to import (MPI) that was employed. A revision of this estimate by Norton to a more realistic level, and the use of the Bradley *et al.* econometric model, gave an export tourism multiplier of 0.7, not inconsistent with Norton's earlier estimate (Norton, 1982). A paper by O'Hagan and Mooney (1983) estimated a multiplier in the region of 0.5–0.6. The authors used the same data as Norton but made different assumptions concerning supply constraints in traded and partially traded sectors.

A recent paper by Henry (1991), based on 1989 data, reports a multiplier of 0.94. He suggests that this value agrees with estimates in several other countries or regions. It is also important to note that a value of 0.94 is seen as being a good outcome by Henry and many other economists in the country. This is certainly different from the prevailing view in the 1970s and early 1980s.

9.3.3 Employment Estimates

In recent years the employment effects of tourism have received considerable attention. A government White Paper on tourism policy (Stationery Office, 1985) outlined the difficulties inherent in measuring employment related to tourism. In the absence of official annual data series on employment in tourism the main source has been Bord Failte. Bord Failte estimates are based on the I–O method. Particular attention has been given to a 1985

Bord Failte study which concluded that 91 000 jobs in the economy were dependent on tourism. The figure was based on the assumption that government tax revenue from out-of-state tourism was re-spent – an assumption which resulted in an extra 40 000 jobs. The reason for this assumption is unclear but certainly it is no longer considered tenable given current economic policies, which do not operate on the basis of a balanced budget multiplier but rather see additional tax revenues as simply reducing the government budget deficit.[3] It is interesting to note that the current figures for employment released by Bord Failte (see Table 9.1) suggest a figure much less than the above. Interestingly the estimate for 1989 is only slightly above the estimate that Deane (1980) and Byrne and Palmer (1981) gave for 1977, when tourism revenue was far less than in 1989. The employment impact of 1989 tourism in Ireland estimated by Henry (1991) using I–O tables implies some 64 000 jobs.

All of the foregoing discussion suggests some concern over the validity of employment estimates in tourism. Ireland is probably no different from many other countries in this regard (see O'Hagan and Waldron, 1987). Nevertheless, the debate has been positive to the extent that the estimates now seem a good deal more reasonable than previously. However, much still needs to be done before confidence in the estimates is appropriate. Even the most rigorous studies undertaken to date cannot provide accurate annual estimates of tourism employment because of the dearth of regularly updated base data. As a result the approach adopted in this study was to use the proportional method. The rationale for this is outlined briefly in the next section.

9.4 METHODOLOGY AND DATA USED

This chapter deals with the direct, indirect and induced employment effects of the projects. These terms have already been described in Chapter 7, but it may be helpful briefly to reconsider them here. Direct employment in the context of this study is the number of jobs generated at the facility itself because of the expenditure of tourists. Indirect employment is generated by the secondary or 'upstream' activities of those supplying goods and services to the facilities. The induced effects result from the re-spending of incomes generated by those directly employed at the sites and in local supplying firms. At the micro level of operation, invoice data can provide figures for the intermediate demand from supplying firms, which can be difficult to estimate in a macro-environment.

The core data used for this study consist of the accounting information supplied by the management at the three sites (House, Caves and Park).[4] The audited accounts and discussion with management provided the necessary information to estimate the direct full-time equivalent (FTE) jobs at the three sites. In addition to the audited accounts, key invoice data of all purchases made during 1989 were used to trace the sector and location for these purchases. The data covered goods purchased for sale and other purchases of an 'overhead' nature, many of the latter being services, e.g. insurance, advertising, electricity.

The use of invoice data involves a number of minor problems. Firstly, the address to which the invoice is sent may not be the address at which the employment was generated. In this study it is assumed that the invoice address is the one at which the corresponding employment occurs.[5] Secondly, it has not always been possible to identify the good or service for which payment was made. As a result 'miscellaneous' or 'unknown' have been used as categories for such expenditure. Fortunately, only minor amounts are involved. Thirdly, the invoices available to the authors can provide estimates of first-round indirect employment only. Further rounds would require access to invoices of suppliers further down the supply chain. Such further rounds would require considerable resources beyond the scope of the study. It is unlikely that the costs of such an operation would be justifiable as subsequent rounds become less significant in quantitative terms. Simple 'rule of thumb' measures derived from first-round effects can be employed. Finally, the geographical breakdown of the invoices can cause some problems. In this study any invoice address within a 30-mile radius was deemed 'local'.

In addition to the above, data from the Labour Force Survey, National Income and Expenditure and the Census of Industrial Production publications were used to calculate the output–employment ratios necessary for estimating the employment effects of first-round purchases. Finally, original survey data were collected at each of the three sites on three sampling dates in July, August and September 1990. This exercise was designed to provide some idea of typical spending patterns at these sites and to establish the consequential spending in the area arising from the visit to the facility. This is a form of 'associated activities' spending, although trying to isolate the impact of the facility on such spending is fraught with methodological difficulties (see Johnson and Thomas, 1990).

9.5 RESULTS

9.5.1 Direct and Indirect Employment

The employment impact of the tourist facilities is subdivided into direct, indirect and induced effects as indicated in the previous section. Direct employment is calculated on an FTE basis in which the basic unit is one person employed for a year. This procedure enables seasonal and other temporary employment at each site to be taken into account on a *pro rata* basis. The totals for 1989 were 29, 18 and 52 FTEs at the House, Caves and Park respectively.

Indirect employment arises in manufacturing and service sub-suppliers in the local area (approximate 30-mile radius), elsewhere in Ireland and abroad. Imports were netted out initially – these were quite low at the House (3 per cent of purchases) and Park (2 per cent) but somewhat higher at the Caves (15 per cent)[6] – and the remaining first-round purchases allocated to local and non-local origins for both manufacturing and services. Total purchases of manufactured supplies for resale or reprocessing (as in the case of food) varied from 41 per cent to 52 per cent of total purchases at the three sites. All VAT payments were excluded from the calculations.

The data available for the manufacturing sector were reasonably comprehensive and up to date, particularly because of the publication of the 1987 Census of Industrial Production (Stationery Office, 1988a). The gross output to employment ratios are thus relatively reliable. The same cannot be said for the services sector ratios, in which a combination of 1988 aggregate national accounts data (Stationery Office, 1989b), 1982 I–O tables repriced to 1989 (Henry, 1990) and the 1988 Labour Force Survey (Stationery Office, 1988b) was used. Turnover–employment ratios for the distribution sector were derived from the 1988 Census of Services (Stationery Office, 1990) and were inflated to 1989 prices. Clearly, further refinement of the output–employment ratios is possible.

Table 9.3 summarizes the indirect employment effects of each of the three facilities under consideration. The principal manufacturing sub-sectors were food and drink, clothing, paper and

Table 9.3 Indirect employment in manufacturing and service sub-suppliers to house, caves and park by location, 1989

	House		Caves		Park		Totals
	Local	Non-local	Local	Non-local	Local	Non-local	
Manufacturing	0.38	3.36	0.22	2.16	0.34	6.15	12.61
Services	1.07	2.85	1.07	1.94	5.84	5.98	18.75
Total	1.45	6.21	1.29	4.10	6.18	12.13	31.36

printing, and crafts, and the highest proportion of local purchases arose in the food and drink sector. The distribution sector (whole-sale and retail trade) represented the main services sub-sector from which purchases were made, representing 57 per cent of all services expenditure at the House, 46 per cent at the Caves but only 26 per cent at the Park. It is quite possible that many of the products purchased from these sources originated as imports but such second-round purchases do not impact on the employ-ment estimation exercise currently being pursued. The employ-ment impact is confined to the jobs arising in the distribution sector itself. Repairs and maintenance represented a major expen-diture item at the Caves (28 per cent of total services expen-ditures), while publicity and advertising was the largest single item of services expenditure at the Park (21 per cent). Mainte-nance costs are also high at the House but, because of financial arrangements with the Office of Public Works, are not reflected in the accounts.

The proportion of indirect to direct employment in the local areas is approximately 9 per cent, which increases to 32 per cent when non-local purchases elsewhere in the Irish economy are added in. Thus 31.4 additional jobs in the economy are deemed to exist on the basis of first-round purchases from the three tourist facilities examined. Put another way, type I ratio multipliers,[7] which relate direct plus indirect employment to direct employ-ment, are 1.09 (local) and 1.31 (Irish economy).

9.5.2 Induced Employment

The main component in this category is the re-spending of factor incomes earned by those directly employed at the facilities. In addition there is induced employment from salaries and wages earned in the local and other Irish sub-supply industry and ser-vice sectors. The incomes arising from purchases from local manufacturing firms are estimated to be IR£8738 and those from manufacturing firms elsewhere in Ireland to be £97 117. It is more difficult to estimate the corresponding figure for incomes generated in services.[8]

The jobs generated in distribution were first estimated at 0.52 (local) and 1.78 (non-local). Census of Distribution data were used to convert these figures into incomes: £4026 (local) and £13 783 (non-local). The balance of service sector jobs (i.e. the total for services in Table 9.3 less the jobs in distribution) was 7.46 (local) and 8.99 (non-local). The incomes earned in these jobs were estimated on the basis of the arbitrary assumption that they were, on average, 80 per cent of the average industrial wage for 1989, i.e. £9002 per person employed. This gave rise to incomes of £67 155 (local) and £80 928 (non-local) generated in the services-supplying firms outside the distribution sector. The total wages and salaries arising at the facilities were deemed to be spent locally and were added to incomes generated in locally supplying manufacturing and services firms to determine the induced employment close to the facilities (i.e. within a 30-mile radius). Incomes arising in supplying firms elsewhere in the economy were deemed to generate employment in the same geographical zone based on the spending proportions and mix. The I–O model developed by Henry (1990) was used to estimate the employment effects of the household expenditure arising from the direct and indirect incomes dependent on the tourist facilities analysed. Only the direct employment (from first-round spending of these incomes) was estimated, based on sales of £56 593 per FTE job. The induced employment arising is estimated to be 3.6 additional local jobs for the House, 1.7 for the Caves and 9.1 for the Park; additional non-local jobs were 0.9 (House), 0.6 (Caves) and 1.8 (Park). Second-round effects have not been calculated but would be significantly less than this owing to various leakages through savings, taxes and imports.

9.5.3 The Gross Employment Impact

Table 9.4 brings together the direct, indirect and induced employment generated by the tourist facilities. It summarizes the outcomes arising from expenditures at each location.

In summary, this gross employment total arises from the following expenditure categories: direct expenditures by visitors to the facilities; the consequential purchases of supplies (manufacturing and service) by the facilities' management; and the

Table 9.4 Total (or gross) employment effects of the three tourist facilities

	Direct	Indirect		Induced		Totals
		Local	Non-local	Local	Non-local	
House	29	1.45	6.21	3.58	0.94	41.18
Cave	18	1.29	4.10	1.72	0.42	25.53
Park	52	5.27	8.19	9.11	1.81	76.38
Totals	99	8.01	18.50	14.41	3.17	143.09

spending of wages and salaries earned both by those employed at the facilities and by those employed in the firms supplying goods and services to the facilities. The ratio of total to direct employment is 143.1/99 or 1.45 to 1. The ratio for total employment generated locally is 121.4/99 or 1.23 to 1. These ratios may be compared to the 'type II' employment multipliers estimated in Henry's (1991) paper for the whole economy.

9.5.4 Net Employment Impact

The above figures need to be adjusted for any displacement effects which arise, i.e. it is necessary to deduct from the gross employment figures any employment which arises from purchases that would have occurred in the area in any case. Such employment, it is assumed, would have arisen elsewhere in the locality (or in Ireland) had the facilities not existed. Displacement may be considered at two levels: first, that of the local areas of the tourist facilities, and secondly, elsewhere in Ireland. In the local areas, any spending diverted from other parts of Ireland would represent additional employment but if diverted from other facilities in the locality (tourist or otherwise) would represent displacement. From the perspective of the Irish economy as a whole, foreign tourists would represent additional employment while Irish tourists would simply reflect displacement from elsewhere in Ireland.

To estimate the net employment effects data are needed on the origins of tourists to the three facilities, supplemented for Irish visitors by information on the nature of their trips there, i.e. whether these are part of a tour passing through the areas or are specifically designed to visit the facilities. Full local displacement is assumed for Irish visitors to the sites who have come from their home or holiday bases. Foreign visitors holidaying in the areas are assumed to generate no displacement. Surveys were

Table 9.5 Net and gross employment effects of the three tourist facilities: local and national levels

| | Gross employment | | Net employment | |
	Local	National	Local	National
House	34.03	41.18	27.56	25.53
Caves	21.01	25.53	17.02	15.83
Park	66.38	76.38	53.77	47.36
Totals	121.42	143.09	98.35	88.72

conducted to obtain information on visitors, and estimates by management at the three facilities, based on visitor books and commissioned surveys, on the foreign–Irish breakdown of visitors were useful in grappling with the displacement problem. Local displacement effects were estimated to be 19 per cent, while total Irish displacement effects were 38 per cent. When allowance is made for both of these effects (differentially at each facility) the total employment effect was reduced to 98.4 locally and 88.7 for the national economy (Table 9.5). The ratios of total to direct employment or direct plus indirect to direct employment, of course, do not change. Local employment generated was greater because the displacement effects were lower than when the total economy was the reference area used. Generally the smaller an area the lower will be the displacement arising within that area.

9.5.5 Employment in Associated Activities

The final component of employment that depends on the tourism facilities arises from the complementary purchases made in the area during visits to the sites. These purchases may be of a 'pure' tourist nature, e.g. accommodation and meals while in the area, or of a general commercial nature, such as purchases of goods and services in the locality. The critical issue in estimating the employment generated is the proportion of the total expenditure which ought to be attributed to the facility in question. Johnson and Thomas (1990) addressed this issue but did not attempt estimations.

As part of the current study a survey was undertaken of 100 visitors to each site. The sample was randomly chosen on each of the interview days, all of which were in the peak tourist season (July, August, early September 1990). Interviewers were instructed to ensure an even distribution of young/old and

Table 9.6 Mean daily expenditure and total annual expenditure on associated acitvities

	Mean daily expenditure (IR£)			Total annual expenditure (IR£)		
	House	Caves	Park	House	Caves	Park
Transport costs	3.09[a]	2.73[a]	4.77[a]	333 720	212 940	944 460
Accommodation	13.23	6.86	8.61	1 428 840	535 080	1 704 780
Food meals	12.04	10.76	5.72	1 300 320	839 280	1 132 560
Drink	5.54	5.59	3.69	598 320	436 020	730 620
Other goods	10.16	6.47	7.44	1 097 280	504 660	1 473 120
Total	44.06	32.41	30.23	4 758 480	2 527 980	5 985 540

[a] Not daily mean but travel to and from the facility divided by 2.

foreign/Irish respondents. The purpose of the interviews was to collect and analyse information on the expenditure patterns of visitors to the facilities. The expenditure categories were as follows: transport costs to and from the facilities, accommodation (bed and breakfast) costs, other food and drink expenses, admission fees and other purchases at the sites themselves and other expenses incurred in the area where the tourist facility is located. Mean daily expenditures were estimated under each of these headings (Table 9.6).

It is assumed that spending on associated activities, including accommodation, that might reasonably relate to the facility is confined to a single day's expenditure, plus half the transport costs noted.[9] To obtain the total annual expenditure estimates shown in Table 9.6 the mean daily spend figures have been multiplied by 75 per cent of the total number of visitors to the sites (to allow for children and school tours where spending would be considerably lower), i.e. by 108 000 for the House, by 78 000 for the Caves and by 198 000 for the Park. However, only a proportion of the total expenditure can be attributed to the facilities themselves. Respondents were asked whether the existence of the facilities was the primary reason for their visits there: 21 per cent answered in the affirmative at the House, 44 per cent at the Caves and 67 per cent at the Park. These percentages were taken as the proportions attributable to the existence of the facilities. For example, the total attributable expenditure at the House was 21 per cent of £4.758 million, i.e. £999 281; corresponding expenditures for the Caves and Park were £1 112 091 and £4 010 312 respectively. Estimates of indirect taxes were deducted from the gross amounts spent to determine the relevant expenditure for employment generating purposes. Output–employment ratios were then applied to the resulting total expenditure estimates to give the employment effects.

These amounted to 16.49 in the House locality, 18.17 in the Caves area and 67.93 near the Park. Allowing for the displacement in each area reduces these results to 13.36, 14.71 and 55.02 respectively, making a total of 83.09. No estimates were made of the indirect and induced employment effects arising from the attributable expenditure estimates.

The numbers employed in the associated activities appear quite high and, if they are accurate, suggest that a major impact of tourist facilities in employment terms arises from the additional spending in the local areas. The crucial question of how much of this spending to attribute to the existence of the facility has been attempted here in a manner that may need to be modified as further probing of the survey results is completed and evidence from other similar studies becomes available.[10] A key influence on the attribution factor used here is the attractiveness of the prime facility to the visitors – the relatively larger employment impact at the Park results from the fact that 67 per cent of visitors gave its existence as the primary reason for their visit there, compared with only 21 per cent at the House.

9.6 CONCLUSIONS

The results presented in this chapter depend critically upon a number of working assumptions that may be altered with subsequent research. However, in the absence of relevant published work, the assumptions adopted do not appear unreasonable.[11] The overall survey results corroborate previous findings carried out by management at the three facilities. The displacement proportions adopted in this chapter are based on an analysis of survey results generated specifically for this study at the three sites.

The choice of a 30-mile radius to define the 'local areas' was based on an examination of invoice data. The analysis of these data confirmed that purchases were either locally based as defined here or from distances well outside the local area. Travel to and spending at the sites from areas outside these 30-mile radii can be reasonably assumed to be non-local. Consequently if the local areas as defined were to be extended the displacement factor would be larger and the local employment impact smaller.

Despite these reservations the approach adopted in this paper has a number of obvious benefits. First and foremost, since the allocation of scarce resources is critical not only to tourism projects but to all forms of economic activity, this type of approach can be utilized in evaluating state investment or subsidies to any initiative which has employment generation as a goal. Secondly, the study demonstrates the importance of distinguishing between the local and the national impact of tourism. Displacement effects are less in the former. Thirdly, it is important to consider whether proposed projects are complementary or competitive. If they are competitive, then displacement will be greater, which is important in the context of the allocation of scarce resources. However, it should be recognized that different sectors of the economy are not of equal labour intensity. Thus even where there is a 100 per cent diversion of demand to tourist attractions, the latter may still experience a net employment gain because they have a higher labour intensity compared with the industries from which demand has been diverted. Fourthly, the results presented in this chapter suggest only modest employment gains from *direct*, *indirect* and *induced* expenditures arising from the tourist attractions themselves.

The main impact appears to arise from associated spending. While we are less certain of the robustness of the attribution factor employed, the results, if correct, suggest that the main employment impact does not occur at the facilities themselves but elsewhere as a result of this associated spending.

Four final points are noted for further study. Firstly, this paper has ignored impacts that are not directly measurable. Preservation of the 'national heritage' may bestow immeasurable benefits on future generations. Secondly, the existence of a facility may make an area more desirable for inward investment, extra spending and employment, which might not otherwise occur. Thirdly, not all jobs created are identical in their economic characteristics. Many of the direct jobs created at the sites are of a part-time and seasonal nature and may to some extent give a misguided impression of employment creation. Fourthly, it may be noted that additional tourist expenditure may not necessarily create extra employment if some sectors of the economy experience under-employment.

All the foregoing suggests that a great deal remains to be undertaken in the tourism employment arena, which is rather surprising given the emphasis that many governments have been placing on tourism over the past ten years.

Notes

The authors are extremely grateful to Breda Aldridge and John Coakley, University of Limerick, for research support in the preparation of this paper; and to Eamon Henry and Brian Deane for comments on an earlier draft; the usual disclaimer applies.

1 For a more detailed outline of the three facilities considered in this paper see Dineen and Deegan (1990).

2 The ESRI and Department of Finance are currently updating the model to include a discrete tourism sector.

3 The assumption that no additional employment or output arises from the taxes generated by the industry is now considered to be perhaps too extreme as the implied reduction in the borrowing requirement and repayment of the national debt have some positive output and employment effects. These effects are built into the Department of Finance/ESRI macroeconometric model of the economy. This point was clarified by an official of the Department of Finance, Dublin.

4 The co-operation of the management at the three sites was of inestimable value in conducting this study.

5 Preliminary research has suggested that this problem is very minor in the present study.

6 Since most imports are of manufactured goods it is interesting to note that the proportions of manufactured imports were: House, 3 per cent; Park, 4 per cent; Caves, 27 per cent.

7 For a discussion of 'normal' expenditure multipliers and type I (and II) employment ratio multipliers applied to the Irish tourism sector see Henry (1991); type II employment multipliers relate direct plus indirect plus induced to direct employment.

8 This is because no regular Census of Services, analogous to the annual Census of Industrial Production, is undertaken in Ireland. This could give data on average wages and salaries earned in specific sub-sectors of the service economy; the only sub-sector for which these data are available is the distribution (wholesale and retail) sector based on the annual Census of Distribution.

9 For this purpose expenditure at the sites is not included as it would involve double counting any employment impact.

10 One possible argument is that all the spending on associated activities would have occurred in any case and therefore no additional employment arises that can be attributed to the existence of the tourist facility.

11 A recent paper by Johnson and Thomas (1990) provides a framework for the estimation of the employment impact of a tourist attraction. This paper dealt with a single site, the Beamish Open Air Museum in the north of England. The 'local area' chosen was the entire north of England and the results cannot be compared easily with the much more narrowly defined 'local areas' in the present study.

References

Bradley, J., Digby, C., Fitzgerald, J.D., Keegan, O. and Kirwan, K. (1981) *Description, Simulation and Multiplier Analysis of the Model – 80 Econometric Model of Ireland*. Research Paper 2/81. Dublin: Department of Finance.

Byrne, J.P. and Palmer, N.T. (1981) Some economic aspects of Irish tourism. *Irish Journal of Business and Administration Research*, **3**, 87–93.

Deane, B. (1980) *Tourism Policy*. National Economic and Social Council Publication no. 52, Prl. 8701. Dublin: Stationery Office.

Deane, B. (1986) Tourism in Ireland: an employment growth area. *Administration*, **35**, 337–49.

Dineen, D.A. and Deegan, J.G. (1990) The employment effects of tourism projects – some Irish case studies. Paper presented to conference on Tourism Research: into the 1990s, held at University College, Durham, 10–12 December.

Edwards, A. (1985) *International Tourism Forecasts to 1995*. London: The Economist Intelligence Unit.

Henry, E.W. (1990) Estimating Irish 1989 GNP and employment multipliers by input–output modelling. A research report for Bord Failte, Dublin.

Henry, E.W. (1991) *Estimated employment and gross national product impacts of 1989 tourism in Ireland*. Paper read before the Statistical and Social Inquiry Society of Ireland, Dublin, 9 May.

Johnson, P. and Thomas, B. (1990) Measuring the local employment impact of a tourist attraction: an empirical study. *Regional Studies*, **24**, 395–403.

Norton, D. (1982) Export tourism input output multipliers for Ireland. *Quarterly Economic Commentary (ESRI)*, May, 34–50.

O'Hagan, J. and Mooney, D. (1983) Input–output multipliers in a small open economy: an application to tourism. *Economic and Social Review*, **14**, 273–80.

O'Hagan, J. and Waldron, P. (1987) Estimating the magnitude of tourism in the European Community. *Journal of the Statistical and Social Inquiry Society of Ireland*, **25**, 89-119.

Stationery Office (1985) *Tourism Policy* (White Paper). Dublin: Stationery Office.

Stationery Office (1988a) *Census of Industrial Production, 1987*. Dublin: Stationery Office.

Stationery Office (1988b) *Labour Force Survey, 1988*. Dublin: Stationery Office.

Stationery Office (1989a) *National Development Plan (1989-1993)*. Dublin: Stationery Office.

Stationery Office (1989b) *National Income and Expenditure, 1988*. Dublin: Stationery Office.

Stationery Office (1990) *1988 Census of Services*. Dublin: Stationery Office.

Williams, A. and Shaw, G. (eds) (1988) *Tourism and Economic Development: Western European Experiences*. London: Belhaven Press.

10 The Economic Impact of Tourism and Recreation in the Province of Antwerp, Belgium

Dirk Yzewyn and Guido De Brabander

10.1 INTRODUCTION

Belgium is not a highly popular international tourist destination, nor is its tourism policy and planning well developed. Yet the need for a more systematic approach to tourism policy is increasingly being recognized, especially at regional and local levels. As a consequence, there is a growing demand for tourism-oriented empirical research. This chapter provides a contribution to this research by examining the economic impact of tourism in the Province of Antwerp.

The City of Antwerp occupies a central position in the tourist activities of the Province. In the sixteenth century the city was the northern counterpart of Venice and one of the most prosperous towns in Europe. It is less prominent today but it is still renowned for its major sea port and leading position in the international diamond trade. The city contains numerous testimonies to a rich and exciting history (such as one of the finest cathedrals in Europe and many links with Rubens and other Flemish painters) as well as a large variety of cultural facilities, industrial attractions (e.g. the Antwerp diamond industry and sea port), sporting infrastructure, shopping opportunities, dining facilities and night-life.

Notwithstanding the province's many and varied attractions and facilities, tourism currently only represents a small part of the local economy and is certainly not of vital importance to it.

Nevertheless, the role of tourism in the Province of Antwerp is attracting increasing attention from policy-makers and planners. It is against the background of this growing interest and of the absence of firm, empirical evidence on the economic impact of tourism that this study was undertaken. It was also thought that without a study of this kind it would be difficult, if not impossible, to raise financial support from either the public or private sectors for tourism development. An initial research study on the City of Antwerp (De Brabander, 1987) proposed a broader provincial analysis.

The research on which this study is based was supported financially by the Regional Development Authority of Antwerp and carried out in 1989-90 (Yzewyn and De Brabander, 1990). The first part of the research was entirely devoted to methodological issues. Since no regional or macroeconomic impact analysis in the tourism field had previously been undertaken in Belgium, it was necessary to draw up an inventory of alternative techniques and their implications in terms of data requirements and costs. This part of the study was particularly valuable in that it identified a number of suitable alternative approaches that might be used for the empirical component of the research. In addition to established methods for impact measurement, the 'minimum requirements' approach proposed by De Brabander in 1987 was further developed. This method first estimates the employment in each of the relevant sectors that is required to meet local needs. Employment additional to this 'minimum requirement' is attributed to tourism and non-local recreation. The method relies almost exclusively on *secondary* data sources providing spatially and sectorally disaggregated employment statistics. It not only permits the computation of the overall employment impact, but also provides insights into the structure and evolution of tourism employment in specific localities.

The second part of the study was an empirical analysis of the economic importance of tourism in the Province of Antwerp. A broad definition of tourism was adopted. This definition includes the following categories:

1 Business and convention tourism in the province.
2 Leisure tourism in the province. The following categories of leisure tourism are identified.
(a) Non-local recreation. Trips of more than two but not more than four hours duration made by residents of the province to destinations within the borders of their own

regions. ('Region' here is defined as the impact area of medium-sized or large cities. The Province of Antwerp has three such regions.)

(b) Day trips. Trips not involving an overnight stay. Day trips are further subdivided into the following components.

(i) Direct day trips. Trips starting from home. A distinction is made between:
- extra-regional day trips (those of more than two hours duration made by residents of a given region to destinations outside that region); and
- intra-regional day trips (those of more than four hours made within the region of residence).

(ii) Indirect day trips. Trips starting from a temporary place of residence.

(c) Staying visits. Visits involving at least an overnight stay.

Local recreation – leisure trips undertaken by the province's residents near to their homes and lasting less than two hours – is not included in the definition of leisure tourism. The above terminologies are used throughout this chapter.

The full impact analysis included the analysis of expenditure volumes and patterns, the measurement of tourist investment and the computation of direct, indirect and induced effects on employment and income. Because of space constraints, however, the discussion here is confined principally to employment issues.

In the next section the methodological framework used in the study is discussed. The empirical results are presented in Section 10.3.

10.2 THE METHODOLOGICAL FRAMEWORK

The basic methodology used for the measurement of the economic impact of tourism is well established (see, for example, Archer, 1977; Henderson and Cousins, 1975; Oosterhaven and Van der Knijff, 1987; Vaughan, 1977). The main challenge arises over how this methodological toolbox is applied in specific situations, where researchers are frequently constrained by the availability of recent and disaggregated data, financial resources and time. Thus a key objective is to find a working method, which may perhaps not be ideal from a methodological point of view, but which takes account of these constraints. Such a method inevitably means that any results are likely to be subject to a margin of error, although it is hoped that they will be sufficiently robust to retain their usefulness as estimates.

In the Antwerp case study the employment impact of tourism was examined from both the demand and supply sides. The two approaches are complementary, and the application of both serves as a counterbalance for data constraints and other research restrictions.

10.2.1 The Demand-side Approach

One way to determine the economic impact of tourism is to take tourist spending in a given area as a starting point, and then to translate this spending into, say, the employment, income and tax revenues created in the local, provincial or national economies. This approach stems from economic base theory, the Keynesian multiplier model and input–output theory. The last of these is clearly superior – for reasons given below – and has frequently been used for the purposes of tourism impact and multiplier analysis.

The use of input–output models essentially involves (a) the measurement of visitor numbers, tourist expenditure volumes and consumption patterns (i.e. demand-side information) and (b) the incorporation of these data into a model of the economy, which contains information about the interrelationships between the inputs and outputs of the constituent industries. Input–output analysis is extremely useful since it allows the estimation not only of primary but also of secondary impacts. These secondary effects include the impact of tourist spending that occurs outside the various sectors of the tourism industry itself, as a result either of the existence of inter-sectoral relationships (indirect effects springing from intermediate sales flows) or of the re-spending of income that is directly or indirectly generated by tourist activities (induced effects). Thus input–output analysis is able to yield a relatively comprehensive picture of the impact of tourism.

In the Antwerp case study calculations were based on a national 54-sector input–output table. The main results of the analysis refer to:

- the total direct, indirect and induced employment effects;
- the distribution of these effects by industry;

- the distribution of the employment impact by type of visitor;
- tourism (employment) multipliers.

Although, in methodological terms, input–output models are superior to other tourism impact models, it is important that the underlying assumptions and operational limitations associated with the application of the technique should be appreciated (see Archer, 1977, pp. 33–44). With respect to the Antwerp tourism study, particular attention should be drawn to:

- some well-known limitations of static input–output models (concerning, for example, the use of linear technical production functions, the existence of supply constraints and the transactions velocity of the economy);
- the lack of accurate and up-to-date input–output tables in Belgium (the most recent dates from 1980);
- the absence of inter-regional input–output tables; and
- the high level of aggregation across sectors, especially with respect to tertiary activities such as those relating to the tourist industry.

It should be clear from the above that, at least in a Belgian research context, input–output models can help to reduce the level of uncertainty about the scale and nature of economic impacts, but will never be able fully to eliminate it. This statement is likely to be especially valid for the estimation of indirect effects and even more for that of induced effects.

The reliability of the results of impact analysis also depends on the quality of the information about tourist expenditure volumes. Here, three elements are of importance: average expenditure per person and per day (or per visit); tourist spending patterns; and the number of tourist days (or visitors). The measurement of these three variables is sometimes highly problematic, a fact that is not often recognized. The main problem is how to obtain a sufficiently representative sample for the destination area and period under study. This difficulty is particularly acute for destinations that show a great variety and spatial dispersion of attractions and facilities, and/or significant temporal fluctuations in the volume and structure of tourist demand. Other problems include the measurement of visitor expenditures and day trips. It is not intended here to give a detailed exposition of how the tourist survey methodology was applied in the Antwerp study. Instead a number of suggestions which might be of use in future applications of this research tool are made.

Firstly, there is much to be said for establishing separate surveys for the main tourism market segments. Overnight visitors could perhaps be most appropriately interviewed near their accommodation, with the size of the samples reflecting the proportions of visitors staying overnight in different types of accommodation. People spending more than one night might be invited to record all their expenditure during one or more days of their stay. For commercial types of accommodation this would, of course, require the full co-operation of the management. In the Antwerp study it was found that the promise of feedback from the study improved the level of co-operation obtained.

Where non-local recreation and intra-regional day trip demand are thought to be important – which was the case in the Province of Antwerp – they can best be surveyed by means of home interviews. Home surveys can also provide useful information about stays with friends and relatives and in second homes. Quota sampling is likely to offer the most representative results. As far as extra-regional day trips are concerned, destination surveys will remain the only effective option because home surveys would be prohibitively expensive.

Provided that staying visits are measured as suggested above, the following equation, proposed by Burkart and Medlik (1974, pp. 88–9), is likely to lead to acceptable estimates of the total number of day trippers to a destination:

$$D = S \times a \times d/s$$

where D is the number of day trips in a given period; S is the total number of staying visitors in this period (obtained from accommodation surveys); a is the average length of stay of all staying visitors; d is the number of day trippers in the survey sample; and s is the number of staying visitors in the survey sample. When intra-regional day trips are estimated through a home survey, the above formula should be restricted to extra-regional day trippers only to avoid double counting.

Secondly, interview locations should be sufficiently representative of the attractions and facilities in the area under study, and the number of interviews at each location should more or less correspond with its relative importance in terms of visitors. Thirdly, surveys should cover a full year in order to allow for temporal variations in tourist demand. A frequency of three surveys a year might be regarded as a minimum. Finally, survey analyses should be subject to sensitivity analysis, thereby providing an indication of the robustness of the results.

One final caveat is appropriate. Research on the economic impact of tourism is often undertaken as a first step in the formulation of a future development policy. At this stage, however, the resources available for research are usually very limited. Under these conditions good research becomes very difficult, especially given the frequent lack of data even about essential market characteristics, such as tourist expenditure. Because tourist profiles and consumption patterns show so much spatial variation (Van den Berg, 1984, p. 12), available studies of tourist expenditure undertaken on an economy-wide basis are unlikely to provide reliable estimates for any particular area. Specially designed visitor surveys may therefore be required (University of York/Leeds Polytechnic, 1988, p. 18). Such surveys are expensive.

10.2.2 The Supply-side or Minimum-Requirements Approach

The economic significance of many industries can be estimated fairly easily, especially if attention is confined to the direct effects. Provided the right set of statistics is selected, it is relatively straightforward to read the number of employed persons, turnover or value added from the relevant tables. This is often the approach used when public-sector decision-makers need to be convinced that a particular industry deserves special attention.

A similar supply-side approach is sometimes applied with respect to tourism. Official figures of Belgian tourism employment, for instance, have until now been calculated on the basis of the number of employees and self-employed persons in a group of tourism-related industries, such as restaurants, hotels and recreational services. This procedure, however, leads to a definition of tourist activity which is different from that implied by the demand-side approach. On the one hand, local recreation is treated as if it were a kind of tourism activity. On the other, a number of elements in the tourist destination mix (e.g. retail business and transport-related services) are excluded. In this way the crucial question of what proportion of total employment in these industries is related to tourism is not addressed. There is, of course, no clear-cut answer to this question, and in any case the situation is likely to vary across local economies. Nevertheless, there is value in developing a general procedure that would provide some indication, for each industry or sub-sector involved, of the importance of tourism and consequently, by aggregation, of the overall tourism impact.

As far as the Antwerp study is concerned, the supply-side approach to the estimation of tourism employment may be described as follows. Firstly, a matrix was constructed representing total employment per group of economic activities (at the three-digit level of the NACE classification, the classification of economic activities used in the European Community) for each municipality of the Province of Antwerp and for each tourism-related activity (mainly hotel and catering, retailing and recreational and cultural services).

Secondly, an estimate of the employment devoted to the satisfaction of local needs was made for each activity. This estimate was obtained by relating the employment of a given activity in a selected reference group of non-tourist municipalities, defined at the lowest level of local authority government, to the number of inhabitants in that group. In this way, the employment per inhabitant required for the satisfaction of local needs may be estimated. Finally, these data are used to estimate the employment required to meet local needs in each cell of the activity-municipality matrix referred to above. Any surplus employment may be attributed to tourism.

This minimum requirements approach is partially abandoned in three cases. Firstly, some sectors, such as hotel accommodation and concert halls, may be seen as depending for almost 100 per cent of their trade on tourism or non-local recreation. Accordingly, all jobs directly related to these activities are characterized here as tourism employment. Secondly, in some activities, mainly retail business, the procedure outlined above is likely to generate an overestimate, as it will lead to the inclusion of all effects of shopping trips, whether these are undertaken for tourism purposes or not. Thus only a proportion of the employment impact estimated via the above method is attributable to tourism. In the Antwerp case, this proportion was derived from results of economic impact studies that have examined the balance of activities in retailing and other tourism-related services. Thirdly, there are some activities in which there is no continuous relationship between employment and population size. Public transport is a good example. Here, a supply-side approach offers little insight, and separate enquiries are needed in order to estimate the number of tourism-related jobs.

It is not difficult to see how the supply-side approach may be subject to criticism from a methodological viewpoint. Clearly the results will depend heavily on (a) the composition of the reference group of municipalities used as a basis for calculating non-local employment and (b) the proportion of employment in certain activities that are classified as primarily non-tourism. Given these limitations, it is important that the methodological approach is fully spelt out and that any results should be subject to sensitivity analysis. Such analysis would show the way in which changes in the underlying hypotheses would influence the results.

At the same time the supply-side approach has a number of attractive features:

- it has a sound theoretical background (namely urban economic base analysis and central place theory);
- it is a relatively simple method that requires little primary data collection;
- it can be applied to both more restrictive and more comprehensive definitions of tourism by varying the hierarchical level of the municipalities that serve as a reference group;
- it may yield a good picture of employment structure;
- it permits the tracking of the development of tourism employment over time.

In the Antwerp study the supply-side approach was used primarily to complement input–output analysis, since the latter did not allow for business tourism and only partially measured employment relating to short cultural and shopping trips, evenings out and sporting activities. The supply-side approach also provided information (not obtainable from the input–output analysis) on the spatial distribution of direct tourism employment and on its development over time.

10.3 MAIN FINDINGS

This section discusses some of the main results of the study, particularly those relating to the number of visitors, tourism expenditures and the impact on employment that such expenditures generate. Inevitably, as the previous discussion has implied, the empirical results are subject to error. However, the estimates presented here are the best available and may be considered sufficiently robust to serve as general indicators of the economic importance of tourism in the Province of Antwerp.

Table 10.1 Tourist demand in the Province of Antwerp by type of visitor, 1989

Category	Person days or nights (thousands)	Average daily expenditure	Average length of stay
Leisure tourism			
Non-local recreation	7 875–10 125	330	–
Day trips			
Direct	5 056–9 101	720	–
Indirect	513	460	–
Staying visits	2 655[a]	1 450	–
Hotels, guest houses	464	2 930	1.7
Camp-sites			
Tourism[b]	296[a]	1 600	2.9
Seasonal[c]	1 288	1 410	7.5
Friends, relatives	68	1 720	3.2
Other accommodation	540	610	2.8
Business and convention tourism (overnight stays only)	662	4 500[d]	2.3

[a] Minimum estimate.

[b] Relates to campers staying for only a short period or single vacation.

[c] Relates to pitches rented by the same individual or family for the whole season.

[d] Assumed daily expenditure, based on current tariffs of accommodation, restaurants, transport etc.

Source: Regional Development Authority Antwerp.

10.3.1 Tourism Demand

The only form of systematic registration of tourist demand in Belgium applies to the number of nights spent by visitors staying in commercial accommodation. As far as the Province of Antwerp is concerned, this accommodation is mainly in hotels and camp-sites. In 1989 about 2 676 000 nights (7 per cent of the Belgian total) were officially registered. This figure represented an increase of 75 per cent over that for 1974.

A more complete picture of tourist demand is given in Table 10.1. This table shows that tourism demand in the Province of Antwerp is dominated by non-local recreation and day trips. Overnight stays represent only a small part of the tourism market. Moreover, for those visitors who do stay, the average length of stay is relatively short. Business and convention tourism is an important segment of the tourism market, representing about 20 per cent of total person-nights. Finally, it should be noted that there is considerable uncertainty over the yearly volume of both non-local recreation and day trips, with the estimate for the total number of trips ranging between 13.4 and 19.7 million. This uncertainty arises primarily because of the lack of consistent information on the spread of these visits throughout the year.

People visiting tourist destinations or leisure facilities in the Province of Antwerp were found to spend on average 690 BF per person-day (100 BF = 2.3 ecu). This estimate relates only to expenditures within the province and does not take account of business tourism. For the latter market segment, the estimates must be regarded as highly speculative. Table 10.1 also shows that average daily spending varies significantly between the various types of tourism.

Utilizing the data in the first and second columns of Table 10.1 the total turnover of the Antwerp tourism industry in 1989 may be estimated at 10.3–14.0 billion BF (i.e. 240–330 million ecu, inclusive of VAT). Business tourism expenditures are not included in these figures because of the lack of empirical evidence. However, if attention is restricted to overnight business visits only and if it is assumed that the average expenditure on such visits is 4500 BF per person-day, then business tourism turnover can be roughly estimated at some 3 billion BF per year.

Forty-seven per cent of the expenditure of leisure tourists was concentrated in the retail trade. Leisure and cultural services accounted for only about 8 per cent of expenditure.

As indicated, these figures include only leisure tourism. Total tourism turnover is probably much larger. Turnover statistics show, for instance, that the total sales of the accommodation and catering industries and cultural and leisure services amounted to 27.5 billion BF (exclusive of VAT) in 1988. Even if half of this figure is assumed to be related to local recreation, as defined earlier, the remaining turnover still exceeds the sum of all expenditures revealed by the 1989 tourist survey. Thus business tourism constitutes an important segment of the Antwerp tourism market.

10.3.2 The Employment Impact of Tourism

With the help of input–output analysis it was estimated that the total tourism demand of 10.3 to 14.0 billion BF generates some 4320–5950 direct jobs, i.e. jobs in the sectors that go to make up the tourism industry itself. To this direct employment must be

167

added some 1210–1630 indirect jobs (i.e. jobs generated in the chain of suppliers serving the tourism industry) and 2840–3990 induced jobs (i.e. jobs generated by the increased incomes in the tourism industry and its suppliers). Thus, overall, employment from tourism is likely to lie somewhere between 8380 and 11 460, a far from negligible figure.

Since national input–output tables have been used to make these estimates, they inevitably include not only tourism jobs within the Province of Antwerp, but also those in other Belgian provinces. This wider impact is likely to be particularly relevant to indirect and induced employment. However, since the Antwerp economy is very diversified it is reasonable to assume that leakages from the local economy are relatively small. It is likely that at least 50 per cent of the secondary effects occur within individual provincial boundaries (compare with, for example, Henderson and Cousins, 1975, p. 69). It must be stressed again that the figures mentioned above only include leisure tourism. Thus even maximum estimates of the impact of such tourism must be considered as a lower limit to the impact of all tourism activity.

From a sectoral point of view, the impact of tourism on employment was heavily concentrated. Such a finding closely reflects the distribution of tourism spending. About 83 per cent of direct and 76 per cent of direct plus indirect employment is generated in three sectors: hotel and catering, trade and services. The indirect impact, however, was found to be much more evenly spread than the direct effect. Indeed, tourism spending affects industries, such as agriculture or the food industry, that at first sight have little or nothing to do with tourism.

One of the advantages of the demand-side approach is that the impact of different groups of tourists can be identified. In the input–output analysis, there is an employment impact vector for each final demand vector. Table 10.2 shows the results of this disaggregated analysis. Generally speaking, the distribution of the direct and indirect employment impact and of expenditures by type of visitor are broadly similar. Some 75 per cent of direct and indirect employment stems from non-local recreation or day trips, which is only slightly more than this group's share of total expenditure. Among staying visitors, camp-sites have a slightly larger impact than hotels.

Although the differences in the distributions of expenditures and of direct and indirect impacts are small, they are nevertheless of some interest. This is illustrated in the last two columns of

Table 10.2 Expenditure, employment impact and multipliers by type of visitors: Province of Antwerp, 1989, maximum values

| Type of visitor[a] | Expenditures (A) | | Employment impact[b] | | | | Type I multipliers | |
| | | | Direct (B) | | Indirect (C) | | 'Orthodox' $\frac{(B)+(C)}{(B)}$ | 'Unorthodox' $\frac{(B)+(C)}{(A)}$ |
	Million BEF	%	Full-time jobs	%	Full-time jobs	%	(B)	(A)
Non-local recreation	3 330	23.9	1 550	26.0	380	23.5	1.25	0.58
Day trips	6 814	48.8	3 000	50.4	770	46.8	1.25	0.55
Direct	6 579	47.1	2 900	48.7	740	45.2	1.25	0.55
Indirect	235	1.7	100	1.6	30	1.6	1.26	0.55
Staying visitors	3 813	27.3	1 400	23.6	480	29.6	1.35	0.50
Hotels	1 359	9.7	600	10.1	190	11.6	1.31	0.58
Camp sites	1 895	13.6	600	10.2	230	13.8	1.37	0.44
Tourism	627	4.5	200	3.4	80	4.7	1.38	0.45
Seasonal	1 268	9.1	400	6.8	150	9.1	1.37	0.43
Others	560	4.0	200	9.3	70	4.2	1.35	0.47
Total	13 957	100.0	5 950	100.0	1 630	100.0	1.27	0.54

[a] For terminology, see notes to Table 10.1.
[b] Figures rounded to the nearest ten.

Source: SESO-UFSIA, University of Antwerp.

Table 10.2, which provide estimates of some employment multipliers. Following Archer (1976, p. 71), 'orthodox' and 'unorthodox' multipliers are distinguished. If induced effects are ignored, the value of the former multiplier for leisure and tourism as a whole is 1.27. This means that for every 100 jobs in the tourism industry, related intermediate spending generates about 27 indirect jobs. This compares remarkably well with a recent impact study in the Netherlands, where a similar multiplier value of 1.28 was found (NRIT, 1990). The unorthodox multiplier is defined quite differently. It relates the total employment impact to tourism expenditures. Table 10.2 shows that, overall, every million BF of tourist spending generates 0.54 jobs. To put it another way, some 1.9 million BF of tourist spending is required to create one additional job.

The above results, of course, capture only part of the picture. Some tourism expenditures were not measured at all and hence the employment figures are underestimated. However, a supply-side approach enables a more complete picture to be obtained, at least for direct impacts. A starting point is the official employment statistics disaggregated by municipality and NACE-3 sector. These statistics show that for the Province of Antwerp total employment in the ten groups of activities, covering accommodation, catering and cultural and leisure services, is about 23 000 on a head count basis, without allowing for variations in the number of hours worked. However, about 9000 of these jobs relate to local recreation and should therefore be excluded. The remaining 14 000 can be categorized as the employment effect of all types of tourism, including business and convention tourism, on the provincial economy. In addition, there are some 2940 tourist jobs in the retail business and service sector, and a further 820 jobs in communications and related activities. These data suggest a figure for total direct tourism employment of 17 760, or almost 3 per cent of total employment in the province. Clearly the tourism industry is an important employer. These figures should be interpreted in the light of the assumptions underlying the supply-side approach, and should be regarded as indicating orders of magnitude only. Nevertheless, it is worth noting that even when a sensitivity analysis is carried out with 48 (slightly) different sets of assumptions, the employment impact still ranges between 16 060 and 18 580 jobs.

The demand-side and supply-side approaches yield significantly different results. Indeed, the direct impact according to the input–output approach is about three times smaller than that indicated by the supply-side approach. This difference clearly confirms the importance of business and convention tourism and those segments of the leisure market, such as night-life and sporting activities, that were only partially covered by the demand side. The discrepancy may also partly reflect an underestimation of tourist expenditure – turnover statistics suggest the same problem – and of the proportion of employment associated with servicing demand. Further research is necessary to establish how important these factors are and the ways in which the methodology – in particular the minimum requirements approach – can be improved.

Despite these difficulties, the results of the minimum requirements approach remain of interest since they can yield useful additional insights into the structure of direct tourism employment. For example, in the Antwerp case it was shown that one-quarter of direct employment consists of self-employed persons, another quarter of white-collar workers and the remaining half of blue-collar workers. The frequently observed dominance of relatively low-skilled employment in tourism clearly applies in the Province of Antwerp.

The supply-side approach also provides good information on the spatial distribution of direct tourism employment. According to the calculations made in this study no less than 50 per cent of the jobs in the tourism industry are located in the City of Antwerp. The second and third most important concentrations are in the cities of Malines (7 per cent) and Turnhout (3 per cent). The remaining 40 per cent is located mainly in a number of municipalities in the Antwerp suburban zone in the west, and in the Campine triangle Turnhout–Mol–Herentals in the east.

10.4 CONCLUSIONS

This analysis suggests that tourism must be considered an industry of some significance in the economy of the province. Its impact on employment, for instance, is about as large as that of the financial and insurance sector. This impact is all the more remarkable given that the province does not have a clear tourism image and given the absence of any systematic policy to encourage tourism. At the same time, however, it may be argued that the development of tourism in Antwerp cannot be left simply to market forces. In view of the intense commercial pressures that exist in the tourism market, there is a good case for a well-formulated strategic plan, which integrates and directs the efforts of both public and private decision-makers towards an agreed set of realistic objectives. In this context the comparison of future expenditures, impacts and multipliers with those estimated for 1988–9 could serve as a useful assessment tool.

The impact analysis in this chapter has also shown that more attention should be given to business and convention tourism. This sector was shown to be of considerable relative importance in the Antwerp tourism industry and it offers a number of growth possibilities. Furthermore, the analysis has demonstrated that the highest employment effects per unit of expenditure are to be found in the markets of non-local recreation, day trips and stays in hotels or guest houses. This suggests *inter alia* that a good case can be made for the further development and increased promotion of hotel tourism in the province. This inevitably implies that more attention should be given to the City of Antwerp as a tourist destination, thereby further reinforcing the dominance of the city in the province. However, this concentration might be offset by the development of high quality tourist products in the rest of the province, such as health and fitness oriented stays in the Campine.

The impact analysis reported in this chapter is only a first step towards the development of a tourism policy. Its main purpose was to estimate the present economic importance of the tourism industry, and thereby to create more goodwill and support for the tourism sector. The direct relevance of the findings for policy purposes is rather limited and further research will be necessary if the future development of tourism policy and planning is to be soundly based.

References

Archer, B. (1976) The anatomy of a multiplier. *Regional Studies*, **1**, 71–7.

Archer, B. (1977) *Tourism Multipliers: The State of the Art*. Bangor: University of Wales Press.

Burkart, A. and Medlik, S. (1974) *Tourism. Past, Present and Future*. London: Heinemann.

De Brabander, G. (1987) *Antwerpen en het toerisme*. Antwerp: SESO.

Henderson, D. and Cousins, R. (1975) *The Economic Impact of Tourism. A Case-Study in Greater Tayside*. Edinburgh: University of Edinburgh.

NRIT (1990) *De economische betekenis van toerisme en recreatie in Nederland*. Breda: NRIT.

Oosterhaven, J. and Van der Knijff, E.C. (1987) On the economic impacts of recreation and tourism: the input–output approach. *Built Environment*, **2**, 96–108.

University of York/Leeds Polytechnic (1988) *Tourism and Regional Development*. Final report. Report submitted to the Directorate General for Transport of the EC Commission.

Vaughan, R. (1977) *The Economic Impact of Tourism in Edinburgh and the Lothian Region*. Edinburgh: STB.

Van den Berg, L. (1989) Urban development and tourism: a discussion focusing on the place of tourism in urban revitalisation. *Contributions to the 7th Congress of the European Leisure and Recreation Association on 'Cities for the Future'*, Rotterdam.

Yzewyn, D. and De Brabander, G. (1990) *De economische betekenis van het toerisme en de recreatie voor de provincie Antwerpen*, volumes 1 and 2. Antwerp: SESO.

11 Timeshare: The Policy Issues

Brian Goodall and Mike Stabler

11.1 INTRODUCTION

Although timeshare or interval ownership, the purchase of the periodic right to occupy holiday accommodation, constitutes a very small proportion of total tourism activity, accounting for just under 3 per cent of overseas holidays taken by UK residents in 1989, it is one of the fastest-growing sectors of the industry and has the potential to become a major form of holiday accommodation. This chapter considers the policy issues raised by its continued rapid growth from its conception in the mid-1960s to the present day, there being 1.585 million owners in 2340 locations worldwide (197 000 owners and 77 locations in the UK) in 1989.

Policy issues can be categorized as intra-timeshare, inter-industry and wider-economic. The first covers those internal to the timeshare industry itself, concerning its promotion, marketing, organization, operation, management and legal characteristics, particularly *vis-à-vis* purchasers. The second category, internal to the tourism industry as a whole, relates to the position of timeshare as a holiday form. Issues of importance are the degree to which it is in competition with other forms or integrated into the industry in terms of its comparative cost or advantage, its requirement for tourism resources and services and its extension of product width and depth. The wider policy issues arise from timeshare's economic, environmental and socio-cultural impact and associated planning policy.

To appreciate fully the policy implications of timeshare's growth and current status, it is necessary to understand its organization and structure and the evolution of its selling methods, the exchange system, and the development and management of resorts. An outline of the structure of the industry and the interrelationship between the organizations involved is given in Figure 11.1. For a detailed account of the legal arrangements and operation of timeshare see Stabler and Goodall (1989) and the Office of Fair Trading (OFT) (1990).

What emerges from an examination of timeshare is that it is a sound concept but has suffered from a poor image. This stems largely from its infant industry character and its phenomenal rate of development. The latter has outpaced its capabilities to conduct and regulate its marketing and operations effectively. Indeed some aspects of its operation have bordered on the naive.

The discussion here of policy issues relating to consumers' interests is mostly confined to UK residents purchasing timeshare. Likewise, the investigation of wider economic, particularly spatial, issues also concentrates on resorts located in the UK.

11.2 THE ECONOMICS OF TIMESHARE RESORT MANAGEMENT

Conventional economic analysis is not appropriate at this infant industry stage because the more fundamental issue for the timeshare industry is to establish and develop itself. The focus here is on the product, with particular reference to the position of potential and existing owners.

The principal issues raised as a result of claims by either the industry itself or purchasers have been timeshare's:

- attributes as an investment asset;
- benefits as an inflation-proof means of securing future holidays;
- cost advantage *vis-à-vis* other forms of holiday;
- resale value;
- possibilities of being rented out;
- terminal value;
- management and maintenance costs.

In promoting and marketing the product, the first three items listed above have been put forward by the timeshare industry as advantages. The remaining four are concerns expressed by

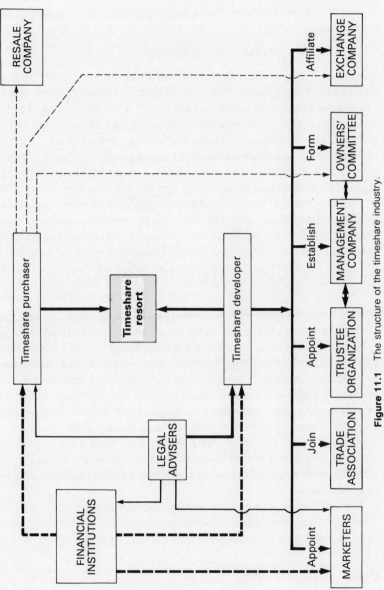

Figure 11.1 The structure of the timeshare industry.

purchasers over the true cost of ownership and the likelihood of recovering a proportion of those costs, both capital and recurrent. All are interrelated and are relevant to the appraisal of the benefits and costs of owning a timeshare.

11.2.1 The Comparative Costs of Timeshare

In principle the appraisal decision rule should be that if the present value of the capital cost and discounted holding costs minus the discounted resale price and any rental revenue is less than the discounted costs of alternative equivalent holidays over the same period, then a timeshare purchase is worthwhile.

In practice there are acute difficulties in ascertaining whether or not timeshare does indeed confer a comparative advantage, given the long time period over which benefits and costs have to be projected. Heroic assumptions have to be made regarding estimates of price inflation for travel, accommodation, maintenance and management, exchange and interest rates, property values, the period for which loans run if borrowed funds are used to purchase timeshare, the size and quality of units, the on-site facilities, location and the terms and conditions of ownership.

Avis and Gibson (1983, 1984) have conducted a rigorous appraisal of timeshare. As their appraisal was essentially a property valuation exercise, they concentrated on resale and terminal values, the present value of which they argued was rather low. The OFT (1990) has questioned the industry's claim that purchasing a timeshare is cheaper than renting a villa, showing that it had failed to discount benefits and costs, that the estimated final value of the property was over-optimistic and that the costs of renting were over-inflated. The extent to which a timeshare can be rented out when not used by the owner and the quality of timeshare as a form of holiday have not been taken into account in any analysis.

The claims by the industry and counter-claims by its critics turn on the assumptions concerning these key variables, and on the rates of discount and inflation chosen to make comparisons.

11.2.2 Management Fees

The OFT (1990) survey revealed an average management fee of about £90 per week (range £70–£125), but some evidence indicated fees as high as £150. What is difficult to establish is the exact composition of these fees and whether they are a true reflection of the costs incurred. Developers are reluctant to release details, perhaps because they do not wish to reveal their financial structures to rivals.

Running costs included in the management fee cover cleaning and maintenance of accommodation and facilities, energy, water, insurance, taxes, rental and exchange services. What is less clear is whether a sinking fund for replacement of equipment, furniture and refurbishment also includes more fundamental structural repairs and amortization of the buildings themselves. This last factor has important implications for fees in the future, especially as accommodation and facilities get older and leases, where applicable, expire.

To make resorts more marketable developers often subsidize the running costs in the early years. They may also do so where a significant number of units are unsold. According to the OFT (1990) some owners had nothing in their agreements to indicate the basis for charging fees in the future; others reported increases of over 100 per cent within three years and even supplementary specific charges for extraordinary items such as facility trading losses. Quite large charges may be imposed on owners by developers as and when major accommodation and facilities reconstruction work is required.

11.2.3 Resale and Termination Values

The timeshare valuation done by Avis and Gibson (1983, 1984) was based on feasible simulation and probability distributions for various scenarios. What they were unable to do, through the lack of evidence of such transactions, was to consider resale market data emanating from developers and brokers.

Evidence of first-time prices, given appreciable discounting at the time of sale, let alone second-hand values, is very scanty. Moreover, it is difficult to relate the latter to the original selling price of specific properties. The only way in which sufficient and reliable data can be obtained is via owners who have disposed of their holdings. The price they will obtain will clearly depend on demand and supply. Given that the marketing costs average 40 per cent of the total first-time sale price (Mendoza, 1986; Miner, 1987) and that if an agency, e.g. Primeshare in the UK, is employed a commission of up to 20 per cent or more can be charged, the second-hand price may well be at least 60 per cent lower than the original purchase price.

Leasehold timeshare values inevitably fall as the termination date approaches. Currently there has been virtually no discussion of this aspect by either the industry or commentators. This inattention is understandable because, for most timeshare, leases are still very much in the early phases of their specified time period. It is clear that research in this area is needed.

11.2.4 The Policy Implications of Timeshare's Operational Economics

Appraisal of timeshare is clouded by uncertainties and lack of data, and the claims made for the concept are misleading. With respect to management fees there is a suspicion that in some instances developers are deliberately devious but in other cases do not possess the necessary expertise. With regard to resale, developers have understandably concentrated on selling new units and appear simply to have ignored the second-hand market.

In general the industry has developed in a piecemeal and uncoordinated fashion. However, that does not explain or excuse sloppy business practice. For example, information on the comparative costs of timeshare could easily have been compiled to give a fair view of timeshare purchase. Furthermore, it is difficult to explain the absence of clear formulas for management fees and resale from the purchaser's contract. The calculation of such formulas should be a normal part of long-term business planning, with capital appraisal techniques being used, in conjunction with cash flow analysis, to establish the life cycle of accommodation and facilities.

11.3 CONSUMER PROTECTION

Timeshare is an infant industry, supplying a rapidly developing but unregulated product. As a concept, it is too new for general acceptance by consumers. Consequently timeshare has attracted bad publicity in the UK, although most criticism has been from non-purchasers.

11.3.1 The Need for Consumer Protection

If ever a situation in which the maxim *caveat emptor* applies it is timeshare. Much criticism concerns the marketing techniques used, in particular the persistently aggressive selling methods and the misrepresentation of sales claims. This holds whether the marketing takes place on-site (the resort location) or off-site (the consumers' home region). At tourist destinations, off-site personal canvassers, working on a commission-only basis, seek to persuade holiday-makers to attend sales presentations in the timeshares they represent. They harass holiday-makers at arrival airports, in hotels and restaurants and on the beach. In tourist origin areas, direct mail activities are controversial because of the promise of 'awards' for attending sales presentations. Awards often have expensive strings attached, such as free flights but an obligation to pay for accommodation in expensive hotels. Invitations are frequently sent to ineligible recipients, such as those who do not meet the joint-income criterion.

Sales presentations are unduly long and the consumer is pressured, by unscrupulous sales personnel, into purchasing immediately to obtain same-day discounts. No opportunity is given to think over the purchase or to seek legal advice. Purchasers who change their minds incur cancellation charges and a long wait before payments are refunded. Misrepresentation takes several forms. Exchange limitations and resale difficulties are overlooked. Low maintenance charges may be a marketing ploy. Investment analysis using formal financial principles suggests that conventional holidays are better value. Cases of fraud are not unknown, developers selling units to which they do not hold clear title or selling the same unit to several purchasers. Developers have contravened planning laws, by building without permission, or taken out mortgage agreements unbeknown to their purchasers. Late completions and developer bankruptcies also give rise to problems of protecting the purchaser's finance and title.

Undoubtedly, many purchasers do not investigate timeshare fully before committing themselves: for them it is an impulse purchase. Thus consumers need protection against their own folly as well as against the sharp practices of some timeshare developers.

11.3.2 Regulation of the Timeshare Industry

Property laws rarely apply to timeshare and consumer legislation and other controls, such as those over direct mail and advertising, offer only limited protection. Consequently, the OFT (1990) argued for controls that would:

- deter the use of unacceptable selling techniques;
- eliminate the use of false or misleading statements;

- ensure that the public have adequate information and time to consider it;
- minimize the risks to purchasers' money;
- clarify the purchasers' position during the term of the time-share agreement.

Clearly implied is the need to regulate the timeshare industry. Many timeshare developers understand that it is in their common interest to improve timeshare's public image. Thus, self-regulation has been attempted in the UK. The Timeshare Developers Association (TDA) was formed in 1987 by the merger of three hitherto separate organizations representing developers. It had a dual role as a developers' trade association and a self-regulation consumer protection organization. Membership implied that the developer accepted the TDA's code governing marketing and sales practices and members' financial and legal status was checked by the TDA's admission rules.

Membership was voluntary and 'cowboy' developers did not join. At the peak of its membership the TDA represented only 70 per cent of British timeshare developers. In 1990, before publication of the OFT report, major developers like Barratt International Resorts withdrew from the TDA because of growing impatience at the latter's slow progress towards consumer protection and its failure to take action against member firms who broke its rules. The TDA's representation of the British timeshare industry dropped to 40 per cent and it went into solvent liquidation in October 1990. It has been replaced by The Timeshare Council (TTC) which aims to represent all interests in the timeshare industry and has draft rules based on the OFT recommendations. Self-regulation by the UK timeshare industry has yet to provide the levels of safeguard of consumer rights expected by the government. Government action to regulate the industry may be on the way.

Consumer protection cannot be foolproof as TTC rules and government action can only apply to British-based timeshare developers. Residents signing contracts at overseas resorts of British-based developers will be covered but those purchasing from foreign timeshare companies will not. Increasing pressure therefore exists for pan-European regulation of the industry (European Communities, 1988). This is a complex matter since, under the Treaty of Rome, the European Commission has no rights over a member nation's property laws and timeshare is regarded as property in some countries, such as Portugal. At best, progress towards European regulation is likely to be slow, although an EC regulation could emerge as part of a directive on unfair contract terms.

Regulation, imposed by the industry or by government, is necessary to establish public confidence in the product and so to ensure the industry's continuing growth. Tighter control of both the marketing and the operation of timeshare will almost certainly bring change. Marketing strategies may be re-thought, there may be a slowdown of sales and profitability may be reduced. The industry will be concentrated into fewer firms as some developers turn away from timeshare. Regulation is therefore a prerequisite to the emergence of a mature timeshare industry.

11.4 STRUCTURAL ADJUSTMENT IN THE TOURISM INDUSTRY

Timeshare is now being sold as a holiday option, rather than as a property investment. It therefore has to be taken seriously by the tourism industry. In terms of product width, timeshare extends the range of holiday accommodation and the opportunity to take independent holidays. With regard to depth, timeshare is a heterogeneous product and the market can be segmented, for example, according to socio-demographic characteristics in which timeshares based on hotel conversions are targeted at the over-50 age group while those with integral sporting facilities are intended for families with children.

11.4.1 Timeshare Creates New Firms

The growth of timeshare has generated new types of firm: timeshare developers, exchange companies and specialist management companies (see Figure 11.1). Since timeshare resorts have generally been developed in tourist destinations receiving high volume flows of holiday-makers, these firms are competing with suppliers of other forms of holiday accommodation. Initially firms developing timeshare resorts were small, independent, newly formed companies but increasingly the developers are corporate interests from the hotel trade – e.g. Marriott and Sheraton in the USA, Granada and Stakis in Europe – or from the construction industry – e.g. Barratts, Wimpey, Costain and Laing. The latter type of developer is important in the UK, being responsible for one-third of timeshare developments.

Timeshare owners are normally resident in the major tourist-generating countries. In these countries timeshare developers and exchange companies compete with other tourism firms marketing holidays. Exchange is pivotal to the timeshare industry, providing a mechanism for owners to holiday in a different place at a different time of year. Moreover, it is duopolistically organized on a global scale as most resorts are affiliated to either Resort Condominiums International (RCI) or Interval International (II). The exchange companies have become increasingly sophisticated in their operations. Firstly, they have expanded into other services required by holiday-makers, providing exchanges with facilities such as discount price flights, airport transfers, preferential car hire and destination sightseeing tours as well as arranging travel insurance. This business would, in their absence, have gone to travel agents and tour operators. Secondly, they facilitate further resort development by helping to arrange finance for timeshare developers, and also act as a check on the quality and security of the resort.

11.4.2 Reactions of Existing Tourism Firms

Timeshare developers compete with suppliers of other tourist accommodation and attractions in destination areas and, along with exchange companies, with tour operators and travel agents in tourist-generating areas. Business may be diverted from package holidays and away from conventional forms of serviced and self-catering accommodation. Since tourism is a highly competitive business one response of traditional tourism firms is to integrate timeshare into their operations. Linkage has been witnessed first in the travel field, since exchange companies have exact knowledge of where people are holidaying. For example, Viking International has established a 'seat-only' subsidiary, Unijet, to offer low-price flights to RCI members; II is linked with Holidayfax to provide its members with flights.

Tour operators have been slower to get involved: a few are diversifying into timeshare accommodation. Tour operators may acquire timeshare resorts, integrating vertically backwards into accommodation supply; for example, Club Méditerranée bought out Club Hotel (a French timeshare developer) and Tjaereborg took over the Club La Santa timeshare (Lanzarote, Canary Islands). Other tour operators, such as Thomas Cook and Horizon (Thomson), are experimenting with timeshare resort-based package holidays by renting unsold units. If timeshare continues to grow and is increasingly recognized as a quality product, and if the holiday-maker continues to move away from cheap inclusive tours, then tour operator involvement is likely to increase.

In tourist destinations, independent hotels and self-catering enterprises view timeshare as an 'enemy', either competing for potential visitors or disturbing existing ones because of persistent soliciting by timeshare canvassers. Larger hotels, as noted above, have moved into timeshare but usually these are national or international chains ultimately controlled from outside the destination region. Such hotel groups are also showing an interest in timeshare resort management; for example, Grand Metropolitan offers a specialist service via its GIS Hotel and Leisure Management subsidiary.

There is now increasing evidence that destination tourism authorities are accepting timeshare as a valid and desirable part of the overall tourism product mix. Moreover, the integration of timeshare into the tourism industry of both destination and generating regions brings added respectability to the product and allows further market development.

11.5 THE ENVIRONMENTAL IMPACT OF TIMESHARE

The environmental impact of timeshare has been largely ignored to date, mainly perhaps because it has not pioneered new tourist destinations. Timeshare developments proliferate along coasts with established volume tourist inflows, such as the Spanish Costas or English Riviera, but are also drawn to scenic areas, such as the Lake District, often in association with ski resorts, as in the French Alps or the Cairngorms in Scotland. These are all 'destination' timeshare resorts and distinguishable from 'regional' resorts catering for owners within easy driving distance (Miner, 1987). Regional resorts are dependent on the range of on-site activities provided to attract purchasers but there is no evidence to suggest that destination resorts are less well equipped (except for timeshares in capital cities, where little more than accommodation is provided).

Of the 90 timeshare resorts in the UK in 1991, most are destination resorts and some three-quarters are located in upland Britain, with nearly two-thirds to be found in Cornwall, Devon, the Lake District and the Scottish Highlands. This regional distribution masks even greater spatial concentrations: there are 11 timeshare developments in the vicinity of Lake Windermere in the Lake District. These locations confirm the attraction of proven tourist destinations but also demonstrate a preference for the very best scenery. Nearly three-quarters of the developments are located in national parks, heritage coasts and areas of outstanding natural beauty in England and Wales or corresponding areas of great landscape value in Scotland. Are timeshare developments compatible with such protected landscapes?

Generally, UK timeshare developments offer a luxury product: high-quality accommodation integrated into a leisure complex providing both indoor and outdoor recreation facilities. Internal site design and landscaping are to a high standard and local materials are used for building in order to blend the development into the local environment. Nearly two-thirds of developments are based on the conversion of existing buildings, leading, in some cases, to the restoration of those buildings and the reclamation of derelict land; for example, the Langdale timeshare converted an old watermill, gunpowder works and caravan site. It is also claimed that timeshare reduces the demand for second homes; certainly it is space-saving compared to a situation where each holiday-maker has an independent second home.

On the negative side timeshare brings large-scale development, in the form of a self-contained leisure complex on the scale of a village, to these areas of 'protected' landscape. The modal size for UK developments is now 80 accommodation units. Thus if each unit is sold for 50 weeks and an average occupancy of four persons per week is assumed, the resort would cater for 16 000 holiday-makers each year, with traffic flows involving up to 650 persons changing over each weekend. Moreover, the sites developed may be segregated from existing settlements – this is particularly so where the development is new rather than based on existing buildings, as is the case for half of the Lake District's timeshares.

If the nature and scale of timeshare are so out of character with these protected landscapes, especially national parks, why did planners allow developments to proceed? Building for tourism and recreation is acceptable because of the prospect of 'planning gain' in the form of reclamation of derelict land, renovation of old buildings and provision of facilities that can be used by locals (Nobbs, 1988). Given the absence of national planning policy on timeshare, each proposal has been dealt with 'on its merits' at the local level and only localities pressured with many applications will consider formulating a policy towards timeshare (this is reminiscent of the way second-homes policies emerged in the 1960s). Once planning permission has been granted, developers have applied for permission to expand, going to appeal if necessary.

The tourism industry generates income not only from tourists who come to enjoy these protected landscapes but also, in the case of timeshare, from visitors attracted by the facility itself, for whom the protected landscape is a non-essential, additional bonus (Nobbs, 1988). Since owners of UK-based timeshares consider the provision of on-site recreation facilities to be more important than off-site opportunities (Ragatz Associates, 1987) it may be argued that such artificial leisure complexes could be located anywhere. Planning policies should therefore seek to discourage timeshare in designated areas such as national parks, especially totally new development. Timeshare developments could then be steered to other, environmentally less vulnerable locations, like the Barnsdale timeshare on Rutland Water.

11.6 TIMESHARE'S IMPACT ON THE LOCAL ECONOMY

A fundamental justification for tourism development is the assertion that it stimulates local economies by generating income and employment. The concepts of tourism multipliers and input–output analysis have been extensively researched and applied (see Pearce, 1989). Although these concepts are appropriate and numerous case studies exist of their application, there are virtually no examples of a comparison of different forms of tourism with timeshare in a single study area. For an effective comparative analysis, timeshare should at least be considered alongside other self-catering accommodation, such as second homes, holiday homes, caravan and chalet parks. Ideally it should also be compared with serviced accommodation, such as hotels, guest houses, Center Parcs (holiday villages developed by a specialist leisure company of that name, providing all-weather, all-season facilities) and health farms. There are, however, no locations in which all of these types of accommodation exist. Thus valid comprehensive comparisons are difficult to make. Nevertheless, in the more rural and upland areas of the UK useful but limited comparisons of impact can still be made between timeshare and those types of accommodation most likely to be found in locations where timeshare has been developed or is proposed, namely second homes, hotels and guest houses.

It can be hypothesized that timeshare accommodation built

on a larger scale, to high specifications with associated facilities, securing high occupancy rates, attracting purchasers in higher-income groups whose expenditure on local goods and services is higher, will have a more beneficial economic impact on destinations than other self-catering or serviced accommodation, particularly second homes. Such homes are likely to be unoccupied for long periods. Even when they are in use, they do not involve employment of local inhabitants or result in high levels of expenditure locally. Some information on the local impact of timeshare in destinations can be found in the Ragatz Associates (1987) survey and the repeat, though not comparable, survey in 1990 (Ernst & Young, 1990).

Purchases by UK residents at home resorts show a fairly even distribution of periods, suggesting a similarly even distribution of holidays taken over the year. Occupancy rates of timeshare are difficult to ascertain simply because the industry does not need such statistics. Evidence from owners (OFT, 1990) suggests a 70 per cent occupancy rate, but this figure does not include either the renting of unused units or exchanges. In any event, as developers charge management fees irrespective of whether accommodation is used, they will only be concerned about occupancy if they wish to generate income through owners' use of the facilities for which payment is made, such as restaurants, bars and certain sporting facilities. (Allowing non-owners and local inhabitants to use facilities obviates this need.) Reliable evidence of occupancy rates for second homes, many of which are never rented out, and for serviced accommodation are equally difficult to establish. Letting agencies dealing with better-quality properties in tourist areas and hoteliers outside popular locations, particularly if there are no associated facilities, do not expect occupancy rates much above 50 per cent per year.

Statistics on expenditure in UK destination areas by timeshare owners were collected in the Ragatz Associates (1987) survey. They reveal that the mean and median expenditure per owner per week were £463 and £375 respectively (all resorts) and £293 and £200 (resorts in the UK). Given that nearly 90 per cent of owners had no children living at home this suggests a mean expenditure per person per week of £232 (UK £147) compared with £83 per week (including accommodation) for all types of holiday taken by UK residents at home. In any particular location, therefore, for an 80-unit development generating 16 000 visitors the total annual spend in the area, based on these UK figures, would be of the order of £2.344 million.

The re-survey of UK timeshare owners in 1989 (Ernst & Young, 1990) indicates that expenditure per party in the north of England was £714, yielding a per person average of £265 (average party size of 2.7). Ernst & Young combine these data, suitably grossed up, with statistics on capital outlay expenditure, to suggest that timeshare in the UK supports 1500 jobs. This estimate assumes that one full-time job is created for every £20 000 expenditure.

Surveys of the occupations of timeshare owners (Ragatz Associates, 1987; Ernst & Young, 1990) confirm the view that they are drawn from the higher-income and higher-spending sectors of society. Almost two-thirds held professional, management, government or technical posts and 18 per cent were retired, for whom no former occupation was ascertained. Their average income was £19 600 (£22 425 in 1990), 203 per cent of the UK mean.

Existing evidence supports the hypothesis of timeshare generating more income locally than other forms of self-catering accommodation. The size and quality of timeshare developments and on-site facilities also suggest that its employment impact is higher than that of other tourism forms. The Department of Employment (OFT, 1990) has certainly expressed a view that timeshare benefited regional economies by creating employment throughout the year and spreading it more widely.

Clearly, currently available data on the economic impact of timeshare are extremely aggregative and sketchy. We are now undertaking further research on the issue in representative areas. This research will apply standard multiplier analysis to both the construction and operative phases of timeshare. It will also examine the wider economic effects of timeshare, such as its influence on local housing markets.

11.7 CONCLUSIONS

Timeshare has developed so rapidly that sound business and marketing practices have not kept pace with that development. Inherently, timeshare is a good product, albeit one with an exceedingly poor public image at present. Even so, in 1983 the English Tourist Board welcomed timeshare as follows: 'there is a growing need for up-market, luxury accommodation and the Board sees timesharing as a way of achieving this high standard to meet the demand' (quoted in Timeshare Developers

Association, 1989). Five years later Lord Strathclyde, then Minister of Tourism, stated: 'quality timeshare developments in the UK are playing an important part in meeting the highest expectations of today's holidaymaker. . . . Realising timeshare's full potential should bring benefits to the tourism industry and the country in general' (quoted in OFT, 1990).

Can that potential be realized in a way that not only brings benefits to the timeshare owners but also protects the environment and acknowledges the needs of host communities? To do so the timeshare industry must espouse unimpeachable business procedures, achieve full integration into the tourism industry and acknowledge its responsibilities towards destination environments and local economies. If the industry is regulated and if hotel chains and tour operators use timeshare public confidence in the product will grow, the more so where it is part of multi-purpose tourism developments like the French EuroDisney. Integration into mainstream tourism will facilitate product development, increasing timeshare's flexibility to cater for second holidays and short breaks with split week and day timeshares and more floating weeks and seasons. Product development could also include the development of urban timeshares, thereby providing easier access to historic and cultural cities, and of business timeshares for travelling executives. Thus timeshare is likely to be a tourism growth area of the 1990s, and to increase its market penetration, particularly in European countries.

Where should additional timeshares be located? The wider environmental and socio-economic issues associated with location concern government departments, local authorities, economic development and tourism bodies, as well as environmental organizations. Policies must be formulated to give clear guidance to the timeshare industry. If there is a strong presumption against 'high profile' timeshare development in areas of protected landscape, there must be an equally positive direction towards locations where development will be permitted, such as forested lowland areas, existing coastal resorts and urban areas.

References

Avis, M. and Gibson, W. (1983) Valuing timeshare interests: 1. *Journal of Valuation*, **1**, 377–85.

Avis, M. and Gibson, W. (1984) Valuing timeshare interests: 2. *Journal of Valuation*, **2**, 240–57.

Ernst & Young (1990) *An Independent Timeshare Industry Review*. London: Timeshare Developers Association.

European Communities (1988) *European Parliament: Report for the Committee on Legal Affairs and Citizens' Rights on the Need to Fill the Legal Gap in the Timeshare Market*, Series A, Doc. A2-199/98. Luxembourg: Office for Official Publications of the European Communities.

Mendoza, L. (1986) A decade in timeshare. *Leisure Management*, **6**, 41–2.

Miner, S.S. (1987) Timesharing in the USA. *Travel and Tourism Analyst*, August, 15–27.

Nobbs, A. (1988) Tourist complexes in national parks. Discussion paper. London: Council for National Parks.

Office of Fair Trading (1990) *Timeshare: a Report by the Director General of Fair Trading under Section 2(3) of the Fair Trading Act 1973*. London: HMSO.

Pearce, D.G. (1989) *Tourism Development*, 2nd edn. Harlow: Longman.

Ragatz Associates (1987) *United Kingdom Timeshare Purchasers: Who Are They, Why They Buy*. London: Timeshare Developers Association.

Stabler, M. and Goodall, B. (1989) Timeshare: a new dimension in tourism. *Built Environment*, **15**, 101–24.

Timeshare Developers Association (1989) Draft submission of evidence to the Office of Fair Trading Review of Timeshare. London: TDA (mimeo).

12 Economic Adjustment Policies and the Hotel Sector in Jamaica

Steve Curry

12.1 INTRODUCTION

In the 1960s and early 1970s, many countries pursued policies of industrialization intended to re-orient their economies away from production for the international market. However, the growing and persistent recession in the industrialized countries re-emphasized the role of production for the world economy. Recently, policy programmes designed to enhance the rate of growth through the international supply of commodities have been implemented. In some cases, these policy programmes have been undertaken under 'structural adjustment' lending conditions, where substantial inflows of conditional capital from international institutions have been involved.

Tourism plays a minor role in this process. It has been affected by the policy programmes although these effects have not been considered in their design. However, in some countries tourism is of considerable economic significance and the effects of the policy programmes on tourism need to be explored.

This chapter outlines the effects of the structural adjustment policy programmes of the 1980s on tourism in one country, Jamaica, where tourism has played an increasingly important role in foreign currency generation. Specifically, it outlines the possible effects of the policy programmes on the hotel sector. The two principal questions are as follows. Firstly, what has been the effect of policy changes made under the structural adjustment loan programmes on the tourism sector, and hotels in particular? Secondly, has the tourism sector in Jamaica, through quality and innovation, been able to maintain its prices in a competitive setting?

The first section makes some comments on common methodologies for analysing the economic effects of tourism. The second section provides an overview of the Jamaican tourism industry in the 1980s. The third section gives an outline of the main policy programmes implemented in that period. The fourth section outlines the main consequences for the hotel sector. The fifth section takes up the issue of pricing. Some general conclusions are drawn in the sixth section.

12.2 THE EFFECTS OF TOURISM INVESTMENT

A common approach to tourism analysis that has been applied, particularly in small open economies, is the calculation of economic impact measures. These impact measures can be expressed in the form of multipliers for output, income, employment, government revenue, imports and other economic indicators (Fletcher, 1989). A multiplier estimates the ratio between the ultimate effect of tourist activity in an economy and the immediate expenditure made by the tourists themselves, and can be used to indicate the extent to which an economy is directly and indirectly dependent on the tourism sector. At least two such studies have been carried out for Jamaica (Curry, 1971; WTO, 1986).

There are a number of technical problems with the calculation of tourism multipliers. Firstly, they need to be calculated for extra tourists using marginal coefficients where possible, in order to correspond to the short-run, under-utilized capacity focus of the methodology. Secondly, they can be calculated at different levels depending on whether the induced effects of additional re-spent incomes are included or not. Thirdly, they may need to be adapted to take account of specific capacity constraints, particularly in small, open economies suffering foreign exchange shortages or with declining agriculture (Wanhill, 1988). Fourthly, the estimated effects of tourism are found to be as sensitive to the ownership of the sector as to its productive structure (Bryden, 1973). Fifthly, multiplier measures are invariably limited to the economic impact of annual expenditures by the tourism sector and do not consider investment expenditures.

Tourism multipliers have been used for basically two policy-related purposes. The first is to draw comparisons between different types of tourist, for example between holiday and business categories, in order to determine investment and marketing priorities. However, it has been pointed out that the impact of different types of tourist is not as significant as differences in expenditure levels (Curry, 1986). The second is to make comparison with other economic sectors to determine sector priorities at the national level (O'Hagan and Mooney, 1983). However, frequently tourism multipliers have been calculated as an end in themselves, outside this broader context.

It can be seen that tourism multipliers have their limitations for decision making purposes. In the context of investigating the effects of policy changes on tourism, and especially the hotel sector, a form of analysis is required that looks at the effects of investment as well as annual expenditures, for example through investment or project analysis. Specific investments can be analysed in terms of their investment, operating and working capital costs and revenues, written out over the full period of investment. Applying conventional project criteria in such analysis involves a number of assumptions: that specific investments are independent of each other; that there are no adverse or positive external effects on supplies; and that no investment will have an identifiable effect upon prices of inputs or outputs.

With the exception of Bryden (1973, Chapter 10), existing studies confirm that hotel investments in particular are more valuable from the point of view of the national economy than from that of the owner. Forbes (1976) shows this for an international hotel in Trinidad and the illustrative examples in Powers (1980) confirm the same result. Adhikari (1986) goes further to show that hotel investments are more favourable nationally than commercially when distribution issues are also considered. Curry (1987), while confirming the basic result, concludes that this is true for town hotels as much as hotels oriented to the international holiday market.

The fact that returns to the national economy generally exceed returns to the owner in international hotel investments suggests that there may be circumstances where investments are delayed or abandoned by owners that would be worthwhile on an economy-wide basis. A substantial difference between national and owner returns may indicate an inappropriate incentive or cost structure. In circumstances where foreign exchange shortages are intense, incentive structures must provide for projects that will be nationally worthwhile in the longer term. For the 1980s, when policy programmes set out to change the relative incentives for export-oriented as opposed to domestic-oriented production, it is pertinent to analyse hotel projects from the financial point of view, to see whether they benefited from policy changes and what might have been the inhibiting factors.

12.3 TOURISM IN JAMAICA IN THE 1980s

World tourism arrivals were estimated at 405.3 million in 1989 and their growth over the 1980s at 4 per cent per annum. This growth was faster in the later years of the decade. World tourism receipts are estimated to have grown at 8 per cent per annum in the 1980s to reach US$209.2 billion in 1989, 7 per cent of total export receipts (EC, 1990). The growth rate of arrivals in developing countries was faster than average in the 1980s, at 5.9 per cent per annum, but the growth rate of receipts in developing countries was only 6.5 per cent per annum.

Tourism is particularly important in the Caribbean, where visitor expenditure in 1988 was 25 per cent of export receipts (EC, 1990, p. 54). In 1988 there were more than 10 million arrivals in the region plus 6 million cruise ship arrivals, and total visitor expenditure stood at more than US$6.5 billion. Jamaica has one of the largest tourism sectors in the Caribbean. In 1988 visitor expenditure was 24 per cent of gross domestic product, and ranked fourth among the islands behind Puerto Rico, the Dominican Republic and the US Virgin Islands. In arrivals and cruise ship arrivals it ranked third, and in the number of hotel rooms second (Holder, 1990, p. 79).

Tourist arrivals in Jamaica grew at 8.8 per cent per annum from 1980 to 1989 (Table 12.1). However, this includes cruise ship arrivals. Stopover arrivals grew at 6.8 per cent per annum, greater than the average for developing countries. The increase in stopovers was interrupted in 1988 by Hurricane Gilbert, which hit the island in that year, but the significant recovery in 1989 is expected to continue, with stopovers projected to increase to over one million by 1993 (PIOJ, 1990, p. 117). The average length of stay in hotels of 8.4 nights in 1989 is less than in other accommodation (15.4 nights). However, hotels account for the bulk of all nights spent in the island. The average length of stay is longer for European tourists. Their share of total arrivals grew through the decade but the bulk of tourist arrivals are still from the USA (67

Table 12.1 Tourism in Jamaica, 1980–1989

	1980	1981	1982	1983	1984	1985	1986	1987	1988	1989	Average annual growth rate (%)
Arrivals											
Stopover arrivals (thousands)	395	406	468	566	603	572	664	739	649	715	6.8
Total arrivals (thousands)	543	552	670	783	844	847	955	1 037	1 020	1 163	8.8
Receipts											
Foreign travel receipts (J$ million)	430	507	601	818	1 655	2 237	2 838	3 273	2 888	4 151	28.6
(US$ million)	242	284	338	399	407	407	516	595	525	593	10.5
Exports (J$ million)	1 715	1 735	1 294	1 392	2 897	3 128	3 226	3 874	4 559	5 571	14.0
Imports (J$ million)	1 840	2 270	2 140	2 841	4 510	6 147	5 322	6 791	7 901	10 370	21.1
Foreign travel to exports (%)	25	29	46	63	57	72	88	84	63	75	
Foreign travel to imports (%)	23	22	28	31	37	36	53	48	37	40	
Balance of trade (US$ million)	(76)	(323)	(442)	(439)	(335)	(436)	(248)	(358)	(395)	(552)	
Rooms											
All accommodation	10 092	10 231	10 327	11 015	11 505	12 218	13 371	14 010	14 029	14 952	4.5

Sources: IMF (1988, 1990); Ministry of Tourism (1990); World Bank (1989).

per cent of the total in 1989) and Canada (15 per cent) (Ministry of Tourism, 1990, p. 15). Tourism to Jamaica by stopovers is all by air and 80 per cent of tourists arrive on the north coast at Montego Bay. Compared with some other destinations, Jamaica attracts tourists who are neither old nor young, with 60 per cent of all tourists in the age range 25–50, the majority travelling as couples (Ministry of Tourism, 1990, pp. 34, 36).

Foreign travel receipts grew at nearly 29 per cent per annum in the decade, and exceeded the growth of both exports and imports. By 1986 tourism receipts were nearly 90 per cent of export receipts, but with the subsequent decline in tourism receipts because of the hurricane, and the increase in other exports, this remains a peak level. Nevertheless, the percentage contribution of tourism to foreign exchange receipts is much higher than at the beginning of the 1980s. As with many other countries, Jamaica's imports grew much more rapidly than exports in the 1980s. In 1989 they stood at nearly double the level of exports, and tourism's contribution was correspondingly smaller.

These figures relate to tourism receipts measured in local currency. If measured in US dollars the growth rate over the decade declines from 29 per cent to 10.5 per cent. However, this is still a rapid rate of growth, faster than average for developing countries. The balance of trade deficit has in several years been covered by receipts from tourism.

Tourism receipts have been important for another reason. As put by Kitchen (1989, p. 89): 'The rapid build-up of debt in the early 1980s, combined with the fall in exports, meant that by the end of 1983 debt had become a severe constraint on the Jamaican economy.' By 1986 total debt service had grown to 30 per cent of exports of goods and services. Moreover, long-term debt service is projected to continue at a rate above US$300 million per annum until 1997 (Kitchen, 1989, p. 92), despite some success at rescheduling.

The Jamaican economy as a whole did not perform well in the 1980s. GDP growth in real terms averaged 1 per cent per annum, with consumer prices rising at 14 per cent per annum. The increase in prices was partly the cause of, and partly in response to, the decline in the exchange rate (Table 12.2). The incentive effects to export sectors of a depreciating currency were partly vitiated by domestic inflation. When compared with world inflation (measured by a US consumer price index) there was a real effective decline in the exchange rate from J$1.78 to J$2.97 over

Table 12.2 Real effective exchange rate 1980–1989

	1980	1981	1982	1983	1984	1985	1986	1987	1988	1989
Exchange rate[a] (J$ to US$)	1.78	1.78	1.78	3.28	4.93	5.48	5.48	5.50	5.48	6.48
US consumer prices (1980 = 100)	100	110	117	121	126	131	133	138	143	150
Real effective exchange rate[b]	1.78	1.73	1.74	2.96	3.63	3.34	2.94	2.88	2.74	2.97

[a] Principal rate, meaning official rate and auction rate in different periods.
[b] Exchange rate adjusted for relative international and domestic price movements.

Sources: IMF (1988, 1990).

the period, confirming the partial effectiveness of devaluation in changing the real rate of exchange in the longer term in Jamaica found by Shafaeddin (1990). In itself, this should have encouraged investment in the tourism sector.

There was considerable investment in the tourism sector, and particularly in accommodation, in the 1980s. By 1989 there were 10 000 rooms in hotels and 15 000 rooms in all accommodation (Table 12.1). Investment in the early 1980s was particularly concentrated in the Negril area at the west end of the island where a new tourism area was being consolidated. At the end of 1986 the withdrawal of hotel incentives (see below) was preceded by a large number of incentive applications that are likely to sustain the expansion of accommodation in the future. In addition, a debt-equity swap programme introduced in March 1987, aimed at increasing investment by providing local currency discounted debt purchases by investors, and targeted at export manufacturing and hotel construction, should help to sustain an interest in tourism investment (Davis, 1988).

The predominant form of ownership has been private and Jamaican. Public funds have been mainly in the form of loans. For example, since 1983 the National Development Bank has invested J$180 million in tourism projects. The major part of these funds, comprising the foreign exchange element, are on-lendings of multilateral lending programmes, from the Inter-American Development Bank or the European Investment Bank, for example. Nevertheless, a significant feature of the expansion of tourism in Jamaica has been the continued shift to Jamaican ownership.

The shift to private Jamaican ownership has been enhanced by a public-sector divestment programme. At the beginning of the 1980s the government owned or leased long-term 17 hotels, both business and holiday hotels, representing 60 per cent of hotel capacity (World Bank, 1989, p. 5). The decision to divest was not implemented until 1988, and ten hotels remain in public-sector ownership. However, the major interest has come from Jamaican sources, particularly financial institutions anxious to obtain access to a source of foreign exchange. In February 1990, the Minister of Tourism claimed that on completion of the divestment programme 77 per cent of all rooms in the hotel sector would be owned by Jamaicans and Jamaican institutions.

Jamaican tourism contained a distinct specialism in the 1980s, that of the all-inclusive, pre-paid holiday. All-inclusive hotels achieved a much higher occupancy rate than non-all-inclusive hotels, and captured virtually the whole of tourist expenditure. This form of tourism might well have sustained tourism receipts in Jamaica when other forms could not. On the other hand, it has affected considerably the distribution of tourism receipts within the country, the concentration in hotel hands being matched by a loss of receipts outside the hotels.

12.4 ADJUSTMENT POLICIES

Jamaica has been the object of both stabilization programmes associated with IMF agreements, and structural adjustment programmes associated with World Bank loans (Looney, 1987, Chapter 8). IMF agreements were made in the late 1970s and three more were signed in the early 1980s, each of them specifying performance targets for the economy. The general policies embodied in the agreements of 1981, 1984 and 1985 included stricter control of the fiscal budget and restrictions on central bank lending and commercial credit. A more detailed listing of the major changes in 1984 will give the flavour of the approach being adopted: unification of the exchange rate and introduction of an auction system; tax increases; reduction in public-sector employment; further import liberalization; reduced bank liquidity; increased interest rates. As Davies (1986, p. 96) points out, 'these policies were being implemented at a time when export earnings were decreasing, due in the main to the continued downturn in the bauxite/alumina industry'. At the same time there was an unprecedented increase in international debt.

Exchange rate policy had to combine the two objectives of stabilizing the exchange rate and prices on the one hand, and shifting incentives to foreign exchange sectors on the other. Major changes involved the abolition of the dual exchange rate system of January 1983 and the introduction of the auction system already referred to, which gave the government the ability to manipulate the rate on a weekly basis. The effect of these changes in 1983–5 was to bring about a considerable shift in the real effective exchange rate. As Bullock (1986, p. 152) concludes, 'it is thus apparent that relative profitability between export and non-export activities has been shifted in a fundamental way, perhaps unprecedented in the history of the country'. This should have brought an expansion in the foreign exchange sectors such as tourism.

Interest rate policy has also been influential at certain times.

The tightening of liquidity in 1984 was designed to reduce demand and generate extra savings. Indeed, the simultaneous increase in interest rates and the exchange rate in the mid-1980s achieved a significant change in economic conditions. Inflation and unemployment rose, the balance of payments situation did not improve and growth was not maintained except at the lowest of rates. In relation to exchange rate and interest rate changes, it was concluded that 'the evidence suggests that the price signalling process has been more successful in inhibiting demand than in stimulating supply' (Bullock, 1986, p. 167).

Jamaica was an early, intensive adjustment country in terms of its negotiated policies but one of the weakest at implementation. Increased savings and exports were not converted into more rapid growth and there was no improvement in per capita food production (Corbo and Webb, 1990, p. 6; Stewart, 1990, p. 24). Moreover, 'In the 1980s, tough stabilisation programmes have caused declining incomes and rising food prices and have cut deeply into social services' (Cornia *et al.*, 1987, p. 115). The adjustment policy has been predominantly contractionary with the vulnerable not being well protected, very substantial declines in real incomes for most of the population, and increases in child and female malnutrition (George, 1988, pp. 185–7). Changes in the exchange rate and internal prices, particularly in the mid-1980s, were met by demonstrations and strikes and declining popularity for the government, which was defeated in a general election in 1989. Meanwhile, debt built up to per capita levels well above those of the large debtor countries like Brazil and Mexico.

In relation to the effect of adjustment policies, however, a World Bank assessment pointed out that 'nowhere has the positive impact of the reform program been more manifest than in the tourist sector' (World Bank, 1989, p. 1), while acknowledging that given the competitiveness of the sector and the need for government support in the form of infrastructure and training, elements of the economic adjustment programmes could be detrimental to the sector. A related conclusion was that 'the government must take an active interest in price and profitability trends within the industry. This will require a careful monitoring of the real exchange rate, as well as a focus on the cost structure of inputs into the sector' (World Bank, 1989, p. 1). The positive impact of the adjustment programmes on tourism is probably a correct conclusion; however, the way in which economic policy changes have affected tourism as a whole and hotels in particular needs more careful investigation.

12.5 ECONOMIC POLICY PROGRAMMES AND HOTEL PROFITABILITY

The hotel sector is the main component of Jamaican tourism. The profitability of hotel investment and operation will have been affected by the changing economic conditions of the 1980s and more particularly by the changes in economic policy under the stabilization and structural adjustment programmes. The purpose of this section is to outline the way in which hotel profitability is likely to have been affected. Table 12.3 provides an overall framework. It identifies the main elements of hotel investments in the broad categories of investment costs, operating costs and revenues. Given the importance of foreign transactions in international tourism these are subdivided between foreign and local costs and revenues. Apart from the basic resources entering hotel investments there are financial transactions relating to long-term and short-term loans, also divided between foreign and local transactions. Payments associated with management agreements, marketing contracts and leases are collected under operating costs.

These elements of hotel investments will be affected by changes in specific economic policy instruments. The main influences will be the exchange rate and tariff reforms, tax changes, utility prices and the interest rate. There are also some more general effects related to the policy programmes, such as government expenditure reductions and credit controls, which should be considered. Finally, hotel profitability will be affected by inflation and relative inflation; this should also be included in any analysis of changing economic conditions on the hotel sector.

What was happening to these specific measures and general effects in Jamaica in the 1980s and how are they likely to have influenced hotel profitability? It is evident that where direct foreign exchange costs are estimated at 30 per cent of hotel costs, and the bulk of the revenue is from foreigners, a depreciation of the currency will create a windfall gain to hotels. Where a currency depreciation is converted into a real effective devaluation, as in Jamaica, the net beneficial effects should be permanent, as was found for Indonesia (Booth, 1990, p. 48). However, these beneficial effects have not always been used to best advantage. Hotels were allowed to retain 20 per cent of their foreign exchange earnings for expenditure on operating assets and annual cost items, but these funds have not all been used. Moreover, the full benefits of currency depreciations were not available to hotels until after the unitary exchange rate system was introduced in

Table 12.3 Economic policy programmes and hotel investments

	Specific measures					General effects		
	Exchange rate	Tariff reforms	Tax changes	Utility prices	Interest rate	Expenditure reductions	Inflation	Credit controls
Investment costs								
Foreign	●	●						
Local								
Operating costs								
Foreign	●	●				●	●	
Local			●	●		●	●	
Revenues								
Foreign	●		●			●	●	
Local			●					
Loan transactions								
Foreign	●				●			
Local					●			●

204

1983. Before then, hotels had to sell foreign currency to the Central Bank at the official exchange rate while purchasing imports using foreign exchange purchased at parallel market rates, thereby bearing a penalty of roughly 40 per cent on import transactions. Nevertheless, the nominal and real devaluations in Jamaica in the 1980s should have been of considerable benefit to the profitability of hotels. The important issue, then, is the other effects of policy changes that offset these beneficial effects.

Another consequence of exchange rate changes relates to loans. Where interest and loan repayments have to be made in foreign currency, the revenue in domestic currency required to service loans increases with depreciation. This is not a problem if revenue also rises with a depreciation, but could become problematic where there is constraint on the maintenance of prices or a deliberate decision to lower them (see the next section).

The purchase of imports by hotels has been affected by availability and price and not just by access to foreign currency. Several steps towards import liberalization were taken in the 1980s, and this made more imports available to the hotel sector. At the same time, hotel imports were influenced by the Incentive Acts for hotels and resort cottages. The Hotels Act of 1968 and the Resort Cottages Act of 1971 specified certain imports on which normal duties and tonnage taxes could be waived for licensed enterprises. The duty waivers could be allowed for between 10 and 15 years, but were combined with surcharges on some types of luxury foods. Undoubtedly, the duty waivers were of importance to hotel profitability. However, they were suspended in 1986 on the grounds that economic policy changes had benefited the hotel sector substantially and so they were no longer needed. This suspension was met with dismay by the hoteliers' association, who argued, firstly, for their reinstatement so that hotels could maintain quality standards in the face of intense competition and, secondly, that at the same time the schedule of allowed items should be updated to reflect changes in hotel technology. This element of the incentives legislation was reintroduced in 1990.

The other major part of the incentive legislation was waivers of profit and dividend taxes, combined with guarantees of remittance for foreigners, again over a 10–15-year period depending on the type of accommodation. This tax incentive partly offset taxation levied on the sector in the form of an annual licensing tax per room and a room tax per occupancy. The latter represents the main form of taxation on the hotel sector and is levied at three fixed rates per occupancy, related to the room price. The fixed nature of the room tax is an obstacle to price reductions following a devaluation: with price reductions the tax becomes a higher proportion of revenues. However, on the point of implementation is a scheme for a general consumption tax which would operate in the economy as a whole and replace the room tax in the hotel sector. This would allow more flexibility as a proportional tax, but the minimum rate of 10 per cent would tend to raise hotel prices.

As significant for hotels are the rates of commission paid to tour operators. These have risen to as high as 20 per cent of the revenue and represent a substantial drain not only on hotel revenues but also on the foreign exchange sent to the country. For all-inclusive hotels where the whole of the expenditure is captured by the operators as a single payment in the country of origin, the commission is unusually high and can be reduced only by a reduction in the price of the all-inclusive holiday itself.

Hotel costs and services have been affected by policy in relation to public utilities, involving a cut-back on centrally funded investment and an increase in charges, particularly for electricity, water and sewerage. An added problem has been the unreliability of supply at times. Telephone rentals and charges have also been increased substantially. In the face of persistent increases in costs, hotel managers have attempted to negotiate two-year labour agreements to give at least some stability to that part of costs; but as the World Bank points out, 'the Caribbean hotel industry has very high operating costs by world industry standards. . . . The reasons for this are various: high imported input costs, utility costs, maintenance and property management costs, and commission payments to wholesalers (World Bank, 1989, p. 4).

Interest rate changes have added further to operating costs, especially in the mid-1980s. Within a 15-month period from January 1984 to April 1985 the bank rate was raised from 11 per cent to 18 per cent. There were several other changes (up and down) during the 1980s but this period was the most significant. To the extent that hotels are leased and not owned, extra interest costs fall on the owner not the lessee. Where agreed capital expenditures are also involved, these take the form of expenditures by the lessee as a loan to the owner at an agreed interest rate, the extra interest costs again falling on the owner. Overall, the interest rate increases would have affected short-term debts rather than long-term debts, but given the relatively low occupancies of the early 1980s this would have affected most hotels.

Hotels have, of course, been affected by the general increase in domestic prices, averaging 14 per cent per annum through the 1980s, the main increases again being concentrated in the middle of the decade. This rate of increase has affected costs considerably. However, the effects should not be exaggerated. There has also been a depreciation of the currency in real terms to sustain the liquidity of hotels. More important has been the cut-backs in real terms in government expenditure. The government has supported tourism in Jamaica through a number of institutions, and is responsible for major infrastructure developments in tourism areas. The associated expenditures have not always been sustained. Indeed, there has recently been a shift of emphasis, with the government expanding promotion expenditures while trying to get private investors and non-governmental organizations to finance a larger part of infrastructure and training programmes.

It is necessary to pull all these effects together to see the overall effect on hotel profitability. The main parameters to monitor in this context are:

Revenue
- exchange rate;
- tax structure and rates;
- commissions.

Costs
- exchange rate;
- import prices and duties;
- licences and other government charges;
- tax structure and rates;
- incentive waivers;
- interest rate;
- domestic prices, including utilities.

Different types of hotel will be affected to different extents. Table 12.4 shows the way in which hotel capacity has grown in Jamaica. It can be seen that half of the existing bed capacity was there before 1971 and that very substantial increases were made in the 1970s in very large hotels, compounding problems of inadequate demand and leading to the government purchase of hotels. Despite the growth of tourism in the 1980s, there has been very little increase in bed capacity; only 8 per cent of all

Table 12.4 International hotels, rooms and beds to 1988: additions

		Before 1971		1971–80		1981–4		1985–8		Totals
Kingston	Hotels	12		2		1		1		16
	Rooms	756	(51)	650	(44)	13	(–)	70	(5)	1 489
	Beds	1 159	(44)	1 300	(49)	26	(–)	169	(7)	2 654
Montego Bay	Hotels	28		6		4		1		39
	Rooms	2 519	(62)	1 463	(36)	92	(2)	21	(–)	4 095
	Beds	5 062	(62)	2 961	(36)	159	(2)	42	(–)	8 224
Ocho Rios	Hotels	14		8		1		2		25
	Rooms	1 384	(54)	1 141	(44)	17	(–)	30	(2)	2 572
	Beds	2 993	(52)	2 603	(45)	51	(1)	76	(2)	5 723
Negril	Hotels	–		7		1		9		17
	Rooms	–		581	(58)	23	(2)	400	(40)	1 004
	Beds	–		1 130	(59)	33	(2)	765	(39)	1 928
Other	Hotels	10		1		–		2		13
	Rooms	244	(67)	25	(7)	–		96	(26)	365
	Beds	496	(68)	40	(5)	–		192	(26)	728
Totals	Hotels	64		24		7		15		110
	Rooms	4 903	(51)	3 860	(41)	145	(2)	617	(6)	9 525
	Beds	9 710	(50)	8 034	(42)	269	(1)	1 244	(7)	19 257

Figures in parentheses are percentages of row totals.

Source: Ministry of Tourism (1989).

beds were opened in 1981–8. The investments that have taken place have been in small units and reflect the changing ownership pattern in the sector. The Negril area represents an exception. Serious investment only started in the 1970s, and although there was a period when little investment took place, 40 per cent of the bed capacity in this area has come in the past few years. A high proportion of this capacity is all-inclusive, and for environmental reasons has been restricted to relatively small, low-rise hotels.

It is difficult to devise an optimal capacity for the hotel sector (Carey, 1989). With tourism and occupancy rates continuing to grow, it is likely that hotel investment will expand again in the early 1990s and make the sector more competitive. In this context, it is necessary to monitor prices and costs and to predict the effect of economic policy changes on them. On the basis of the types of tourism in Jamaica, the recent changes in the pattern of demand and the data available, it seems that three types of hotel could be chosen for detailed investigation. The first would be a

Kingston business hotel, away from the holiday tourism of the north and west coasts. The second would be an all-inclusive hotel in the Negril area to reflect this recent type of operation and recent scale of investment. The third would be a conventional holiday hotel in one of the older areas of Montego Bay or Ocho Rios, because this form of tourism continues to be important and, because of the wider distribution of benefits within the country, is in some quarters preferred.

12.6 HOTEL PRICES

Overall, the hotel sector should have benefited from the economic policy changes in Jamaica in the 1980s. These benefits would have accrued to existing owners and operators given the excess capacity at the beginning of the decade. They may have influenced several to invest later in the decade. However, the net beneficial effects would have accrued only if price levels could be sustained, thereby deriving windfall benefits from the real exchange rate changes.

It is not clear whether price levels in foreign currency could have been sustained. Firstly, many prices are contracted at less than publicized rates even before commission. Secondly, hotels have had to compete with a growth in villa and apartment accommodation. Thirdly, hotels in Jamaica have had to compete with hotels offering similar services in other Caribbean islands. This may have held prices down on top of the continued instability of tourism earnings (Sinclair and Tsegaye, 1990).

In Table 12.5 the increases in prices in foreign currency between 1980 and 1989 for three selected hotels, corresponding to the three categories identified above, are compared with US and domestic inflation. The rate of increase of prices relative to US inflation, representing the price of imports, is a main factor in the extent to which tourism earnings expand the economy's import capacity. The rate of increase of prices relative to domestic inflation is a main influence on the financial performance of hotels.

The results are surprising and indicate the need for further investigation. For business and holiday hotels Table 12.5 suggests that the increase in hotel prices in foreign currency has considerably exceeded the increase in import prices. If this was the case, then the opportunity for price reductions with a real devaluation was not taken. The exception is for the all-inclusive hotel, where prices have risen at broadly the same rate as US

Table 12.5 Hotel prices inflation and import prices 1980–1989 (indices)

	1980	1989[a]	1989[b]
Kingston hotels, business	100	235	392
Negril hotels, all-inclusive[c]	100	145	242
Ocho Rios hotels, holiday	100	259	432
Consumer prices	100	327	
US prices[d]	100	150	

[a] US$ per head, double occupancy, winter, Jamaica.

[b] Adjusted for real depreciation of the currency.

[c] Adjusted for change from modified American plan 1980 to all-inclusive 1989.

[d] Used as a proxy for import prices.

Sources: Jamaica Tourist Board rate sheets; IMF (1990).

inflation. This lower rate of increase yielded windfall gains anyway, given the real devaluation of the currency, and may have been sufficient for a relatively new market segment.

The price increases for the business and holiday hotels do not seem so large when compared with domestic inflation. However, given the real devaluation, these prices have risen faster than prices in general, tending to improve financial performance. The exception is again the all-inclusive hotel, where prices converted to domestic currency rise at a rate less than prices in general. As nearly two-thirds of holiday hotels are now all-inclusive, this result suggests such hotels needed to steer a course between meeting domestic cost increases and ensuring foreign currency prices were not rising too fast.

This discussion of hotel prices suggests that hotels have probably compensated for cost increases through price increases and the windfall effects of real devaluation. The profitability of hotels should have been higher at the end than at the beginning of the 1980s. It also suggests that as capacity expands again an alternative strategy of price reductions and increased occupancy may be tried to sustain profitability and foreign exchange inflows.

12.7 CONCLUSIONS

Tourism grew in Jamaica in the 1980s to become the major foreign exchange earner. The growth of arrivals and expenditure early in the decade prompted a resumption of hotel investment in more recent years. The hotel sector is predominantly Jamaican owned and has incorporated a new form of all-inclusive holiday tourism.

Jamaica was also subject to considerable economic changes in the 1980s. In part these changes were the consequence of economic adjustment programmes implemented under international loan agreements. Changes in economic policy instruments, designed to shift production incentives towards the foreign exchange earning sectors, should have had a beneficial impact on the tourism sector. However, certain features of these programmes will have had a negative impact on hotel profitability.

The effects of economic policy changes will be different for business hotels, for all-inclusive hotels and for conventional holiday hotels. Moreover, hotel profitability will be influenced by price policy, firstly in relation to import price changes and secondly in relation to increases in domestic costs. The effects of economic policy changes on hotel revenues and costs should be monitored as a background to tourism sector policy and pricing.

References

Adhikari, R. (1986) Efficiency and social analysis of projects in the Nepalese economy. *Industry and Development*, **17**, 91–109.

Booth, A. (1990) The tourism boom in Indonesia. *Bulletin of Indonesian Economic Studies*, **26**, 45–73.

Bryden, J.M. (1973) *Tourism and Development. A Case Study of the Commonwealth Caribbean*. London: Cambridge University Press.

Bullock, C. (1986) IMF conditionality and Jamaica's economic policy in the 1980s. *Social and Economic Studies*, **35**, 129–76.

Carey, K. (1989) Tourism development in LDCs: hotel capacity expansion with reference to Barbados. *World Development*, **17**, 59–67.

Corbo, V. and Webb, S. (1990) Adjustment lending and the restoration of sustainable growth. In *Policy-based Lending*. Manchester: Manchester University.

Cornia, G.A., Jolly, R. and Stewart, F. (1987) *Adjustment with a Human Face*; Vol. 1: *Protecting the Vulnerable and Promoting Growth*. Oxford: Clarendon Press.

Curry, S.R. (1971) Tourist expenditure project: preliminary report. Kingston: Central Planning Unit, Government of Jamaica.

Curry, S.R. (1986) The economic impact of the tourist industry in the United Republic of Tanzania: an input–output analysis. *Industry and Development*, **19**, 55–75.

Curry, S.R. (1987) Hotel investments in Tanzania: an evaluation using accounting prices. *Project Appraisal*, **2**, 221–30.

Davies, O. (1986) An analysis of the management of the Jamaican economy: 1972–1985. *Social and Economic Studies*, **35**, 73–109.

Davis, N. (1988) Debt conversion: the Jamaican experience. *Social and Economic Studies*, **37**, 151–69.

EC (1990) *The Courier*, **122**, 50–86. Brussels: European Community.

Fletcher, J.E. (1989) Input–output analysis and tourism impact studies. *Annals of Tourism Research*, **16**, 514–29.

Forbes, A. (1976) The Trinidad Hilton: a cost–benefit study of a luxury hotel. In Little, I.M.D. and Scott, M. (eds) *Using Shadow Prices*, pp. 15–42. London: Heinemann.

George, S. (1988) *A Fate Worse than Debt*. London: Penguin.

Holder, J. (1990) The Caribbean. Far greater dependence on tourism likely. *The Courier*, **122**, 74–9. Brussels: European Community.

IMF (1988) *International Financial Statistics, Yearbook*. Washington, DC: International Monetary Fund.

IMF (1990) *Monthly Statistics, September*. Washington, DC: International Monetary Fund.

Kitchen, R. (1989) Jamaica's external debt: its origins and management. *European Journal of Development Research*, **1**, 78–96.

Looney, R.E. (1987) *The Jamaican Economy in the 1980s. Economic Decline and Structural Adjustment*. Boulder, CO: Westview.

Ministry of Tourism (1989) Hotels at end 1988, Internal Memorandum. Kingston: Ministry of Tourism.

Ministry of Tourism (1990) *Annual Travel Statistics 1989*. Kingston: Ministry of Tourism.

O'Hagan, J. and Mooney, D. (1983) Input–output multipliers in a small open economy: an application to tourism. *Economic and Social Review*, **14**, 273–80.

PIOJ (1990) *Draft Jamaica National Five Year Plan*. Kingston: Planning Institute of Jamaica.

Powers, T.A. (1980) Using accounting prices to evaluate international tourism projects in developing countries. In Hawkins, D.E., Shafer, E.L. and Rovelstad, J.M. (eds) *Tourism Planning and Development Issues*, 411–28. George Washington University.

Shafaeddin, M. (1990) The effectiveness of nominal devaluation in developing countries in the 1980s. In *Industry and Trade Liberalization*. Bradford: Development and Project Planning Centre.

Sinclair, T. and Tsegaye, A. (1990) International tourism and export instability. *Journal of Development Studies*, **26**, 487–504.

Stewart, F. (1990) The many faces of adjustment. In *Policy-based Lending*. Manchester: Manchester University.

Wanhill, S. R. C. (1988) Tourism multipliers under capacity constraints. *Service Industries Journal*, **8**, 136–42.

World Bank (1989) *Jamaica: Adjustment under Changing Economic Conditions. Annex VI, Tourism.* Washington, DC: World Bank.

WTO (1986) *The Contribution of Tourism to the National Economy.* Madrid: World Tourism Organization.

13 European Community Tourism Policy

Gary Akehurst

13.1 INTRODUCTION

Should the European Community (EC) have a tourism policy? Such a question would have been dismissed as at best irrelevant even a few years ago. Now, as past President of the European Commission Roy Jenkins observed in 1989, there is 'a new wave of European momentum' (Jenkins, 1989). By the year 2000 the EC may have grown to 18 or 20 members, including East European and Scandinavian states; it may have developed a Central European Bank with a common currency. Together with an expanded European Monetary System, the institutions of the EC may have significant control over European macroeconomic policies and it is not now inconceivable to consider the possibility of some kind of directly elected European government with, in effect, regional or national assemblies. Given the momentous events of the past three years such scenarios should not be dismissed. A key question now is whether the EC has or should have a tourism policy, given the economic significance of the tourism sector in the economies of each member state.

The Treaty of Rome, which formally established the European Economic Community in 1958, set out to establish a 'common market' by removing all restrictions on the free movement of goods, persons and capital between member states. Tariff barriers to trade between members were to be dismantled and a common tariff imposed on non-members, thus creating a protected free trade area. This formation of a customs union was conceived to be the first stage in the creation of an economic union, in which member states' national economic policies would be harmonized. The formation of the EC and subsequent legislation (most notably the Single European Act in 1986) has created a 'domestic' market of some 320 million people, with all the possibilities of economies of scale in the production of goods and services. Up until 1986 the EC appeared to have achieved modest progress but was dogged by internal budgetary disputes and arguments, particularly over the Common Agricultural Policy. Was the economic growth of West Germany and France, for instance, due to the EC or in spite of it? Jenkins believes that there was an impression that the Community had 'lost both its dynamism and its idealism' (Jenkins, 1989, pp. 3–4).

The Single European Act has added a new momentum and has to some extent fired the imagination of politicians and business people. The creation of a single internal market is concerned with the dismantling of those domestic regulations in each member state that restrict the free movement of people, goods and capital. This means the removal of physical, technical and fiscal barriers. Considerable obstacles – not least the national differences in legal and fiscal systems – will remain for years to come and member states may be reluctant to agree to a transfer of responsibility for macroeconomic policies. They will also be wary of moves that may lead to national identities and cultures being submerged into some kind of European super-culture. However, it should be noted that a single internal market, if it is to be successful, will need stable exchange rates and some kind of common monetary policy; that is, a Community-wide monetary policy. This ultimately implies a common currency and a European Central Bank. The EC agreement reached in Maastricht in December 1991 will lead to a common currency by 1999 at the latest. The Delors Report on Economic and Monetary Union published in 1989 recognized that completion of the internal market will increase economic integration in the EC (Committee for the Study of Economic and Monetary Union, 1989). National economic policies will need to be increasingly compatible with one another or there will be exchange rate tensions. Co-ordination of both domestic and EC policies will thus be required (Mair, 1991).

Given all these developments and the fact that tourism is a significant activity in the Community – it accounts for 6 per cent of total employment in the EC and 5 per cent of EC GNP

216

(Eurostat, 1990) – the question of the desirability or otherwise of an EC tourism policy or strategy comes very much to the fore. A tourism policy is here defined as a strategy for the development of the tourism sector at Community level that establishes objectives and guidelines as a basis for what needs to be done. This means identifying and agreeing objectives (what are the policy problems and what is the EC seeking to achieve?); establishing priorities; placing in a Community context the roles of national governments, national tourist organizations, local governments and private-sector businesses; establishing possible co-ordination and implementation of agreed programmes to solve identified problems, with monitoring and evaluation of these programmes. Kendall (1988) argues that tourism planning falls broadly into two principal areas: strategic planning and master planning. Strategic planning has just been described. Master planning is concerned with translating objectives into a programme of action that establishes when things get done, how and by whom. For further discussion of what constitutes a tourism policy, see OECD (1989).

The EC has been slow to develop a tourism policy. Given the bigger issues that the EC has had to consider, it is perhaps not surprising that such a policy has had a low priority. There are different views about the role, forms and extent of intervention by national governments, let alone supra-national organizations like the EC intervening in the economies of sovereign states. At one extreme there are interventionists who believe that governments should intervene strategically, via state agencies, state ownership and subsidies, throughout an economy at industry and firm levels, because of imperfections and failures in the market-place. At the other extreme there is the *laissez-faire* approach, which believes that every economic activity should be left to market forces. This means a smaller public sector, deregulation, reduction and finally withdrawal of industrial subsidies, enhanced competition policies and so on.

There are persuasive arguments for why the EC should not intervene in the tourism industry or regulate its activities. These arguments relate to the very *raison d'être* of the Community; that is, the development of free markets without artificial restrictions or intervention. Given that the tourist industry in Europe is a diverse mixture of private enterprises with public-sector involvement there is perhaps a need not for regulation but for a European sense of direction, of vision within the Council of Ministers supported by a well-briefed European Commission

217

Table 13.1 Tourism in the economies of the member states

Country	% share of travel receipts in exports of goods and services (1989)	% share of travel expenditure in imports of goods and services (1989)	% GNP (1988)	% employment (1988)
Belgium	2.3	3.1	3.0	3.9
Denmark	6.0	8.3	4.5	5.3
France	5.5	3.5	9.0	6.9
Germany	2.9	7.9	4.6	5.2
Greece	16.3	4.3	7.3	7.2
Ireland	6.3	7.3	6.2	6.3
Italy	7.2	3.9	4.5	6.4
Luxembourg	n.a.	n.a.	n.a.	5.2
Netherlands	3.1	7.2	1.3	2.3
Portugal	17.3	2.9	6.0	8.6
Spain	22.7	3.5	9.4	9.3
UK	6.0	7.0	4.0	6.0

n.a., not available.

Source: Eurostat (1990, p. 11).

which understands the tourism phenomenon. It is insufficient to believe that tourism is important in employment generation, balance of payments and GNP. What is needed is a policy framework at Community level within which the tourism sector can prosper.

This chapter sketches the emergence of a tourism policy in the European Community, particularly since 1988, and looks for pointers to the kind of tourism policy that may be in existence following completion of the single internal market at the beginning of 1993. The chapter brings together for the first time information from a diverse range of sources.

13.2 THE SIGNIFICANCE OF TOURISM WITHIN THE EC

According to the World Tourism Organization the number of registered tourist arrivals in 1990 rose to 415 million worldwide, of which 63 per cent relates to Europe. In addition, the total international income from tourism in 1990 was US$230 billion, of which 51 per cent accrued to Europe.

Table 13.1 lists four main indicators of the relative position of the tourism sector in the member state economies. In terms of GNP the share of tourism in the EC is around 5 per cent. In

Table 13.2 Tourism receipts and expenditure in the balance of payments of member states (billion ecu)

	Receipts 1989	Expenditure 1989
Belgium and Luxembourg[a]	2.9	3.8
Denmark	2.1	2.7
France	15.0	9.4
Germany[b]	11.5	26.0
Greece	1.8	0.7
Ireland	1.3	0.9
Italy	10.9	6.2
Netherlands	2.7	5.9
Portugal[c]	2.0	0.4
Spain	14.8	2.8
UK	10.3	14.0
EC	75.3	72.8

[a] Based on the period January to October. Some non-tourist items included.
[b] Including transport.
[c] Based on the period January to October.

Source: Eurostat (1990, p. 7).

Spain the share is 9.4 per cent and in France 9 per cent. On average the tourism sector provides 6 per cent of total EC employment although in Spain the share rises to 9.3 per cent. The share of travel receipts in the total exports of goods and services shows the considerable importance of tourism to Spain (22.7 per cent), Portugal (17.3 per cent) and Greece (16.3 per cent).

Table 13.2 illustrates the relative importance of tourism receipts and expenditures. In 1989 the EC received tourist receipts of 75.3 billion ecu, an increase of 9.5 per cent in current price terms over 1988, when receipts totalled 68.7 billion ecu. In 1989 EC tourism expenditure was 72.8 billion ecu, an increase of 9.1 per cent in current price terms over 1988, when expenditure reached 66.7 billion ecu. Clearly, these summary statistics show that the tourism sector in the EC is a highly important activity.

13.3 DECISION MAKING IN THE COMMUNITY

To understand some of the history of tourism policy development in the EC it is necessary first to describe the decision making bodies of the Community. (For further details, see for example British Tourist Authority/English Tourist Board, 1990.) The European Commission ensures that Community rules are followed by member states. It also makes proposals for policies and laws and carries out policies of the Community. There are 23 Directorates-General, each with specific responsibilities. The Tourism Unit was transferred in February 1989 from Directorate-General VII Transport to a new Directorate-General XXIII for Enterprise Policy, Tourism and Social Economy, but such is the fragmented and diversified nature of tourism that several Directorates-General develop measures and policies that may affect the tourism industry. These include the following:

DG III   Internal Markets and Industrial Affairs (e.g. 1992 impacts)
DG IV   Competition (competition policy)
DG V   Employment, Social Affairs and Education (e.g. European Social Fund, free movement of labour)
DG VII   Transport
DG XI   Environment, Consumer Protection and Nuclear Safety
DG XII   Science, Research and Development
DG XVI   Regional Policy (European Regional Development Fund)
DG XXI   Customs Union and Indirect Taxation
DG XXII   Co-ordination of Structural Instruments (Mediterranean programmes)

The existence of all these Community 'departments', each of which may promote policies that could profoundly affect tourism, strengthens the argument for an overarching and co-ordinating tourism policy with not just a medium-term but also a long-term outlook.

The Council of Ministers comprises ministers from each member state. Having considered European Parliament and Commission proposals it establishes laws by a voting system. The European Parliament discusses proposed EC legislation and proposed amendments to legislation, and has a loose consultative and supervisory role within the Community.

13.4 TOURISM PLANNING

It can be argued that the tourism sector should be left to determine its own prosperity. If tourism markets are working satisfactorily (with societal welfare enhanced or maximized by an optimum allocation of resources) then intervention is clearly undesirable. However, tourism activities have profound economic and social consequences within local, regional and national communities. Imperfections in tourism markets, such as restrictive trade practices, or harmful externalities, such as noise pollution, give rise to market failures that may require corrective action or an externally generated solution of a second-best nature (recognizing that an optimal allocation of resources is a desirable but theoretical ideal). For these reasons it can be argued that tourism activities require very careful planning not just at national level but also at supra-national and product or service supply levels.

A tourism policy can itself fail for a number of reasons. Firstly, there may be insufficient identification and articulation of policy problems (objectives) that are agreed by all parties, at supra-national, national, regional and local levels. Secondly, all parties may not agree as to what a policy or policies are seeking to achieve or, indeed, whether there should be a policy at all. Thirdly, there may be disagreement about which policy problems are most important. Fourthly, there may be disagreement on how each problem can be solved and on the roles to be played by public and private sector organizations. Finally, there may be disagreement about how to monitor and evaluate implementation and action programmes.

Kendall (1988) has succinctly identified the principal failures of tourism planning within Britain. He argues that a weak organizational structure, which fails to identify who does what, when and how, leads to planning failure. This weak organizational structure fails to establish the roles that should be played by the public and private sectors in implementing a policy, especially in developing, marketing and monitoring the tourism sector. He further argues that inadequate financial support for the national tourism organization also leads to weak marketing and promotional activities. In Britain, tourism has been seen as an essentially private-sector activity with public-sector involvement concerned with marketing and promotional support and pump-priming investment, even though this is considered by some to be rather ineffective public-sector support.

Is it possible, then, to develop criteria for a successful tourism policy? I believe that certain factors are critical for success; they must be considered in the development of a policy and can be used to assess policies. The following five sets of questions must be asked before these criteria can be highlighted.

1 Are there persuasive arguments in favour of an EC tourism policy in terms of identifiable benefits to the Community, member states, organizations and individuals? If so, what form should EC involvement take and what should be its scale?

2 What are the tourism objectives of the EC? Is the EC seeking (for example) employment creation, revenue generation, regional development and/or social benefits?

3 What should be the precise role of the EC? Should it involve regulation only, or should it entail active financial investment, the promotion of investment incentives, support for promotion and marketing and/or stimulation of training? Do these roles enhance, support, duplicate or damage national governmental roles? Are all roles clear and all channels of communication in place?

4 How is the tourism sector organized in each member state? Who develops, delivers, manages and promotes the different tourism products and services?

5 What is known about the tourism product and services in each member state? What are their strengths and weaknesses and their projected growth of supply? What is the nature (e.g. purpose of visit) of current and future tourism demand? Are there growth inhibitors, such as lack of infrastructure, organizational weaknesses and investment difficulties?

Answers to these rather basic but nevertheless fundamental questions will generate a well-designed tourism policy that will:

- identify the policy problems within the Community with a clear understanding of the nature of the tourism product;
- agree and establish objectives (the policy problems) as a basis for what needs to be done and what the EC is seeking to achieve;
- establish and agree clear objective priorities;
- establish and place into a Community context the roles of national governments, national tourist organizations, local governments and private-sector businesses (including funding agencies);
- establish the effective co-ordination and implementation of agreed programmes to solve identified policy problems;
- monitor and evaluate action programmes by identifying the precise personnel and time scales involved.

To meet these criteria, tourism statistics that use consistent bases need to be collected in each member state.

13.5 AN EMERGING EC TOURISM POLICY?

The EC may be slow in developing a tourism policy but there are certain signs of one emerging. However, given the criteria above there is still a long way to go. It is instructive to piece together the developments of the past five years or so in an attempt to identify possible central policy themes, if they exist. Statements of policy have appeared from time to time although the emphasis has not always been consistent. In March 1986 the Commission published a paper entitled 'Community action in the field of tourism'. The conclusions of this paper led the Council of Ministers to adopt the following measures.

1   A resolution on the promotion of a better seasonal and geographical distribution of tourism (adopted 1986). Member states were called on to measure the capacity of tourist and transit areas and to assess the effects of saturation during peak traffic periods of the year; to discontinue incentives for tourist development in areas and sites that have reached saturation; to discourage or prohibit further construction in these areas; to encourage measures to reduce the causes of saturation; and to encourage tourist facilities in areas and sites where the risks of saturation are low.

2   A recommendation on standardized information on hotels (adopted 1986). Standardized information systems would be implemented and monitored by national tourist organizations and hoteliers' associations.

3   The establishment of a consultation and co-ordination procedure in tourism (adopted 1986). This decision provided specifically for an Advisory Committee on Tourism to be established, so providing a formal framework for co-operation between member states. Each member state is required to send the Commission an annual report on the most significant measures taken, and those it intends to take, to provide services for tourists that could have consequences for travellers from other member states.

4   A directive on the harmonization of legislation on package travel (draft proposed in April 1988, amended 1989, following European Parliament amendment adopted by the

Council in June 1990). The directive harmonizes national provisions with the express aim of encouraging the free circulation of travel packages (by ensuring that consumers have knowledge of and access to all marketable travel packages) and improving consumer protection.
5 A directive on the easing of controls and formalities applicable to nationals of the member states when crossing intra-Community borders (proposed 1985 and subsequently taken up in internal market legislation).
6 A recommendation on fire safety in hotels (adopted 1986).

These decisions can be classified under three closely related headings: information, quality of services and promotion. These themes have been followed through in further statements and actions. The Commissioner for Directorate-General XXIII, in a speech marking the inauguration of the European Year of Tourism in Dublin in January 1990 (Cardoso e Cunha, 1990), asked whether the Community has a role in tourism policy that goes beyond the control of state aid and competition policy within member states. In affirming this he argued for:

• the marketing of Europe as a whole and the importance of ensuring that the product 'Europe' is a consistent, high-quality product;
• integrated information and reservation systems;
• co-operation between member states' governments, national tourist boards and the tourist industry, with the Community as a partner of national governments.

This emphasized again the three main themes which, taken together with a speech the Commissioner made at Mont St Michel in 1989, suggest a higher profile for tourism activities when decisions are made about Community policies. However, judgement must be reserved on this at the present time.

The designation of 1990 as European Tourism Year could have been regarded as a belated realization of the economic, social and political importance of tourism, but it can also be seen in retrospect as one further manifestation of a developing EC tourism policy (Commission of the European Communities, 1990). In December 1988 the ministers responsible for tourism in member states' governments held their first formal meeting and adopted a programme for European Tourism Year that had two main objectives:

- to stress the integrating role of tourism in working towards a single internal market, facilitating a greater knowledge of European life styles and cultures among citizens of member states, especially young people;
- to emphasize the economic and social importance of tourism.

Again the range of co-ordinated activities proposed or supported involves information, service quality and promotion, with a sharper focus on promoting novel tourism products, such as rural tourism, and the extension of the tourist season (thus making more effective use of human and capital resources). Some 2.5 million ecu has been made available for this support together with a further 2.5 million ecu to support information campaigns, including competitions and prizes. How successful European Tourism Year has been in meeting its objectives may be debatable. It is doubtful if most Community citizens are really aware of alternative tourist destinations or the advantages of low-season tourism.

Other pointers to the direction of an EC tourism policy can be seen. Firstly, the Deputy Director-General in the European Commission for small and medium-sized enterprises (Alan Mayhew) has recently outlined the objectives for a new tourism strategy based on Council of Ministers' guidelines developed at their meeting in December 1989 at Mont St Michel. Yet again the stress is placed upon improving the quality of European tourism services, stimulating demand from countries outside the EC (or third countries) and working to improve the business environment within which tourism enterprises operate (principally by improving tourism information flows and analysis to aid business decision making and helping the development of new products). Mayhew (1990, p. 4) also states:

The role of Community tourism policy is not to regulate the industry, although this may be necessary when no other way is open to it. The principles of Community enterprise policy, which apply equally well to the tourism sector, aim to achieve administrative simplification and the removal of burdens on business, rather than the regulation of the sector.

Mayhew further called attention to the considerable change that will occur throughout Europe in the rest of the 1990s and beyond. Economic integration and any political integration that accompanies it will have profound effects, which, linked with

225

changing demographics, will change both the demand for and supply of tourism services. It is possible that the Community of 12 member states will be enlarged to 18 or more by the turn of the century with the inclusion not just of Eastern European but also of Scandinavian states. Whether a federal Europe emerges or not the growing realization that nation states are interdependent will continue. Indeed, the very idea of nation states may well be questioned in the long-term future.

The development of an EC tourism policy will not go unquestioned. While it may be accepted that the Community does not seek to interfere or regulate the tourism industry, fundamental questions still remain. Van Hove (1990) has pointed out that 'in the future tourism policy will to a large extent be a matter of national governments or regions'. Van Hove argues that a tourist product is related to one or a few regions and that the north of Europe cannot offer what the south of Europe can supply. Another well-respected tourism writer and industrialist, Stephen Wheatcroft, questions whether the Commission should 'take action in the development of new products or the promotion of demand in third countries'. He suggests that new product development is without question the domain of industry and promotion is already undertaken by the European Travel Commission together with national tourist organizations (Wheatcroft, 1990).

Further indicators of a post-1992 Europe are available. Firstly, because of the single market legislation many obstacles to the free movement of travellers and tourism employees between member states will be eliminated. Intra-Community tourism will be easier. Travellers from third countries will be able to travel with freedom between member states after being checked at one of the Community's external borders. Secondly, use of the ecu for tourism and travel will grow and a Europe-wide electronic funds transfer and point of sale card system will develop. Such developments will greatly simplify payments and money withdrawals throughout the Community (provided the commercial banking system can be persuaded to make the appropriate investment).

Tourism cannot thrive without a strong infrastructure. Although the Council of Ministers has so far failed to agree on a common transport policy it has adopted a number of directives with the objectives of: providing financial support for major infrastructure projects; encouraging a greater integration of national transport policies; eliminating bureaucratic constraints within the European transport system; and creating more competition between and within different forms of transport.

In 1989 priority transport projects for funding support were identified, including high-speed rail networks (Paris–London–Brussels–Amsterdam–Cologne; Lisbon–Seville–Madrid–Barcelona–Lyon) and the improvement of the European air traffic control system. A series of other measures are helping the tourism industry. Decisions taken or being discussed at the time of writing (April 1991) include the gradual liberalization of air transport (fares, market access and competition), which may lead to the development of new air links if not to lower air fares. Trips by coach and bus will be easier following the establishment of European networks and deregulation measures.

As mentioned earlier, in December 1989 the Council of Ministers sketched out some guidelines for the development of a more structured and longer-term approach to EC tourism. These ideas were refined at first by an informal Tourism Council meeting in March 1990, followed by a formal meeting in June 1990. It is worth summarizing again what has become in effect the definitive statement on EC tourism policy and is likely to endure for the next ten years or so.

1 The role of the Community is not to regulate industry unless necessary but to achieve administrative simplification.
2 Member states should work together to devise long-term strategies.
3 The EC should do only those things best done at Community level.
4 The objectives of the Community tourism policy are to benefit the individual tourist and tourism enterprise. For the individual, this means higher-quality tourism services, help for specific groups such as the disabled, young and elderly, and a broadening in the range of people taking holidays; for the enterprise this means the development of new products (especially rural and cultural), promotion to third markets (especially Japan) and the provision of information on tourism to aid business decision making.
5 The EC will encourage investment in human capital and the improvement of tourism industry working conditions, the improvement of professional training for tourism employees including languages, the expansion of exchange programmes, data collection on available training and

education programmes, and the networking of existing training organizations.

6 The EC will stimulate investment in infrastructure. European Investment Bank finance is available for transport, water supply and quality improvement of coastal waters. European Regional Development Fund resources will be more concentrated on least-favoured regions of the Community (often areas of great tourism potential).

7 The EC will encourage a better seasonal and geographical spread of tourism.

8 A statistical action plan (discussed in March 1990 by tourism ministers and the subject of a Commission proposal to the Council in May 1990) is being drawn up. Existing statistics on tourism are unreliable and based on different definitions and collection practices, making comparisons between member states virtually impossible. Eurostat, the statistical office of the EC, is currently assessing the feasibility of a harmonized system.

To support its tourism development programme the Commission has started to carry out studies in certain sectors of the tourist industry to 'establish the bases of its policy'; that is, to determine policy problems. Consequently, invitations to tender for 11 projects were issued in October 1990. These projects are:

- the impact of completion of the internal market on the tourism sector;
- the place of tourism in the policy on structural funds;
- the evolution of holiday travel facilities, the flow of tourism inside and outside the European Community and the identification of innovative tourism products;
- cultural tourism – clientele and specific difficulties, and analysis of supply;
- social tourism – components, evolution of facilities and demand;
- tourism supply in Central and Eastern Europe and the problems and prospects for co-operation;
- tourism clientele in Central and Eastern Europe and development prospects;
- the evolution of tourism-related employment and vocational training;
- all-season tourism – analysis of experience, suitable products and clientele;

- the development of a co-ordinated European descriptive system for rural tourism;
- the establishment of a documentation centre.

Do these developments add up to a clear tourism policy? From the evidence so far it is apparent that certain features of a policy are emerging but other essential elements are lacking and remain to be defined.

The identifiable benefits of tourism to the Community have been rather loosely sketched out; there needs to be a further elaboration and quantification with a well-defined statistical foundation. The EC is attempting to identify the policy problems within the Community but clearly needs to understand far more about the nature of tourism supply and demand. A somewhat rudimentary consultation and co-ordination process has been started but this is still only at an embryonic stage. While the tourism objectives of the EC are slowly emerging some kind of priority order is appearing although it is still rather ill-defined. Novel tourism products, an extension of the tourist season and tourism training are clearly identified priorities. But in defining the roles of the various national organizations, in the public and private sectors and at central and local levels, and the role of the EC itself much work still needs to be undertaken. This is perhaps the area of greatest potential weakness and will be difficult to resolve. Finally, monitoring and evaluation of programmes is at an early stage and needs strengthening.

13.6 CONCLUSIONS

In conclusion, any post-1992 tourism policy will have to be judged on how well it meets a number of criteria and factors, including the following:

1 Is it clearly stated, well communicated and well co-ordinated?
2 Does it identify and prioritize the policy problems?
3 Is there a consistency of approach over time in the implementation, monitoring and evaluation of agreed action programmes, combined with a flexibility to accommodate unforeseen changes?
4 Is it based on a detailed understanding and knowledge of

the tourism phenomenon, with information flows helping business decision making?

5 Does it channel and distribute the impacts of tourism?

Above all, the EC needs to consider and define very carefully its role in the tourism sector and ensure that this role supports national governmental and national tourist organization roles. There must be agreement about the role of the EC and its importance in giving a strategic lead to the tourism sector.

The EC has developed a rudimentary but nevertheless evolutionary tourism policy that is capable of expansion into an effective and timely action programme. It now needs to go further in developing this policy and do so quickly.

References

British Tourist Authority/English Tourist Board (1990) *Tourism and the European Community*. London: BTA/ETB.

Cardoso e Cunha, A. (1990) Inauguration of the European Year of Tourism 1990. Speech made in Dublin, 30 January.

Commission of the European Communities (1990) *1990, European Tourism Year*. Brussels: CEC.

Committee for the Study of Economic and Monetary Union (1989) *Report on Economic and Monetary Union in the European Community (Delors Report)*. Brussels: Commission of the European Communities.

Eurostat (1990) *Tourism in Europe. Trends 1989*. Luxembourg: Office for Official Publications of the European Communities.

Jenkins, Lord (1989) Britain in Europe: left behind again? *Royal Bank of Scotland Review*, **162**, 3–8.

Kendall, P. (1988) Planning the tourism product. In *Tourism: a Portrait*, pp. 43–6. London: Horwath & Horwath.

Mair, D. (1991) Regional policy initiatives from Brussels. *Royal Bank of Scotland Review*, **169**, 33–43.

Mayhew, A. (1990) Towards 1992. Europe in the 1990's. In *The Tourism Industry 1990/91*, pp. 4–5. London: Tourism Society.

OECD (1989) *Tourism Policy and International Tourism in OECD Member Countries*. Paris: OECD.

Van Hove, N. (1990) The Community's strategy. In *The Tourism Industry 1990/91*, pp. 5–6. London: Tourism Society.

Wheatcroft, S. (1990) In search of a policy? In *The Tourism Industry 1990/91*, p. 7. London: Tourism Society.

Author Index

Subject Index

UWCC LIBRARY